Modern Culture and Critical Theory

Russell A. Berman

Modern Culture
and Critical Theory

Art, Politics, and the Legacy of the Frankfurt School

The University of Wisconsin Press

The University of Wisconsin Press
114 North Murray Street
Madison, Wisconsin 53715

The University of Wisconsin Press, Ltd.
1 Gower Street
London WC1E 6HA, England

Printed in the United States of America

Library of Congress Cataloging-in-Publication Data
Berman, Russell A., 1950–
   Modern culture and critical theory.
   Includes bibliographical references and index.
   1. Culture.   2. Critical theory.   3. Postmodernism.
4. Fascism and culture.   5. Avant-garde (Aesthetics)
I. Title.
HM101.B4723   1988   306   88-40426
ISBN 0-299-12080-5
ISBN 0-299-12084-8 (pbk.)

Contents

Acknowledgments

THIS book incorporates issues from aesthetic theory, literary criticism, social history, and political debate. Drawing on the interdisciplinary materialism of the Frankfurt School, it has benefited from an institutional setting that has grown increasingly supportive of interdisciplinary research. The reorganization of the relationship among the disciplines, however, implies a reconsideration of the relationship of the academy to its wider context as well as changes in academic style and institutions.

Among these institutional changes, one of the most important has been the emergence of new types of journals, where earlier versions of several chapters have been published. Chapter 4 appeared in *New German Critique*, no. 29 (Spring–Summer 1983); Chapter 7 in *Cultural Critique*, no. 5 (Winter 1986–87); and Chapters 5 and 11 in *Telos*, no. 62 (Winter 1984–85) and no. 68 (Summer 1986), respectively. I am grateful to the editors for permission to include them here.

I am grateful as well to friends and colleagues for their help and advice which contributed to the shaping of this project. I want to give special acknowledgment to Abdul JanMohamed, Regenia Gagnier, Peter Hohendahl, Martin Jay, Paul Piccone, Mary Pratt, Renato Rosaldo, William Todd, Katie Trumpener, and Richard Wolin for their generosity with criticisms and suggestions in many discussions. Members of the Culture Studies Group at Stanford will recognize some of our shared concerns and ongoing differences, which have influenced considerably the direction this book has taken. I am grateful to Barbara Hanrahan of the University of Wisconsin Press for her enthusiasm and to Susan Tarcov for her skilled editorial assistance. I dedicate this book to Doris Berman, who guided me through some of this material. Her support and encouragement have been indispensable.

Modern Culture and Critical Theory

Introduction

IN the passages in the first and especially second chapters of the *Dialectic of Enlightenment* devoted to an examination of the *Odysee*, Max Horkheimer and Theodor W. Adorno provide not only a rich example of the literary-critical potential of classical critical theory but a compelling political account as well: an examination of the emergence of an occidental imperialism and its embeddedness in a trajectory of rationalized modernity. In a series of episodes, they trace the constitution of the bourgeois sovereign as a putatively coherent ego and the subject of legitimate authority, and they demonstrate the complicity of this process of enlightenment in both the domestic violence of the patriarch and, simultaneously, the cosmopolitan belligerence of the first voyager at the minatory commencement of an age of discovery: the victory over the Sirens, whose voices are henceforth as subdued as are those of the subordinated laborers on Odysseus' vessel; later, the hoodwinking of Polyphemus, treated explicitly as a representative of the relatively underdeveloped mode of production of "hunters and shepherds," always outwitted in international relations because they have not learned to read the fine print in the deceptive contracts of the mercantile bourgeoisie; finally, the lordly retribution exacted brutally from the servant women of Ithaca who opted for pleasure rather than duty, the cardinal sin in the disenchanted age of a Protestant ethic *avant la lettre*. In case after case, the authors uncover a modernizing enlightenment doubling back on itself, reproducing the violence it intended to escape and asserting identity only by destroying it.

The tension between the legacy of the critical theory of the Frankfurt School and some major developments in recent thought—an underlying concern throughout this book—can be highlighted initially by juxtaposing this seminal reading of Homer and Jean-François Lyotard's *The Postmodern Condition*. In order to contrast the two texts effectively, it is crucial to recognize several features shared by both inquiries. Both inquire, first of all, into structures of knowledge; although in each case, knowledge is certainly related to social processes and political power, each text foregrounds (albeit in different ways) the vicissitudes of modes of cognition. Second, the cognitive material scrutinized at the center of both texts is the same, whether it is labeled enlightenment by Horkheimer/Adorno or science by Lyotard; both evidently operate within a post-Weberian critique of occidental rationality that thematizes the performative capacity as well as the deleterious consequences of an institutionalized reason. Finally, Horkheimer/Adorno as well as Lyotard focus on the destructive force modern science unleashes in its confrontation with prescientific modes of knowledge: the imperialist moment when civilization attempts to enforce its supremacy over the primitive, the backward, the barbarian, when, to cite the Occident's own geographical metaphor, Europe constructs Asia in order to subjugate it.

With so much in common, there might appear to be little room for contrast remaining, and one could be tempted to construct the following lineage: Horkheimer/Adorno, critics of modernization, advocate an adversarial aesthetics of modernism but refuse to define a substantive politics—hence, their proverbial pessimism; Lyotard, proponent of postmodernism, might then be seen as building sanguinely on their critique by filling the lacunae with a positive program. Such a hypothetical reconciliation of these thinkers could point additionally to Lyotard's expressed affinity for the earlier Frankfurt School and to arguments by, for example, Albrecht Wellmer regarding a postmodern moment in Adorno's own work. In the end, however, this argument would, I believe, do considerable injustice to both critical positions and ignore the specificities of the texts at hand. At best one could contend that *The Postmodern Condition* borrows from *Dialectic of Enlightenment* a Nietzschean critique of systematic knowledge and certain traces of an anthropological irrationalism derived from Ludwig Klages, and both texts gingerly retain certain Marxist categories in order to construct their neo- or post-Marxist accounts. But these similarities and ties are less interesting than immense differences which open onto important issues in contemporary critical debates, especially the mutual repulsion of the categories "modernism" and "postmodernism."

To engage these terms with reference to this textual selection goes against the grain of Lyotard's own preference, since *The Postmodern Condition* enacts its politics as a critique of Habermas and the consensus theory of truth. It has generated a debate over relativism between a model of communicative competency and a principle of indetermi-

nacy. Yet ultimately a fundamental tension between Adorno and Lyotard is of greater interest. Both—unlike Habermas—are emphatic
critics of institutionalized reason, with Lyotard opting for the paral-
ogy, the transgression against the logic of identity thinking, and
Adorno investigating the consequences of what he terms "logocen-
tric" thought. It is this proximity which highlights the difference, a
difference which is profound, and which I want to profile with regard
to the political differential and the contrasting accounts of an imperialism inherent in narratives of modernity.

While each text claims for itself a theoretical status as a reconsideration of the transformation of cognitive structures, each also dis-
creetly announces its own political allegiances; with allusions and
asides, each refers to a specific context, underscoring its immediate
urgency. Here the differences begin to take shape. For Horkheimer/
Adorno, the analysis of the self-destruction of enlightenment is framed
by the multiple catastrophes of the Second World War, i.e., the political concerns include critiques of European fascism, of the liquidation
of the socialist project in Stalinism, and (in the chapter entitled "Culture Industry") of authoritarian tendencies in the ostensibly democratic culture of the United States. The two-track program, including
both an antifascism as well as a distancing from a naive progressivism,
corresponds to the double judgment on enlightenment: because myth
was already enlightenment, the fascist exhortation to return to myth
is duplicitous; because enlightenment reverts to myth, an unbroken
liberal or socialist faith in progress will not escape the cycle of
violence.

In short, Horkheimer/Adorno, writing as critics of the civilizational
regression they locate in fascism, maintain a loyalty to enlightenment,
whose internal deficiency—a sort of compulsive neurotic inability to
achieve happiness—they seek to remedy in order to initiate a genuine
modernity. The proponent of postmodernism declares an alternative
political commitment. While Lyotard too examines the disappointing
consequences of enlightenment, he comes up with a different diagnosis: the problem is not some ultimately correctable flaw in enlightenment but the very project of enlightenment itself. For Lyotard, any
narrative of emancipation is fundamentally totalitarian, be it liberal
or Marxist, political or cultural. In his "Report on Knowledge" (the
subtitle of the essay), he is therefore only consistent when he argues
against the model of the (as he puts it) "democratic" university with
low tuitions, nonexclusionary entrance requirements, and large stu-

dent bodies, to which he counterposes the desirable alternative of elite institutes for technical specialists.[1] This postmodern politics of higher education, which became so topical in France and elsewhere during the 1980s, derives from a mixture of the anticommunist fear of totality popularized by the *nouveaux philosophes* during the seventies and the supply-side trope of innovative entrepreneurship. At a Marxist moment, the modernists Horkheimer/Adorno refer to the archconservative essayist Rudolf Borchardt as an "esoteric representative of German heavy industry"; in a similar vein, the neoconservative Lyotard would appear as a postmodern pointman for French high tech, providing, with his slogan of "paralogism," a circumlocution for the Eureka project, a West European forced march to the frontiers of the new technologies, while he transforms the free play of signifiers into an account of the flexible deployment of a merely semiotic *force de frappe*.[2]

The proverbial pessimism of Horkheimer/Adorno retains ultimately a barely articulated hope of redemption. The upbeat optimism in Lyotard's new-age account is fundamentally pessimistic, reducing practice to the eternal return of an agonistics of power. This difference is repeated in the contrasting modes of presentation. Horkheimer/Adorno rescue a mimetic fragment, the fable of the Sirens, from the totalizing force of enlightenment conceptualization, while Lyotard's account, lacking any similar allegorical residue, amounts to a collection of just so many separate mininarratives. And these alternative resolutions of the problem of *Darstellung* correspond to antithetical versions of narrative and the construction of imperialism.

Consider first the anterior structure of knowledge, i.e., that which precedes enlightenment and eventually succumbs to the violence of reason. Horkheimer/Adorno focus on this material with their initial literary-critical move in the second chapter, subjecting the Homeric text to a Benjaminian mortification in order to dissolve the superficial coherence of the work into ultimately incompatible moments. The imperialism of epic narration entails the forced reconciliation of the multiplicity of local myths in the totalizing *Bildungsroman* of the single hero. Each episode, each island, each deity is *aufgehoben*—denigrated, preserved, and revalorized—as a subordinate way station in the Odyssean development, corresponding (so the authors suggest) to the establishment of a Hellenic hegemony in the Mediterranean basin: the world market makes world literature.

Criticism moves backward against this self-declared progress in order to disclose a conflationary movement at the beginning of Western culture, but it does so without positing a beginning. For Horkheimer/ Adorno, the local myths consumed by Homeric rationalism in no way represent nostalgic alternatives to the violence of modernization. On the contrary, the origin, which is no home, is the locus of a violent nature and a Hobbesian vision of ubiquitous belligerence. There is no Garden of Eden, no primitive communism. Consequently, the critique of enlightenment is directed not at the transcendence of myth but at the failure to transcend myth successfully. The problem with progress is that it hasn't progressed, trapped in a constant repetition of the savagery it claims to oppose.

One aspect of the dialectic of enlightenment has to do, therefore, with the tension between the pretense of temporal transformation and the constancy of structural violence. Inverting the fascination of modernist artists with primitive material, Horkheimer/Adorno as theoreticians of modernization denounce the primitive reality of modernity. Strangely enough, it turns out to be the postmodernist Lyotard who reproduces the most orthodox account of progress. Of course, he claims to demonstrate the obsolescence of enlightenment metanarratives of emancipation, but at the center of the essay, preserved like a mammoth in a glacier, a surprisingly naive version of *Geschichtsphilosophie* starts to defrost. One finds another, yes, three-part account of the history of human knowledge, beginning with the untroubled coherence of the prelapsarian community, engaged in what Lyotard labels as narrative; passing through the alienation and despair wrought by modern science; and concluding with a postmodernity, returning to some of the ancient pleasures of narration freed from an obligatory legitimation. Winning the postmodern game means hitting a homer, breaking a record, and getting back to the communal dugout where it all began, where no wise-guy umpire or rational lawgiver would dare to tread with his fixation on rigid rules or abstract notions of justice.

Horkheimer/Adorno posit initial violence and conflict; Lyotard dreams of an original community. His primal narrative is the vessel of "customary knowledge," not differentiated into realms of judgment, and shared by a group with no social differentiation: every narratee may become a narrator in an eternal present untarnished by a linear conceptualization of time. More Hegelian than the young Lukács, Lyotard admits as much when he footnotes the ominously unnuanced notion of "the culture of a people" with the remark "The term is preromantic and romantic; cf. Hegel's *Volksgeist*." This indebtedness is problematic, given Lyotard's otherwise acerbic rejection of idealism; the primitivist idealization is unacceptable, drawn from the anthropological romanticism of Mauss and Lévi-Strauss; and the nostalgia is unconvincing, since Lyotard writes unabashedly from the standpoint of "the most highly developed contemporary society," as if an understanding of developmental success were immediately given.[3]

For Horkheimer/Adorno, Homeric imperialism begins with the obliteration of local myths, secularized and disempowered once they are included within the classical epic. Yet the epic which incorporates myth is filled with mythic substance and must repeat the blind violence it thought it had overcome. An adequate critique of domination must therefore address the doubling of domination, but Lyotard flattens out the dialectic. For him, cultural imperialism is the displacement of communal narratives and pristine origins by occidental science, with its universalist references to truth and justice and its perpetual demand for legitimation. He is consequently concerned with the quantitative reduction of language games and not with the legitimacy of any particular ones. The postmodernist critique of imperialism denounces the assertion of any totalizing power but cannot thematize domination or violence as unjust, since any substantive notion of justice will necessarily appear to be universalist and therefore totalitarian. Lyotard's result is a pluralism of competing narratives, which is never resolved and from which one never escapes; Horkheimer/Adorno point toward a genuine escape from the brutality of the agonistic origin which continues to determine an unredeemed social being. The alternative is elsewhere; "*Heimat ist Entronnensein*," home is the state of having escaped, beyond violence and beyond domination.[4]

The critical projects of modernism and postmodernism both foreground the relationship between local practices and an institutionalized master narrative, and both locate imperialism in the moment of this relationship. Both furthermore describe a return of the repressed, either as the reversion of enlightenment to myth for Horkheimer/Adorno or, for Lyotard, as the role of narrative in the nonnarrative mode of science. Both finally underscore the internal lability in these dichotomous forms of cognition, but the accounts of this lability are characteristically antithetical. Again Lyotard turns out to be the more conservative dialectician, arguing a simple double negation: when science turns its compulsion for legitimation back on itself, it can find no answer which would necessarily be both immanent and transcendental; the system collapses leaving a multiplicity of practices with no universal metalanguage. Horkheimer/Adorno present a truncated master-slave dialectic; the very power of the master narrative estranges it from sensuous experience and therefore impoverishes its content, but, pace Hegel, the subordinated actors attain to no superior knowledge which could guarantee emancipation. For there is no guarantee, as Horkheimer/Adorno and Lyotard would agree before shifting attention to language as the realm of a possible criticism. In the case of Lyotard, the focus of attention is the perpetual transgression of the rules of established language games in order to establish new ones, with no claims to universal validity. Postmodernism wants to criticize imperialism but refuses to label domination unjust. Horkheimer/Adorno focus on a surplus of language that might overcome the facticity of violence: the enlightenment that talks too much, Settembrini the organ-grinder. Hence the double character of Homer's imperialism: the founding text of Western culture, like all cultural texts, is simultaneously a document of barbarism; but documents of barbarism by the alienation of their language articulate criticism as a step toward a future culture.

This emphatic notion of criticism, with its concatenation of inquiries into aesthetic culture with questions of societal power, is a central feature of the legacy of the Frankfurt School and one which, I hope, pervades the essays collected in this volume. While all of them address matters of theory and criticism, none is concerned exclusively with an elaboration of the intellectual history of this wing of Western Marxism. Considerable work in recent years by scholars such as Susan Buck-Morss, Russell Jacoby, Martin Jay, and Richard Wolin has helped immensely to illuminate that tradition and has led to somewhat of a minor renaissance, an effort to rethink the questions of the classical Frankfurt School with reference to the culture and politics of the West after 1968. The essays that follow were written in this spirit, posing the questions of critical theory in the context of neoconservatism and the new social movements, the discontents with modernity and the debates on postmodernism, the political hegemony of Ronald Reagan and his allies and the cultural hegemony of structuralism and poststructuralism. Their point is therefore by no means a reinterpretation of critical theory and certainly not a retraction or revision of its central aspects as discussed above with reference to the *Dialectic of Enlightenment*. Their point is rather the changed character of Western society and the subsequent challenge to critical theory to address some of the developments of the past decades.

The initial three chapters discuss theoretical problems that bear on the political specificity of the present: the question of liberty and emancipation as it is thematized by Foucault and Adorno; Benjamin's understanding of fascism and the continued relevance of the formulaic designation of an aestheticization of politics; and a related inquiry into consumerism, aestheticism, and Peter Bürger's description of the avant-garde. Oscillating between political and aesthetic theory, these discussions are motivated by the transformation of political culture during the 1980s, the emergence of an unabashedly spectacular media politics that has gradually become more a matter of art and style and less a public deliberation on issues and policies.

The following five chapters, which occupy the center of the book, trace the prehistory of this aestheticization by investigating the vicissitudes of modernization and aesthetic culture. Chapter 4 takes a look at the restructuring of literary life in Germany during the nineteenth century, i.e., in the context of an increasingly organized capitalist system marked by the emergence of a specifically modern mass culture, or, more correctly, a culture produced for the masses by a commercial culture industry. Chapter 5 examines early twentieth-century modernism, its relationship to social change, and some of the aspects of its obsolescence. In addition, this chapter broaches the question of postmodern culture and its ambiguous political significance in the 1980s, a theme taken up again in Chapter 7. Chapters 6 and 8 each scrutinize texts by single authors which take on paradigmatic importance within this account of cultural change. Beginning with a discussion of Leni Riefenstahl's film *Triumph of the Will,* the former treats Ernst Jünger and fascist modernism—a topic which earlier chapters will have shown is by no means solely historical. In fact, the figure of Jünger, who recently received the Goethe Award of the City of Frankfurt and was honored with a visit by the West German chancellor in the year of the infamous Bitburg commemoration, combines the problems of aesthetics and politics in an emblematic manner. Chapter 8 turns to modernism and postmodernism one last time in an examination of a drama by West Germany's leading playwright, Botho Strauss's *Der Park.* A contemporary retelling of *A Midsummer Night's Dream,* it stages the temporal frame of modernity and its crisis: from the sixteenth century to the present.

The concluding three chapters modify the problem of aesthetics and politics by giving priority to topical political issues, each of which however turns out to be intimately related to aesthetic problems. Chapter 9 discusses the construction of national identity as it relates to the institutionalization of culture in the context of the Hapsburg Empire (and therefore provides a further discussion of European modernism). Chapter 10 turns to a much more contemporary matter, the peace movement of the 1980s and the internal structure of some of its political claims which turn out to share important—and highly problematic—features of the twentieth-century avant-garde. What is the relationship between avant-garde culture and vanguardist politics? Addressing some very specific matters, the final chapter nevertheless returns to issues that have been touched on in earlier passages: modernism, national identity, social movements, and contemporary politics. The pretext for this culminating conclusion is the constellation of interests in Vienna: the cultural fascination with the fin-de-siècle; the intersection of Austrian neutralism and some considerations emerging from the missiles debates of the eighties; and especially the Waldheim election, linking a fascist modernity that refuses to disappear to a neonationalism which not only remains one of the most salient features of Western politics in this decade, by no means solely in Austria, but also elides with notions of national culture and therefore with the aesthetic problems of modernity and postmodernity.

Is Liberty an "Invention of the Ruling Classes"?: Genealogy, Effacement, Autonomy

NIETZSCHE'S judgment on liberty—"an invention of the ruling classes"—is lodged in his critique of nineteenth-century liberalism, the ideological character of which was already being exposed by the rise of social movements in the context of industrial capitalism. Foucault cites Nietzsche in order to exemplify the genealogical method and to demonstrate its refusal to engage in debates over abstract principles, like "liberty"; his point is rather to show their derivation and the network of power in which their invocation is embedded. This constellation of Nietzsche and Foucault in the claim regarding liberty is an auspicious setting in which to raise questions regarding critical theory and politics and to examine the complex of attraction and incompatibility between the legacy of the genealogists and the arguments of the Frankfurt School.[1]

What does the claim mean that liberty is an "invention of the ruling classes?" Understood initially only as a statement of cultural sociology, it associates an identifiable unit of cultural material—here the notion of "liberty"—with a more or less precise social group. This kind of linkage is certainly not controversial, especially from the standpoint of the Frankfurt School; from Benjamin's work on the *Trauerspiel* or the film, through Lowenthal's essays on literary history, to Adorno's *Aesthetic Theory* the location of cultural production in heteronomous social structures has remained a central assumption of this tradition.

The point however may be that liberty is an "invention," i.e., a fiction which, as such, is counterfactual but which nevertheless is asserted by the "ruling classes" for their own pragmatic concerns. In other words: the "ruling classes," in order to continue to rule and thereby to preclude oppositional developments (which might include the establishment of a state of universal liberty), must declare the present to be characterized already by "liberty." In this reading, the enunciation of the fiction turns out to be an ideological practice, in the sense of the propagation of a false consciousness. Here too genealogy and critical theory have no particular bone to pick, although the material would be articulated in unmistakably different philosophical languages. For just as Foucault and Nietzsche may be suggesting a duplicity inherent in appeals to "liberty" by "the ruling classes," the Frankfurt School draws attention to a homologous inversion in the history of occidental rationalization. Enlightenment, not unlike "liberty," turns out to be entwined in elaborate strategies of domination, the apparent opposite of enlightenment; the first chapter of Horkheimer and Adorno's investigation of this dialectic begins by introducing Francis Bacon as an advocate of a scientific enlightenment designed to magnify the power of the state and multiply the wealth of the bourgeoisie, and it is enlightenment (or a version of it), rather than a conservative traditionalism, that leads to Auschwitz.

In fact, with regard to this particular historical material—the complicity of enlightenment as rationalization in the establishment of the modern state to which something like totalitarian power might be accruing—Foucault and Adorno seem remarkably close. In a moment, I will consider their specific responses to what they perceive as at least a tendency toward the totalizing power of the state, and I will trace their differences with respect to the related tropes of effacement and physiognomy and the problem of the mask. For now however I simply note the shared post-Weberian critique of the iron cage, i.e., the expression of anguish over the putative tendency of capitalist modernization to crush creativity and extinguish liberty.

But if "liberty is an invention of the ruling classes," is even this phrase, as an evidently libertarian critique of the iron cage, itself part of the strategy of the "ruling classes"? The writer who, like the genealogists, denounces the invocation of liberty as a ploy of a power which has no exterior can hardly claim to stand outside of power. Genealogical method, which obsessively describes the positivity of complex interrelations but eschews the abstraction inherent in even the most determinate negation, may not be able even to imagine an emphatically critical stance, at least if the method remains internally consistent; one cannot elaborate a critique of power via a Foucaultian writing that wants only to describe and trace. Yet while genealogy cannot articulate emancipation (having just reduced it to an "invention of the ruling classes"), critical theory may not fare much better. Its pessimism is proverbial (a further point of contact with genealogy), although Frankfurt School pessimism is ultimately a very specific political judgment in a precise historical setting: despair over the weakness of the left vis-à-vis fascism and the postwar consumer societies of the West. For Nietzsche and Foucault pessimism is a much more general matter: a metaphysical affirmation that amounts to a joyous celebration of metaphysical homelessness.

Instead of pursuing the matter of fictionality suggested by the term "invention" or the problem of power inherent in the adjective "ruling," I draw attention to the seemingly most innocuous aspect of the phrase, the term "classes." Foucault has chosen to cite Nietzsche at the moment where he sounds most like Marx, that is, the historical materialist Marx rather than the critic of alienation. By emphasizing this point (perversely enough, let me add), I mean to suggest that genealogy is compatible with at least this one descriptive relic of Marxist historiography, while the Frankfurt School, despite its interest in the sociology of culture, refuses to offer anything that orthodox Marxists would be happy to label a class analysis. In fact, within Western Marxism in general, one notes a gradual decline in the centrality of the category of class, especially evident if its current usage is measured against its status in the classical Marxism of the nineteenth and early twentieth centuries. One can explain this decline in the discourse on class in terms of key transformations in Western societies: the atomization of blue-collar communities, changing patterns of industrial organization, a global redivision of labor, and the rise of new social movements not easily described in terms of class.

Yet whether or not these factors significantly influenced the work of the Frankfurt School, the de-emphasis of the category of class is in fact a ramification of a dynamic immanent to its central project, its specific critique of enlightenment. For Horkheimer and Adorno, at least, enlightenment is the tyranny of the concept that reduces the wealthy multiplicity of concrete qualities to the abstract identity of formal homogeneity. Initially operating in the service of self-preservation, enlightenment allows for a control of a violent nature, experienced as life-threatening; however, the same process of enlightenment then demands the control of internal nature—the tyranny of the superego—while flattening individual particularity into the emptiness of class membership. It goes without saying that the Frankfurt School does not surrender the aspect of the Marxist legacy that criticizes social stratification, i.e., that to which the label "class society" refers. Characteristically, critical theory renames the issue "heteronomy," so as not to obscure particularity through an invocation of class similarities, but still retain a loyalty to the political project of achieving a genuine self-determination by dismantling the structures of domination, a project definitively rejected by Nietzsche's aristocratic pessimism. Consequently, for Adorno, "education for autonomy" can be a serious political goal; it is not a matter of a class vanguard seizing state power (I add: thank goodness), but it is the corollary radical move. For critical theory, autonomy as liberty is not just an "invention of the ruling classes."

For Foucault citing Nietzsche, autonomy is liberty which is just such an invention. He can cite a Nietzsche who sounds like Marx anticipating a Leninist attack on bourgeois freedoms and civil liberties as "inventions of the ruling classes" and therefore not worthy of preservation—he can do so, for what is solely at stake is power, perhaps even only state power, to which there is no outside. One can imagine different orders of power or different ruling classes, but no social relations exterior to power and certainly never a social constellation that could do without the coercive force of power relationships. Genealogy therefore describes chains of determination so ineluctable that autonomy is at best a fiction told by adolescents. For critical theory, autonomy is the project of the subject who has not yet escaped heteronomous determination but who might do so, a potential indicative of the openness of history not closed off by the idealism of an epistemic logic of genealogy. Genealogy has no interest in protecting the individual; its goal is the denunciation of the concept of the individual, like that of liberty, at a darkened noon of fiction: Foucault as Gledkin. But critical theory is the critique of the mutilated subject, and these alternative positions are most evident in microstructures of writing (to which, by the way, both the genealogists and critical theorists turn): in the portraits of the labile subject, fiction or not, and in the tropes of effacement and physiognomy.

The dialectic of enlightenment tears at Adorno's prose in two directions. As a critique of representation, it induces a conceptual rigor that precludes any immediate descriptivism, in a manner reminiscent of his own predilection for an aesthetics of abstraction and a poetry purged of the communicative language of the market: hence the melancholy self-discipline with which he refuses to engage in mimesis. Yet the same critique of representation, understood now as a critique of the process of formal rationalization, forces Adorno to undo the abstraction and to rescue particularity, paratactic chunks of mimetic sensuousness not yet dissolved into concepts. Can he do so without reverting to an empiricist reproduction of the merely given? Can he, as writer, embrace mimesis without regression to a conformist imitation of the same—an option which, at best, would only repeat the alienated status quo without calling it into question, and at worst reinforce alienation by robbing the represented material of its not-yet-rationalized particularity? The answer has to do with the construction of appearance and the access to particularity in Adorno's writing.

The construction of particular appearance: Adorno's suggestion is that the particular is never a natural substrate, somehow always given prior to any social or historical process; on the contrary, it comes to appearance only as already constructed, a compromise formation of antinomic forces. Never stable, the image emerges in the oscillation between incompatible differentials. Consider the 1962 essay "Toward a Portrait of Thomas Mann."[2] Adorno has chosen the title carefully. The initial preposition suggests an incompletion that resonates with the full historico-philosophical project: the image of the individual will not be completed before society has a human face. The choice of genre, meanwhile, the "portrait," enacts an ironic dialectic: how to paint the writer, how to render language visible? It is crucial to recall that Adorno is speaking in the context of a documentary exhibit on Thomas Mann, and, as he makes clear in the opening sentences, he considers the cognitive value of the visible document close to nil; not the merely given graven image but only its transformation into conceptual language can provide genuine insight, an argument central to debates with Walter Benjamin thirty years earlier. Similarly he announces that his remarks neither are comprehensive nor function as a window opening directly onto their subject matter; on the contrary, they are directed against another version of the merely given—the merely given, nonrational prejudices regarding the author which the photodocumentary material, left to itself, would only reinforce.

I have reviewed this framing gesture of the portrait in order to underscore two points. First, the portrayal of the individual, i.e., the appearance of the particular, must proceed (in Adorno's account) through language. From the standpoint of enlightenment rationality, Adorno is therefore denigrating the visual image devoid of any verbal moment. As I will try to show in a moment, however, such a thoroughly prelinguistic version of the image is probably only a rhetorical foil, since the image or the appearance or the iconic portrait is always embedded in language, and every face bears the marks of writing.

After refusing the icon, Adorno, second, refuses sense certainty; he commences the portraiture without making a claim to authentic referentiality. Instead of insisting on his own privileged access to the subject matter, he proceeds rather by calling into question competing accounts, designated as document or prejudice. An appeal to material of an equal epistemological status, e.g., alternative documents, prejudices, or a factual claim to have known the "real" Thomas Mann, would have little argumentative value and certainly no philosophical appeal for Adorno. Consequently he criticizes inadequate representations and examines their failings instead of immediately presenting a putatively superior countenance; he paints the portrait, so to speak, without using a model but by pursuing the contradictions in the distorted renderings. The genuine portrait emerges as a correction of distortions, a negation of negation, and not as the accurate reproduction of an original material according to a principle of verisimilitude.

The construction of the particular is therefore a matter not of a direct retrieval of empirical, authentic material but of a critique of its reified representation. Adorno is especially allergic to any effort to confuse the empirical identity of the author with the objectivity of the aesthetic work. Mann is not present in his texts as if they were only so many romans à clef, barely disguised autobiographies. He is present, on the contrary, only as the absence achieved by the rigorous application of a principle of stylization by the performance artist who was Mann. The biographical fallacy misses what Adorno regards as essential in the problem of appearance, especially aesthetic appearance: that it is not at all simply referential, that it is carried by a dialectic of denial and expression, and that it is certainly not the medium of private sentiment. The aesthetic appearance is, if anything, the locus of the disappearance of the private subject.

What links these two materials: Adorno's account of the problem of portraiture and his antibiographical description of the status of the work of art? Neither the portrait, i.e., the secondary description of the author, nor the literary text by the author provides direct access to an authentic identity. Of course identity is itself a problematic notion for Adorno, since it is always socially mediated and, moreover, mediated by an advanced capitalist society that is heteronomous and itself thoroughly mediated. I bracket these matters here, however, in order to address a different issue: the inaccessibility of identity except via the materiality of its appearance. The particular appears in a performative artificiality that conceals empirical substance through ironic simulations of presence; thus Adorno's account of Mann's self-stylization and his refusal to confuse it with the private person stand for a problem that extends far beyond this single author, i.e., the question of the mask. Appearance as a mask corresponds to identity as the tension between empirical facticity and social representation, and the mask is consequently the interface where antithetical processes cross: as the denial of the merely given, it overcomes nature by repressing it; as visible appearance, it names the particular and salvages the same mimetic substance that had just undergone repression.

For Adorno, the mask is not a cipher for an open plurality of identities, such as one might associate with a carnival or a costume party. On the contrary, it is the form that identity must assume in order to appear in repressive society, and it bears the marks of the repression while denouncing them mutely: "The radically individual features are both components in one, the factor that has been able to escape the ruling system and fortunately lives on, and the symptom of the injury by which the system maims its members."[3] Even physiognomic traits, the web of facial muscles and the involuntary habits of expression, constitute a mask, traces inscribed in the face: traces in the double sense of both a material residue of experience and the evidence which, documenting that experience in memory, records it and, possibly, articulates protest, the Ariadne thread of emancipation. Thus, as already suggested, even the image which has not yet been explicitly rendered as words is covered with writing and therefore already lexemic.

A related dialectic occurs in the final passages of the Mann essay. Adorno concludes by embellishing the portrait of the author with a reference to a material that must be regarded as the erasure of appearance: Mann's own extensive exploration of the thematics of death. This is, Adorno insists against a standard reading of Mann, no late-blooming fin-de-siècle decadence but a mortification of the reified identities of administered society; the apparent fascination with death is therefore treated as a heroic injunction never to settle for a life restricted to the categories of bourgeois pusillanimity: better dead than reduced. Death becomes the antidote to the rigor mortis of a deadening totality, and the death mask the metaphor of an appearance that both conveys the experience of repression and, by preserving the features of repressed identity, calls the repression into question.

Identity is present only in the appearance of the mask, which hides identity; only in the effacement of any original features. Indeed an invocation of such original features makes little sense, since they are accessible only in the displacement of the markings of the mask. That is to say that the mask, inscribed with the traits of physiognomy, is always subsequent to an inaccessible origin. The temporal deferral that precedes the mask indicates therefore how the mask is always a death mask, presenting the face of death, Benjamin's *facies hippocratica*, where the melancholy traces of ruination come to the fore. In "Cultural Criticism and Society," Adorno asserts that "today ideology means society as appearance," i.e., ideology is no longer merely some discrete, ideational realm of philosophy, religion, etc., but rather a grand sum of all cultural objects and practices. Yet to read society as appearance means to construct it as a "death mask," while "cultural criticism becomes social physiognomy." [4]

Consequently, this programmatic essay is replete with exhortations to locate the markings and traces of repression in the ideological appearance which is the mask of society. An attenuated freedom of the press, for example, has marked the print media indelibly with "the stigmas of that slavery [*Schandmale der Sklaverei*] within which the liberation of the mind—a false emancipation has taken place." Similarly, only in the self-seclusion of autonomy can culture "conceive of a purity from the corrupting traces [*entstellende Spuren*] of a totalitarian disorder." The more universal socialization proceeds, "the more all spiritual phenomena bear the mark of that order [*wird allen Phänomene die Marke der Ordnung aufgeprägt*]." [5]

Stigmas, traces, mark (*Schandmale, Spuren, Marke*): the appearance of society is not unblemished. It is covered with the markings of repression, the scars of the incisions that divide the social community. It is the duty of the cultural critic to decipher these markings in the "physiognomy of society," markings that have been left by the process of culture itself. For if autonomous culture emerges, as Adorno suggests, as an effort to emancipate humanity, at least in this single dimension, from the exigencies of material production and physical labor, culture is itself a matter of a brutal separation, thriving only thanks to the subordination of the laborers, and therefore always subverting its own cultural pretenses: culture is already barbarism. Without this radical *Trennung* or separation in the social world, culture would be impossible. Yet the gaping wound of this society, split asunder, is recorded in the slashes across its mask; the stigmas of culture are the signs of difference, of violent differentiation.

We have seen Adorno suggest that the appearance (as a portrait) always has the character of a lexemic mask, whose hieroglyphic inscriptions differentiate it from the merely given character of the naive image. In addition, the mask is written over with the markings which record the experience of violence. What remains to be clarified, however, is why particular identity, in whatever form, still bothers to appear at all. For particularity is inimical to the process of civilizational rationalization that quickly marginalized and suppressed the mimetic ability to approximate—rather than to homogenize—the alterity of difference. Yet, as argued in the crucial fifth "thesis on anti-Semitism," mimesis and rationalization both derive from the exigency of self-preservation, and the former survives in the mimic facility, the facial expressivity of the creature in suffering. Of course even the face is historically mediated, and the thoroughly enlightened world produces "the unmoving and unmoved countenance which, with the end of this age, finally degenerates into the 'baby face' of practical men, politicians, priests, managing directors, and racketeers."[6] Nevertheless, atavistic residues of human expressivity remain, an "undisciplined mimicry [which] is the brand [Brandzeichen] of the old form of domination, engraved in the living substance of the dominated and passed down by a process of unconscious imitation in infancy from generation to generation." Expressivity as the marking in the mask is the mimetic reproduction of the mortal danger which the creature would overcome through imitation, playing dead, or appease through lamentation: "Expressiveness is the painful echo of a superior power, of force, voiced in a complaint [Klage]."[7] The primal scene of critical theory is one of force as domination and a simultaneous suffering that names it—with the cry, the magic word, the concept—to make it go away.

The vital claim of critical theory is thus not simply that society is crisscrossed with lines of power and structures of domination; such a claim is hardly original and is fully compatible with genealogy and other conservative accounts that insist on defending the power structures of institutional authority. The point is rather that extraordinarily diverse human activities, from the work of art to the grimace of pain, record the experience of violence and suffering, and by recording it point it out and thereby point to its end. Appearance is the vessel of this expression and therefore the agency of criticism: "In the death struggle of the creature, at the opposite pole from freedom, freedom . . . shines out irresistibly as the thwarted destiny of matter [die durchkreuzte Bestimmung der Materie]."[8] The suffering creature, its mask distorted by pain, gives expression, now as a subject, to the suffering and calls the pain into question. It is not at all the ruling classes who invent liberty but the victim who is able to thwart or at least to articulate the wish to thwart the destiny of matter. Thwart: the German is *durchkreuzen,* cross out; freedom is heteronomy under erasure.

No, scratch that. It is by no means an erasure as an effacement that obliterates the marks of particularity. On the contrary, matter, as it initially exists in its sheer determinacy (*Bestimmung*), is augmented with the incremental mark, crossed through but not crossed out, written over but not wiped clean. The mark in matter negates the immutability of its destiny and emancipates it, as if the mark of the cross had set it free, free at least to give expression to its suffering and to anticipate bringing suffering to an end. And this *x* marks the spot of the crucial distinction between critical theory and genealogy, prior, I suggest, to the many secondary issues such as specificity, consensus, etc.: is liberty the "invention of the ruling classes," or is freedom the mournful expression of the suffering creature?

This political distinction is inscribed in the contrasting accounts of the image. For Adorno, the portrait emerges in the tension between empirical experience and its conceptualization; it combines mimetic and rational components simultaneously, or, in another terminology: imaginary and symbolic dimensions, staging and preserving their unresolved conflicts. The image is covered with writing which the cultural critic, as physiognomist, apperceives and deciphers. As a mask, the portrait conceals and defends, while announcing and expressing. For Foucault, the mask has a different status. It indicates the radical absence of a genuine identity and the constant possibility of the multiplicity of personae. Subjectivity, always a construction of contingent power structures, cannot define itself by appealing to an origin, since history, including biography, begins not with an origin but with radical disparity. "The new historian, the genealogist," therefore can appreciate the eclectic costumes provided by traditional historicism: "He will not be too serious to enjoy it; on the contrary, he will push the masquerade to its limit and prepare the great carnival of time where masks are constantly reappearing." Because no identity is fixed, the masks of "Friedrich von Hohenstaufen, Caesar, Jesus, Dionysus, and possibly Zarathustra" become interchangeable and ought constantly to be available: a shopping mall pluralism of male fantasy costumes.[9]

Similarly, because there is no original identity of the individual, it makes no sense to thematize the individual's freedom. "The concept of liberty is an 'invention of the ruling classes' and not fundamental

to man's nature or at the root of his attachment to being and truth."
Obviously polemicizing against Enlightenment accounts of human
rights, Foucault rejects notions of individual liberty and opts instead
for the free play of identity putatively offered by the rotation of masks.
One can certainly change one's roles often, Foucault suggests, but one
can never escape role playing in order to return to one's genuine identity and thereby become something liberals used to call "free." For
"genuine identity," in the sense of an autonomous subject not subjugated by external domination, is probably, according to Foucault, like
liberty an "invention of the ruling classes." Hence Foucault's conformist exhortation to a "return to masks." Hence the mandated applause
for a "dispersion of man." And hence the trope of the final sentence
of *The Order of Things:* "If those arrangements were to disappear as
they appeared, if some event of which we can at the moment do no
more than sense the possibility . . . were to cause them to crumble,
. . . then one can certainly wager that man would be erased, like a face
drawn in sand at the edge of the sea." [10]

Foucault's effacement is an erasure; he envisions the full obliteration of the face and the end of man. Unlike Adorno, for whom the
face is a mask that conveys the experience of suffering, Foucault treats
the face as merely another particular mask constructed by discursive
constellations and derived from epistemic structures prior to any experience. The mask consequently lacks any expressive character; indeed the question of expression becomes moot after the tidal liquidation of the subject. Given its thorough contingency, the mask is linked
to an imagery of perpetual change; the sea can erase one face in order
to make room for another, another drawing in the sand, equally arbitrary and equally ephemeral. What is lost is the Adornian construction of the face as a palimpsest, bearing the marks of its own history,
never fully erased and therefore the foundation of a complex autonomy. What is also lost is the plausibility of an emancipatory project;
one may or may not concede such a plausibility, but one cannot convincingly argue that genealogy and emancipation are compatible. This
claim alone by no means disproves genealogy, but it does cast a doubt
on the viability of a leftist appropriation of Foucault.

Effacement and physiognomy—no matter how great the differences
between the treatments by Adorno and Foucault, one must nevertheless note a crucial similarity. Both construct the face (antithetically of
course) and subject it to particular practices (physiognomical scrutiny,
watery erasure) in order to pursue a common goal: the articulation of

a critique of excessively rigid identity structures. Adorno calls on the cultural critic to read the writing already inscribed in the face and extrapolate its encoded criticisms of an administered society; Foucault looks forward to wiping away the inherited structure of identity and replacing it with a "masquerade," the open universality of masks. Both display an anxiety regarding the possible restriction of diversity and disparity. In this sense, both are writing "after Auschwitz," i.e., both construct the portrait (as the appearance of identity) with reference to the twentieth-century experiences of totalitarianism. Reading the face for Adorno like erasing the face for Foucault is a gesture directed against the expansive power of the rationalized state, in particular against the power of the fascist state which looms on the horizon of the two accounts of modernization. And it is precisely toward their differing responses to fascism, the different accounts of Auschwitz, that the tropic divergences of the accounts of effacement and physiognomy point.

In other words, the accounts of effacement and physiognomy in Adorno and Foucault turn out to be homologous, despite major differences, insofar as both represent responses to the trauma of the totalitarian state and its ability to obliterate. Indeed only once one recognizes this genetic similarity does the difference between the two models become clear. Moreover it is not surprising that it is precisely this material with which Ernst Jünger elaborates the project of fascist modernism.

Jünger lodges his political program in facial accounts; the teary-eyed bourgeois of the bygone era of interiority has been displaced by the modern type, whose face is described as follows: "It has become more metallic, its surface is galvanized, the bone structure is evident, and the traits are clear and tense. The gaze is steady and fixed, trained on objects moving at high velocities. It is the face of a race that has begun to develop in the peculiar demands of a new landscape, where one is represented neither as a person nor as an individual but as a type." Fascism is the imperious insistence on the end of bourgeois subjectivity: Jünger's modern type has a face wiped clean of any residual nuance or particular features, hidden by a mask that reveals nothing except the compulsion to conceal. Of course precisely that obsession, the compulsive concealing, is a symptom of repression, but Jünger does not name it as such; for his point is that the modern worker-soldier with the metallic face is no subject and shows no expression and no distinguishing facial features. How different from this description is the account of the enemy, the advocates of an autonomy aesthetics whom Jünger regards as a treasonous threat to the stability of the total state: "Therefore in Germany one meets this parasitic art world [*schmarotzender Artistentum*] in close connection with all those forces on whom a hidden or overt treasonous character is written right across their faces."[11]

Jünger goes on to designate these figures as heretics and to predict—he is writing in 1932—that they will soon become victims of an emergent "Dominican zeal." This is rich material to decipher and will be treated extensively in Chapter 6, below. For now only one facet matters, the figures whose "character is written right across their faces." If it is the association with writing that renders the figures treasonous, then the writing burned into the face as *Brandzeichen* is the proleptic punishment, an excruciating demonstration of the materiality of language to the advocates of aesthetic autonomy. Meanwhile it is the writing itself which renders the victims identifiable and available to persecution, just as, from the standpoint of the victim, the writing remains a carrier of memory and a reservoir of potential protest. Any distinctive feature becomes the trace of guilt: the mark of Cain and, simultaneously, a death warrant. Marked by writing as victims, the figures of writing, Jünger promises, will be wiped away by the coming Dominican zeal.

Fascism is the absolute effacement of the victim and, in metonymic conjuncture, the irrevocable disappearance of the body: in the camps, in the gulag, in the modern battlefield. It is the trauma to which both Adorno and Foucault respond in their critiques of the totalitarian state, but their facial tropes, measured against Jünger's treasonous countenance, now display crucial differences. Attacking the markings in the face, Jünger enacts the fascist anxiety that a symbolic order might disrupt the perpetual imaginary of the prelinguistic community of the people; the image, therefore, must be wiped clean of marks and memory. Inverting the fascist practice, Adorno foregrounds precisely these marks, without which the mimetic specificity of the imaginary would remain inaccessible and through which, alone, a symbolic protest might be voiced. For critical theory, the linguistic turn means preserving the subject's speech as *Mündigkeit* or autonomy and writing as documentation of the violence which real subjects endure. In contrast to this redemptive orthography is Foucault's radicalization of the fascist gesture of effacement: it is not at all his point to save the specificity of the suffering creature and its expressive facility but rather to recognize even the most specific particularity as a discursive inter-section and therefore as fully constructed, that is to say written, and consequently susceptible to erasure. Therefore because everything, as mask, might be erased, and because any position, as a function of discourse, is already written, any insistence on the permanence (or naturalism or authenticity) of a particular figure constitutes a hypos-tasis of writing and, hence, a Jacobin terror of the symbolic. Fearful of such a totalitarian resolution, Foucault invokes the sea, figure of the sublime, Freud's antirational oceanic feeling, to wash away the face. Terrified of a radical revolution, Foucault in Paris looks toward the sea, Nelson at Trafalgar, to sweep away the temple of reason and the tablets of the law.

The antinomic relationship between genealogy and critical theory today is an enactment of these divergent responses to fascism, the suc-cessful counterrevolution that still remains the defining experience for European intellectuals, and this divergence is already inscribed within fascism itself. Even for the antidialectician Jünger, the mark "written right across the face" implies the dialectic of the mask. It is crime and punishment in one: sign of particularization and license for particular persecution. Adorno resists that persecution that would erase and ob-literate; he preserves the mark as mnemic trace. Foucault subverts that persecution, which he reads—in contrast to Adorno—as inscriptive and discursive, by relying on an oceanic amnesia to erase the language which in his own account drew the face. To put a fine point on it: Adorno constantly reconfronts fascism in a struggle to define the sta-tus of the trace—hold that line. Foucault tries to outwit fascism by imitating it: even the erasers must be erased. But if this account holds, then common knowledge regarding the current critical landscape needs massive revision, since Foucault, despite himself, turns out to be the practitioner of a conservative—conservative because it only re-peats—double negation, while Adorno, in violation of his own ex-plicit teleological pronouncements, ends up staging in his writing an open agonistics that one may well label dialectic but which lack any synthetic closure.

Refusing to participate in the gleeful euthenasia on the putatively senile bourgeois subject, critical theory remembers a future in which subjects might begin to appear for the first time. This is the one line that critical theory cannot cross. Because fascism annihilates individ-uals on a mass scale, Foucault sacrifices the subject, once and for all. Because fascism demonstrates the coercive efficacy of power, Foucault investigates the relations of power to which there is no outside. Because of the success of power, there is no room left for freedom, and liberty turns out to be an "invention of the ruling classes." Auschwitz renders humanism implausible: ergo the "end of man." Adorno argues otherwise. Human experience is never absolutely indelible, but the ability to remember is not a casual fiction either. "Every reification is a forgetting"; lamentation, recalling the dead, shatters the optical illusion of the present: the epitaph as radical slogan. The sign, the record of violent power—the writing in the face, the scar, the tattoo, the castration—marks it, remembers it, and, the labor of enlightenment, thwarts the brute force of a destiny blind in the excessive glow of power.

CHAPTER TWO

The Aestheticization of Politics: Walter Benjamin on Fascism and the Avant-garde

"THE Italy of our ancestors has, as we know, since the railroads opened it up for traffic, become one of the least known countries of Europe."[1] When Rudolf Borchardt, friend of Stefan George, mentor of Hugo von Hofmannsthal, and translator of Dante, commences his 1907 essay on the Italian villa with this authoritative complaint, he gives voice to the conservative hostility to modernization that frequently accompanied the articulation of modernist cultural programs. An ancestral Italy, Goethe's Italy, is reinvoked as a measure with which to decry the misperception of the landscape by the modern bourgeois tourist, settled comfortably in a train, eager for stereotypical aesthetic experiences and loaded down with the intellectual baggage of the nineteenth century: liberalism, humanism, and an optimistic faith in progress. Borchardt's concern is less with an objective transformation of Italian reality in the wake of capitalism and technology than with the inability of the German tourist, blinded by an idealist veneration of high culture and trapped by a "conspiracy of railroad administrations, Swiss and German hotel owners, tourist industries, tourist cities, tourist guides with Baedeker in the lead," to recognize the authentic reality of Italy and its legitimate forms of expression, foremost among which he ranks the villa.[2] For the traveler, locked in a speeding railway car, will usually make do with a fleeting glimpse of the rural homes and will barely recall the dwellings standing gracefully among the cypresses of San Miniato or mixed with the "lily and ivory colors of death on the mountainous ridge of Fiesole in the evening."[3] In rare cases, the exceptional tourist may visit a famous villa of the Medici nearby, Poggio a Caiano or Careggiana, but—Borchardt is no friend of the *Bildungsbürger* and culture-vulturism—he will do so as if the villa were a museum and can only be disappointed that the "frescos are only by Pontormo and the fountains only by Tacca or Tribolo." In any case, the most noteworthy villas remain undiscovered, beyond the scope of "the tourist, this miserable modern type of traveler in Italy":

27

Who then has seen Artimino, the seat of the Passerini, hours
uphill from the empty Signa, this petrified dream of mountainous isolation fit for a king, with the treetops of protective gar-
dens all around the silent spell? Who knows the villa of Marlia
with its melancholy of wild blossoms and the evil, steep laurels,
the confusion of crumbling terraces and heavy waterfalls, tum-
bling insatiably to their death from the bowls and cornucopia
of bursting tritons?

The railway has brought the German tourist, Borchardt's cipher of
bad modernity, to Italy, but it cannot make him see. The bourgeois
vision is apparently caught between a fetishization of material progress and a reverence for cultural objects, trains and frescos, technology
and museums, the site of both of which is the city. Borchardt may
well couch his argument in a rhetoric of archconservatism and borrow the archaic imagery of romanticism (*königliche Bergeinsamkeit*
[mountainous isolation fit for a king]), but he does so in order to
construct a specifically modernist argument against the bourgeois modernity of the city, and its locus will be the rural villa where agricultural economy and patriarchal architecture converge in an explicit
expression of power. Against the tourist's desire for beauty, he postu-
lates an aesthetic exigency of form, rooted in the soil and tradition,
that has as little in common with a subjectivist culture as does the villa
with a grand hotel.

Like D. H. Lawrence, to whom I will turn in a moment, Borchardt
articulates a cultural criticism of the present by conjuring up an image
of a distant past. This reactionary pose however is merely the medium
for an innovative transformation of the aesthetic project (and it is
therefore proper to discuss this cultural criticism as one version of a
much broader early twentieth-century modernism).[4] The bourgeois institution of art, formulated systematically around the end of the eighteenth century, entailed a set of conventions and expectations defining
the aesthetic object as autonomous (i.e., separate from the material
practice of everyday life); individual (produced and received by isolated subjects); and emancipatory (participating in a historico-philosophical teleology leading potentially to a secular redemption via an
"aesthetic education").[5] By the end of the nineteenth century, the aesthetics of autonomy faced various and increasingly vociferous critiques; in Borchardt's essay, the attack on autonomy takes shape as
the antinomy of culture and form. The liberal tourist, still indebted to

traditional bourgeois assumptions, visits museums in search of individual works of art characterized as beautiful, while Borchardt insists on the superiority of the villa which combines the features of material functionality (it plays a role in the agricultural economy) and ruthlessly rigorous form (it does not try to be "beautiful"). Particularly this second aspect, the formal imperative, fascinates Borchardt; he sets it as a norm and associates it with the desiderata of order and hierarchy which, he suggests, have disappeared in the liberal chaos of the German north. The villa is the victory of form over chaos, power over nature. It is attractive and desirable not, as the tourist might believe, because of some aesthetic intent; rather it becomes aesthetic precisely because of its organic relationship with the landscape and the power manifested in its form:

> The villa is historically one with its landscape and therefore—
> and only therefore—is it also aesthetic. Like a mountain forest
> with a mountain, the villa has shared its fate organically with
> its landscape for generations of continuity and has ruled it and
> formed it, instead of being formed and modeled after it.[6]

If this passage makes explicit the proximity of form and domination (*beherrscht* [ruled]) with regard to nature, Borchardt elsewhere makes the relationship between the aesthetic project and social order equally clear. The priorization of architectural form goes hand in hand with an appreciation for stable social structures, in particular the hierarchy of landowners and peasants, *poderi*. Indeed Italy, Borchardt's true Italy, is marked by the continued viability of its "polar" social ordering, again a contrast to the ominous (and certainly only imagined) egalitarianism of the modernized *Reich* in the north.[7]

In "Villa," Borchardt attempts to teach his reader a new vision that valorizes a nonautonomous art as the practical expression of power, stripped of any commitments to emancipation; he subjects the Italian landscape to an aestheticization not in order to find beauty but, on the contrary, to preserve order. More precisely, it is not the landscape itself but the vision of the landscape which Borchardt reconstitutes in terms of an abstract valorization of form, and this formal order in turn becomes the normative ideal that the aestheticized perception can project and rediscover in Italy. Borchardt therefore breaks with traditional nineteenth-century bourgeois culture in a dual fashion: he rejects the autonomous work and replaces it with an aestheticization of social relations, and he rejects the liberal ideal of progress in the name of a constant stability. This restructuring of the ideological vision suggests that a viable legitimation of the social order could no longer rely solely on the inherited conservatism of traditional privilege but was forced to appropriate a particular aesthetic terminology, the discourse of aestheticism, in order to defend the irrational principle of unquestionable form; the watchwords of aestheticism are lifted out of the aesthetic discourse and become the slogans of a political project.

In order to demonstrate how Borchardt is part of a wide current in early twentieth-century thought, let me point briefly to a passage written some two decades later by an author whose concerns are otherwise hardly compatible with Borchardt's highbrow elitism. Near the center of *Lady Chatterley's Lover,* Lawrence has his heroine travel through an industrial terrain which one can read as the inverse of Borchardt's Tuscany, i.e., the negative image that thrives on the same antinomy of aesthetic form and modern disorder:

> The utter negation of natural beauty, the utter negation of the gladness of life, the utter absence of the instinct for shapely beauty which every bird and beast has, the utter death of the human intuitive faculty was appalling. . . .
>
> Tevershall! That was Tevershall! Merrie England! Shakespeare's England! No, but the England of today. . . .
>
> The miner's cottages, blackened, stood flush on the pavements, with that intimacy and smallness of colliers' dwellings over a hundred years old. They lined all the way. The road had become a street, and as you sank, you forgot instantly the open, rolling country where the castles and big [Elizabethan] houses still dominated, but like ghosts.[8]

Borchardt's tourist had no eye for Goethe's Italy; for Lawrence, Shakespeare's England has been obscured by industrial capitalism. Not only do both modern authors mobilize premodern cultural figures in order to pursue parallel political denunciations of social modernity; their conservatisms intersect insofar as it is the railway bourgeois of Borchardt who, unable to appreciate the formal aesthetic of the villa, pursues a venally conceived progress, the spatial institutionalization of which leads to Lawrence's Tevershall and the marginalization and destruction of the mansions of tradition, corresponding of course to the similar architectural objects that had not even been seen in Italy. Goethe and Shakespeare, the villas and the Elizabethan houses—Lawrence may claim that soot obscures the past but in these texts it is an imagery of art and architecture that obscures the political practice, the goal of which is the return to a lost origin in which form and life are identical.

There are certainly crucial differences between the particular strategies and general projects of Borchardt and Lawrence. Assuming an immutable Italy, Borchardt consequently directs his attention to failures of perception and attempts to enact a subjective regeneration, i.e., a transformation of vision in order to enable the viewer to recognize formal coherence. For Lawrence, on the other hand, the crisis is not merely a matter of consciousness or an inadequate perception of sensuous reality but rather the particular character of reality itself, its sensuous desiccation, the destruction of nature and the loss of beauty. His project therefore takes shape as an objective regeneration of a lost substance which is defined not like Borchardt's form but in terms of a primal glow, an auratic magic, that manages to redeem the atomistic individuals of capitalist alienation in a unity that is both biological and divine. Only an authentic, phallic sexuality, Lawrence argues, ensures humanity's integration in the natural cosmos, the organic rhythms of which were echoed in the genuine traditions of the people. These multiple interconnections have however been destroyed by modernization—Protestantism, capitalism, and science—and with them the significance of circumambient nature has disappeared:

> "Knowledge" has killed the sun, making it a ball of gas, with spots; "knowledge" has killed the moon, it is a dead little earth fretted with extinct craters as with smallpox; the machine has killed the earth for us, making it a surface, more or less bumpy, that you travel over. How, out of all this, are we to get back the grand orbs of the soul's heavens, that fill us with unspeakable joy? How are we to get back Apollo, and Attis, Demeter, Persephone and the halls of Dis? How even to see the star Hesperus or Betelgeuse? [9]

The recovery of an auratic intersubjectivity with nature, which Lawrence presents here in the terms of a mythic cosmos, entails the regeneration of an original knowledge that has been occluded by the superficial "knowledge" of science and enlightenment. Such a project relies on objective techniques capable of escaping the limits imposed by modernity: Mellors' sexual versatility and, equally crucial, Lawrence's redefinition of the novel form. Others have treated Connie like a "person," but only with Mellors does she feel herself addressed as a "woman." The same contradiction between social material and a biological sphere designated as fundamental and auratic reappears in the interpolated aesthetic discussion. Rejecting the conventional form of the novel, which is treated as little more than vicious gossip, the narrator insists that "the novel, properly handled," can surpass the limits of a discourse of social description and reach "the most secret places of life: for it is in the *passional* secret places of life, above all, that the tide of sensitive awareness needs to ebb and flow, cleansing and freshening." [10] In both cases—the representations of sexuality and the programmatic definition of the literary form—Lawrence substitutes for the material of social relations an invocation of an original aesthetic aura. The repressive character of this substitution is evident not only in the misogynist depiction of the heroine but in the extensive denial of any specifically social dimension where political conflict might take place.[11] For politics are henceforth presented as indistinguishable from an aesthetic rejuvenation.

Lawrence pursues an objective regeneration of an original state and the invocation of an aesthetic aura; Borchardt undertakes a subjective regeneration of vision and the valorization of absolute form. Despite these differences however both Lawrence and Borchardt mobilize aesthetic material—for Lawrence aura, for Borchardt form—as substitutes for an explicitly political discussion, or, better: they try to resolve the political tensions of modernity through a practice of denial and aestheticization. Art becomes the means through which the discontents in contemporary civilization are to be answered—or stifled, since each process of substitution and aestheticization is clearly a matter of repression and the forced reconciliation of social contradictions. What Lawrence and Borchardt ultimately share then is a project of repression based on what Walter Benjamin would later call an "aestheticization of politics." This proximity is noteworthy, since, as I have already pointed out, the two have otherwise little in common. Yet Borchardt's supercilious neoclassicism and Lawrence's proletarian neoromanticism respond to the same set of questions that emerged from Max Weber's designations of occidental rationality and modernization: in the context of a separation of competing value spheres, is a coherent structure of meaning possible? Given the dissolution of traditional patterns of legitimate authority, is an intersubjective system of belief compatible with the exigencies of scientific rationalization? Weber's pessimism is well known; the only escape from the "iron cage" of atomistic individuality and capitalist rationality entails an exogenous intervention of "new prophets" with a charismatic message ultimately hostile to the character of Western modernity, a solution which Weber himself of course consistently rejected.[12] Nevertheless the models of Borchardt and Lawrence can be regarded as alternative answers to the same Weberian problematic. At this point it is interesting to note how both figures can be placed on the periphery of Weber's close circle: Lawrence via his connection to the von Richthofen sisters and Borchardt through his relationship to George with whom Weber occasionally met in Heidelberg.[13] More germane however is the shared character of their answers: the hypostatization of art as a solution to the shattered totality of modernity.

This strategic (but ultimately highly problematic) attempt to force art to assume a totalizing function vis-à-vis the fragmentary present was identified by a member of Weber's inner group, Georg Lukács, at a crucial point in his *Theory of the Novel*:

> Henceforth, any resurrection of the Greek world is a more or less conscious hypostasy of aesthetics into metaphysics—a violence done to the essence of everything that lies outside the sphere of art, and a desire to destroy it; an attempt to forget that art is only one sphere among many, and that the very disintegration and inadequacy of the world is the precondition for the existence of art and its becoming conscious. . . . A totality that can be simply accepted is no longer given to the forms of art: therefore they must either narrow down and volatilise whatever has to be given form to the point where they can encompass it, or else they must show polemically the impossibility of achieving their necessary object and the inner nullity of their own means. And in this case they carry the fragmentary nature of the world's structure into the world of forms.[14]

Lukács proceeds to describe the consequences of the lack of totality in the no-longer-closed civilization of modernity for the constitution of the work of art. He provides a basis for a specifically modernist aesthetic that can privilege contradiction, polyphony, and irony against the terms of classicist form. At the start of this passage, however, he rejects the alternative to carrying "the fragmentary nature of the world's structure into the world of forms," i.e., appealing to the world of forms—aesthetics—as a model of a coherence that might be projected onto the fragmentary world. Such a strategy would ascribe to art a priority that it cannot legitimately claim for itself as merely one among several competing spheres of differentiated social activity. That priority would also necessarily have a repressive character, since it would entail an imposition of an aesthetic rationality onto the heterogeneous domains of politics, economics, religion, etc. Clearly what Lukács rejects here is precisely what Lawrence and Borchardt attempt, insofar as each tries to replace an elaboration of sociopolitical dissension (for Borchardt the class conflicts in the Italian countryside, for Lawrence the social costs of capitalist industrialization) with various aesthetic discourses. In both cases, the formation of ideology is not simply artificial, i.e., a socially necessary distortion of real social relations; instead these early-twentieth-century ideological projects characteristically include the emphatic aestheticization of the artifice of ideology, the priorization of art, which Lukács subjects to a Weberian critique as a transgression against the principle of modernization. Benjamin's discussion of the same priorization, to which I now turn, will preserve certain elements of Lukács's discussion, especially the insistence on the repressive moment in an "aestheticization of politics," but the argument will no longer be cast in the Weberian terms of an ineluctable separation of value spheres.

In his seminal essay "The Work of Art in the Age of Mechanical Reproduction" (1936), Benjamin conflates his assumptions regarding aesthetic production and reception, derived from a neoromanticist vitalism and German-Jewish mysticism and increasingly colored by an idiosyncratic Marxism, with a diachronic and dualistically structured account of the historical process of modernization. His goal is the defense of exoteric art forms, in particular the cinema, to which he ascribes an emancipatory potential and which he implicitly relates to features of the Soviet Russian *Proletkult* and French surrealism. This program of an avant-gardist modernism that remains open to popular reception represents the alternative within the neo-Marxism of the Frankfurt School to the classic position of Theodor Adorno, whose suspicion of popular forms in capitalist culture generally led to the canonization of the esoteric modernism of figures like Schoenberg and Beckett; in their works a radical hermeticism purportedly provided the possibility of a thorough critique of alienation and reification.[15]

Benjamin's exploration of the potentials of contemporary popular forms was based on a considerably more optimistic view of the process of modernization than was held by Adorno (or by Benjamin himself a few years later in his "Theses on the Philosophy of History"). The description of the work of art depends on a historical periodization that contrasts an early phase of religion and primitive technology with a later, secular modernity of science and industry. In the premodern context, the work of art, initially an object of cult, always retains a residual sacred character; it has an aura that thrives on the singularity of the work of art and the isolation of the single recipient. In contemporary modernity, culture becomes increasingly profane, while the industrial production of art (film) and its mass reception displace the erstwhile individual actors with collective agents. "That which withers in the age of mechanical reproduction is the aura of the work of art," and this transformation, the ultimate emancipation of art from its cultic origin, emancipates the recipient as well;[16] whereas the auratic work of art demanded a passive contemplation that subdued the irrational individual viewer, the postauratic work permits the collective recipient to adopt a critical and rational stance.

Benjamin's apparently unbroken confidence in technological progress in general and the emancipatory force of the cinema in particular seems odd and no longer tenable fifty years later. One can of course attempt to relativize his judgment by recalling the formal characteristics of film in the twenties and thirties when jump cuts and montage (the crucial category for the aesthetics of left-wing modernism) were much more common than in the Hollywood narrative films that have come to dominate the industry.[17] It is similarly useful to consider the social composition of the audience in the early years of the cinema; Benjamin's constellation of a self-consciously proletarian public appreciating an avant-garde form linked to technological progress could represent a plausible alternative to the bourgeois aesthetic culture of museums and novels.[18] Nevertheless the close reader of the essay will recognize that Benjamin does not insist that the deauraticization of art in the wake of modernization is inexorable; it is only a potential consequence, the revolutionary ramifications of which provoke a reactionary response in both art and politics. In art the collapse of the aura of the actor compels the industry to engage in "an artifical build-up of the 'personality' outside of the studio," i.e., the production of film "stars";[19] in politics, the emergence of the masses as a self-conscious force threatens the anachronistic character of class relations in capitalism. At this point in the argument the discussion of the transformation of the modernized work of art turns into an analysis of fascism.

In the epilogue of the essay, Benjamin politicizes his own aesthetic discussion; the emancipatory potential of social modernization, so he argues, is blocked by fascism which, in a manner reminiscent of the strategies of Borchardt and Lawrence, mobilizes aesthetic categories in order to impede the dissolution of traditional social order. Benjamin documents his claim with an extended quotation from an unidentified manifesto of Marinetti which insists on the beauty of war, allegedly a reference to the invasion of Ethiopia. As useful as the citation is for Benjamin's argument, it is important to note that it is rather exceptional within his overall oeuvre. Nowhere else does he concern himself with the specificity of Italian fascism or with Marinetti. Furthermore, textual evidence suggests that the quotation was borrowed from a French translation and not from an original Italian text.[20] I point this out in order to suggest that the evaluation of fascism at the conclusion of "The Work of Art in the Age of Mechanical Reproduction" is based less on extensive examinations of the Italian culture and politics of the thirties than on the exigencies of Benjamin's argument, his own cultural commitments, and, perhaps, some characteristic assumptions of German antifascist political thought.

Before mustering the passage from Marinetti, Benjamin begins the epilogue with a concise characterization of fascism that combines three independent features: (1) the context of industrial modernization and its social corollaries; (2) the association with capitalist property structures; and (3) the strategy of aestheticization. The first two are of course compatible with standard orthodox Marxist accounts of fascism; the third however is not. When the communist journalist Alfred Kurella entitled his denunciation of fascist Italy *Mussolini without a Mask* (1931), he was drawing on an Enlightenment rhetoric directed against the mendacious character of fascist self-representation, but he did not intend to suggest anything more than a metaphoric relationship between fascist politics and an aesthetic discourse.[21] For Benjamin, on the other hand, the analysis of fascism relies on the emphatic claim of a convergence of aesthetic and political developments; neither the history of aura nor the history of class conflict is dispensable.

For Weber, social modernization implies an increasingly radical separation of value spheres that renders bourgeois culture more and more labile; for Benjamin, it replaces the bourgeois with a new social type, the proletarian, who is the carrier of new cultural forms (in particular, new modes of aesthetic reception) and who is furthermore amenable to collective practices (unlike the essentially individualist bourgeois) and a collectivist economy. Thus the epilogue commences with the claim that "the growing proletarianization of modern man and the increasing formation of masses are two aspects of the same process."[22] The foregrounded distinction between "proletarianization" and "formation of masses" is crucial for the subsequent description of fascism. For fascism, in Benjamin's account, carries out a precarious balancing act, accepting a "proletarian," i.e., postbourgeois and postindividual culture, while endeavoring to inhibit the collectivist claims of the "masses." Therefore he continues, "Fascism attempts to organize the newly created proletarian masses without affecting the property structure which the masses strive to eliminate." The politics of nineteenth-century liberalism had initially positioned the bourgeois entrepreneur as the revolutionary antagonist opposed to aristocratic privilege, but the emergence of an industrial proletariat eventually produced a challenge to that liberalism from "below."[23] Benjamin contends that fascism abandons the politics of the liberal bourgeois era, an individualist politics, while defending the bourgeois principle of private property against the collectivist desires of the "masses." All this of course does not diverge significantly from an orthodox Marxist class analysis of political motivation. In the following sentences however he describes the central mechanism of fascist politics, aestheticization:

> Fascism sees its salvation in giving these masses not their right, but instead a chance to express themselves. The masses have a right to change property relations; Fascism seeks to give them an expression while preserving property. The logical result of Fascism is the introduction of aesthetics into political life. The violation of the masses, whom Fascism, with its *Führer* cult, forces to their knees, has its counterpart in the violation of an apparatus which is pressed into the production of ritual values.

The claim that the aestheticization of politics is the "logical result of Fascism" is based on the preceding opposition between expression (*Ausdruck*) and right (*Recht*), corresponding to form and law, i.e., aesthetics and justice. For Benjamin, fascism opposes justice with aesthetics, as is made unmistakably clear in the final paragraph where he ascribes to fascism the slogan *"Fiat ars—pereat mundus,"* a telling transformation of the motto of Ferdinand I, *"Fiat iustitia et pereat mundus."* The characterization of art as incompatible with justice derives from Benjamin's early thought, before his political radicalization, where the symbolic work of art as an organic imitation of fallen nature is implicated in a sinful disregard of divine justice. Only a melancholy insistence on the lack of redemption might anticipate a messianic intervention, the religious category which always lurks behind the later Benjamin's notion of revolution. An aesthetic representation of this-worldly completeness however remains deaf to a redemptive potential. While the symbolic work of art carries a truth content within itself, it is obscured by aesthetic formation, and the duty of the critic is therefore the "mortification of the work" in order to free the truth—the expression of justice—from aesthetic form.[24]

Benjamin's iconoclastic distrust of aesthetic form explains in part his preference for fragmentary, open genres: the German *Trauerspiel* of the baroque as well as the avant-gardist valorization of montage. His critique of fascism transfers his aesthetic judgment into the political realm; the closed order of the organic work of art, which he regards as a deception that imposes an enervated passivity on the bourgeois recipient, is disassociated from a specifically aesthetic realm (e.g., the museum) and transplanted into a political practice that demands however the same passivity. The traditional sphere of autonomous art has grown obsolete in a "proletarian" context, but the associated modes of behavior—silence, inaction, submission—are reorganized around the fascist state and the natural consequence of its politics, war, which therefore can be regarded as the fascist work of art:

> "*Fiat ars—pereat mundus,*" says Fascism, and, as Marinetti
> admits, expects war to supply the artistic gratification of a
> sense perception that has been changed by technology. This is
> evidently the consummation of "*l'art pour l'art.*" Mankind,
> which in Homer's time was an object of contemplation for the
> Olympian gods, now is one for itself. Its self-alienation has
> reached such a degree that it can experience its own destruction
> as an aesthetic pleasure of the first order. This is the situation
> of politics which Fascism is rendering aesthetic. Communism
> responds by politicizing art.[25]

A politicization of art, Benjamin's progressive alternative to fascism, in no way suggests that art must manifest thematic tendentiousness. On the contrary, within the context of his broader aesthetics, it can only mean an attack on the autonomous work of bourgeois culture, an extension of the avant-gardist campaign of the dadaists (and, for that matter, the futurists as well). In place of the auratic artwork, with its isolated and pacified recipient lost in contemplation, Benjamin proposes a postauratic model that would convene a collective recipient (the "masses") endowed with an active and critical character. This notion of a politicized art, despite its association with "communism," therefore has little in common with the contemporary program for a socialist realism, a model in which inherited bourgeois forms were appropriated and allegedly filled with a new political message. For Benjamin, the political substance has much less to do with the explicit message than with the technical character of the form and the corollary structure of reception. Similarly his critique of fascism does not address the likely ideological themes—nationalism, mythic irrationalism, biologistic racism—but rather the structure of communicative relationships within the political interaction. Fascist politics mobilize the masses and silence them at the same time, for the state claims for itself an untouchable self-containment that permits the public only the same powerless acceptance and submission with which it had previously encountered the autonomous work of art. In this sense, the fascist state and the war it incites are the legitimate heirs of the aestheticism of *l'art pour l'art*—not because aestheticism anticipated fascism in any of its ideological claims but because they are both constructed in terms of a principled refusal to allow any intersubjective communication. Prohibiting criticism, right, and justice, the fascist state and absolute art valorize submission and spectacle.

Benjamin's association of fascist politics with a particular constitution of aesthetic experience as *Ausdruck* does represent a logical extension of his own earlier theoretical paradigms, and "The Work of Art in the Age of Mechanical Reproduction" is by no means the sole text in which this constellation appears.[26] However, as already pointed out, nowhere does one find a concrete discussion of the historical experience of fascism or the specific character of culture in Mussolini's Italy, i.e., the characterization remains a solely theoretical construct. Therefore the precise (if obscure) reference to Marinetti in order to demonstrate the confluence of deautonomization and fascist politics, futurism and the Ethiopian war, comes as a surprise because it breaks with the abstraction of the preceding argument. Yet if one recalls the historical and cultural context of the essay, the significance of the Marinetti citation, the aesthetic force of which threatens occasionally to overpower Benjamin's own rhetoric, may become evident. In the mid-thirties, the continued stability of National Socialist Germany was by no means certain, and Italy remained the natural example of institutionalized fascism. Any theoretical analysis of fascism still had to make its case with reference to Italian fascism, hence the functionality of invoking Marinetti, although in retrospect a discussion of Ernst Jünger or Leni Riefenstahl might have served the same logical purpose.

Furthermore, given Benjamin's designation of fascism as an aestheticization of politics, Italy represented the likely terrain because of particular cultural commitments within the ongoing German antifascist discourse. Consider for a moment Thomas Mann's "Mario and the Magician," a novella cast as a fictional report of a summer vacation in Italy; while the narrator avoids any explicit political discussion—he serves as Mann's alter ego as an "unpolitical" German—the text nevertheless provides considerable insight into the character of fascism: extreme nationalism, aggression, irrationalism, and an elitist class structure.[27] For my purposes however one single aspect of this analysis is crucial, the narrator's suggestion that Italy is the likely locus of fascism because of a privileged Italian access to aesthetic experience; the narrator describes an oppressive sunlight, "proper to the south, it is classic weather, the sun of Homer, the climate wherein human culture came to flower," but it cannot satisfy "the deeper, more complex needs of the northern soul."[28] Associated with Homeric classicism, the naïveté of sensuous appearance, and the constancy of illumination, the Italian south becomes an aesthetic domain, fundamentally different from the latitudes that nurtured the sensitivity and interiority of the "northern soul." This is of course a traditional topos of German culture, now transformed however into the dystopic constellation of superficial aestheticism and brutal domination. Mann certainly allows his narrator to follow this line of speculation in order to suggest to the German audience that fascism, this Italian particularity, may not be appropriate for their "northern souls." Nevertheless there is considerable evidence to suggest that the narrator himself is hopelessly susceptible to the same aestheticizing force and cannot escape the power of fascist domination, despite his own self-assurances, i.e., Mann may be suggesting that a German immunity to the confluence of aesthetics and fascist politics current in Italy is unlikely to last very long. This discussion cannot be pursued any further here; the point however is that Mann anticipates Benjamin's constellation of Italy, fascism, and the aestheticization of politics. The arguments are somewhat different, but both operate with a shared association derived from a long-standing feature in the German cultural tradition.

To the extent that Benjamin's designation of fascism as an aestheticization of politics derives both from this larger cultural tradition and from his own intellectual projects, it ends up too narrow a definition to encompass the full historical substance of fascist politics and culture. Largely ignoring the specificity of Italy in the thirties, he avoids any discussion of National Socialism, and the characterization may not apply at all to the modus operandi of other fascist movements. In addition, by reducing fascism to this single strategy of aestheticization, he is incapable of discussing other features of fascism which are indisputably crucial to a satisfactory profile: police-state methods, an expansively bureaucratic administration, opportunistic alliances, and genocide. Unless these elements are treated abstractly as simple consequences of a preservation of bourgeois class relations, they disappear from Benjamin's model; if one attempts to include them in this manner, it becomes impossible to distinguish between fascism and other forms of the capitalist state.

On the other hand, the equation of fascism and an aestheticization of politics may be too broad in the sense that a politics of spectacle that precludes rational communication appears in many twentieth-century contexts which ought not to be labeled fascist, if the term is to retain any historical specificity at all. The aesthetic packaging of political discourse, the priority of image over substance, and the metamorphosis of the political speaker into an actor for the mass media all point to the continued relevance of Benjamin's insight for contemporary culture in the process of what Jürgen Habermas has labeled "refeudalization," i.e., the demise of a public of rational debate, replaced by a consumerist culture of manipulation and acclamatory politics.[29] The historical episodes of fascism undoubtedly represented a major acceleration of this aestheticization of politics. Yet as little as that theoretical designation captures all the unique characteristics of the thirties, its association solely with that single historical moment underestimates its critical viability forty years after the collapse of the Central European fascist states.

Consumer Society: The Legacy of the Avant-garde and the False Sublation of Aesthetic Autonomy

ISTVAN Szabo begins his film *Mephisto* (1981) by deviating from Klaus Mann's 1936 novel, on which it is based, in a manner which is extraordinarily significant for the vicissitudes of the avant-garde and the contemporary aesthetic discussion. The novel commences with an account of a grand celebration, an official reception in the third year of the Third Reich, when Hendrik Höfgen, the corollary for the acclaimed actor Gustav Gründgens in Mann's roman à clef, is at the height of his power. Having thus recounted the end of the story, the narrator flashes back to the beginning, the early days of the Weimar Republic, in order to trace Höfgen's notorious rise to fame and glory; this disruption of the natural biographical sequence alerts the reader to the foregrounded issue, corruption and careerism, and serves as an almost Brechtian estrangement device to prevent any empathetic identification with the hero. The novelistic text employs a modernist technique, estrangement, in order to scrutinize a bourgeois figure, the venal artist prepared to sacrifice everything for success.

Szabo's film revises this apparently unnatural order by returning the celebration to its proper chronological location at the conclusion of the narrative, which in turn begins at the earliest represented moment of Höfgen's trajectory, i.e., a properly ordered biography is provided. In fact however the film does not commence with Höfgen himself. It opens instead with the representation of an aesthetic event, an operatic performance, a pure case of bourgeois high art; the film cuts then immediately to Höfgen, crying desperately in his dressing room. The film's juxtaposition of these scenes suggests that the actor's anguish refers to the excessively traditional character of the German stage, which he will henceforth attempt to revolutionize and modernize at any cost. While the novel, a function of Mann's desire to denounce the individual Gründgens as a collaborator with the fascist regime, focuses on personal issues, attributing his tears to unrequited love and his theatrical energy to private ambition, the film examines the collective problem of the aesthetic modernist; radically hostile to the culture of the nineteenth century, the bourgeois world of the past, the modernizer Höfgen overthrows a panoply of inherited categories. Szabo is interested in showing the consequences of this sort of cultural revolutionism: political opportunism, ego weakness, and totalitarianism. The film retreats to traditional, premodernist forms, especially its realist construction of cinematic narrative, in order to critique the historical avant-garde.

In its final sequence, the film shows how the Goering figure drags Höfgen to the Olympic Stadium late at night and, blinding him with a giant spotlight, calls out his name again and again, enacting a theater of cruelty reminiscent of Artaud. This reference to the modern stage is placed at the conclusion in order to indicate the bitter fruits of Höfgen's labor: the avant-garde attack on bourgeois culture and the initially represented aesthetic of autonomy (opera) paves the way for the sublation of life and art in the totalitarian spectacle. The artist Höfgen has destroyed bourgeois art and, so Szabo tells us, prepared the ground for fascism as an aestheticization of politics. With the demolition of autonomous aesthetic form, the integrity of the traditional personality has been eroded, and Höfgen has lost any ground from which to resist the overwhelming power of the new regime. Yet Szabo's film is evidently concerned not only with Mann, Gründgens, and the Third Reich but with the consequences of the avant-garde in the countries of really existing socialism. If this is the success of the avant-garde in the East, what of its legacy in the West?

During the past decade the very notion of an avant-garde has been subject to a barrage of attacks from various quarters. After the institutionalization of the aesthetic avant-garde in the fifties (as high modernism) and the repoliticization of an intellectual avant-garde during the sixties, the seventies witnessed the emergence of a widespread denunciation of the avant-garde project. Former liberals blamed the turmoil of the previous decade on the allegedly excessive influence of a "new class" of intellectuals disseminating the "antibourgeois" values associated with the historical avant-garde movements of the early twentieth century. Neoconservative cultural critics argued that the message implicit in the process of perpetual aesthetic innovation was antithetical to the maintenance of a stable social system dependent on the legitimacy of unquestioned norms and the resources of a valid tradition.[1] Meanwhile a shift on the level of aesthetic theory and critical taste has insisted on the obsolescence of the avant-garde by declaring the commencement of a new period, characterized specifically as postmodern, in which the central elements of the project of the historical avant-garde—the emancipation of individual subjectivity and the radical transformation of the social totality—lose their relevance. This is the point at which the various attacks on the avant-garde converge: the denial of the legitimacy, desirability, or even possibility of the participation by an aesthetic or political avant-garde in a process of radical social change.[2] This conservative cultural position can be located—after the defeat of 1968 and the economic downturn of the seventies made the program for an oppositional literature and art appear increasingly implausible—as a corollary to the conservative shift in Western politics evident in the elections of Thatcher, Reagan, and Kohl. The hostility to the ethos of the historical avant-garde, which claimed that aesthetic innovation could be intimately linked to social transformations, is the common denominator among the conservatives, linking the traditionalist conservatism of U.S. Secretary of Education William Bennett, the cybernetic conservatism of Jean-François Lyotard, and the prestabilized positivism of Michel Foucault.[3]

At stake is not merely whether aesthetic production is possible in the present at all, i.e., the problem suggested by a trivial usage of the terms "avant-garde" and "modern" as that which is merely new and up-to-date, but rather whether that production still has a specifically avant-garde character, i.e., whether it consciously and effectively participates in a project of political progress. Focusing on the movements of the early twentieth century, especially dadaism and surrealism, Peter Bürger emphasizes the effort to overcome the separation of intellectual and aesthetic activity from politics and everyday life in order to transform both components of the dichotomy. The displacement of the traditional organic work of art, an object of the atomistic individual's passive contemplation, by the principle of montage, which transported elements of the social context immediately into the aesthetic sanctuary, represented the corollary to the programmatic infusion of values previously sequestered within the works—beauty, autonomy, and freedom—into social life itself. Bürger's account locates the avant-garde at the culmination of the bourgeois institution of art: only when the autonomization of art is complete can the attack on autonomy be articulated fully. Hence the concentration on the early twentieth-century artistic movements, which appear to break with hermetic symbolism, as the essence of the avant-garde.

If this version proves useful in explaining the immanent aesthetic structure of avant-garde works, it tends to overlook a historical connection to a broader concept of modernity, for the insistence that aesthetic and intellectual production be linked to social and political modernization has been symptomatic of much of the self-understanding of the European intelligentsia at least since the period preceding the French Revolution. The activism of the Enlightenment *philosophes,* who soon confronted the prototypical anti-avant-gardist in the figure of Edmund Burke, was certainly associated with a very different aesthetics—and for that matter, a very different politics—than was advocated by the early twentieth-century cultural revolutionaries. Nevertheless the fundamental linkage of intellectual production and social progress was so evident that one of the mentors of the German avant-garde, Heinrich Mann, could invoke Rousseau as a model for the young German writers of 1910, exhorted to emulate his democratic commitment rather than—Mann's counterexample—Nietzsche's alleged acceptance of the status quo. The paradigmatic connection of intellectuality and politics is set up:

> An intellectual who accommodates the ruling caste betrays the spirit. For the spirit is not conservative and grants no privileges. It dissolves; it equalizes; and it pushes through the ruins of hundreds of castles toward the final fulfillments of truth and justice and their completion, even if it is the completion of death.[4]

Enlightenment is thus the nature of the spirit and the duty of the writer; the writer who is not part of the avant-garde stands in contradiction to his own calling. In Mann's account, all writing has an avant-garde component, to the extent that it constantly endeavors to overcome a self-encapsulation of the spirit, which is to be directed toward a thorough transformation of life practice. This conception of the intellectual as agent of social change, radicalized at the beginning of the century but drawing on traditions rooted deeply in postmedieval modernity, is where the contemporary opponents of the avant-garde zero in. In order to ensure the stability of a conservative order, the participation of writers in change is denounced.

Bürger is certainly correct when he underscores the contrast between the model of the organic work of art, characteristic of the bourgeois institution from Goethe to George, and the avant-garde work, fundamentally hostile to the separation of life and art. Yet his presentation suggests that the emergence of the avant-garde can be explained solely in terms of the development of the institution of art, with no reference to broader social transformations: a sort of expanded intrinsic criticism, as if the economic changes around the turn of the century and the subsequent political upheavals bore no relation to aesthetic developments, the relative autonomy of which is never distorted by intrusions from other value spheres. This description is even more Weberian than Weber's, where modernity involves both the separation of rationalized value spheres and their constant conflict, as elaborated in the "*Zwischenbetrachtung*" of the essays on the sociology of religion.

Furthermore, Bürger's account implies that the avant-garde responded to the successful completion of bourgeois autonomy. Yet while autonomy may have represented a norm and perhaps a desideratum, it is at the very least problematic to describe particular works of art as genuinely autonomous and therefore fully devoid of any ideological character. Instead one can inquire into the specifically affirmative character that autonomy assumed within a culture that ascribed it to art which was however always simultaneously curtailed by the exigencies of a heteronomous social organization. The commodification of all relationships induced the fetishization of cultural objects within a cult of sterile veneration. Recall Robert Musil's acerbic description:

> At home these men's works [Kant, Schiller, and Goethe] were
> kept in the bookcase with the green glass panes in Papa's study,
> and Törless knew this bookcase was never opened except to
> display its contents to a visitor. It was like the shrine of some
> divinity to which one does not readily draw nigh and which
> one venerates only because one is glad that thanks to its existence there are certain things one need no longer bother about.[5]

It is not the success of bourgeois culture which is addressed here but its failure, i.e., its inability to live up to its own program. In Weberian terms: bourgeois culture undergoes a process of bureaucratization, its forms grow rigid and perfunctory, and the avant-garde emerges with a project of charismatic renewal, the establishment of an aesthetic community in which the perpetual promises of bourgeois art would be fulfilled as real happiness.

The crisis of twentieth-century values was not, as conservatives claim, a result of avant-garde activity, but, on the contrary, the avant-garde responded to that crisis engendered by the process of capitalist development. Its attack on inherited cultural structures is dialectical in the sense that its destructive strategy is tied to the goal of emancipating an immanent content from ossified forms: the avant-garde protests against the manner in which bourgeois culture has insufficiently realized its own values, and it promises to carry out the bourgeois project in general more successfully by jettisoning one particular feature, aesthetic autonomy. The legacy of that strategy—the sublation of autonomy in the name of emancipation—includes the history of twentieth-century art as well as the major cultural-historical ramification of the avant-garde, an aestheticization of everyday life.

Evidently the relationship of the historical avant-garde to the bourgeois institution of art is not merely an external attack but rather a sublation (whether successful or not will be discussed in a moment): the avant-garde intends to negate the contradictory character of the bourgeois institution through an eradication of autonomy; it will preserve the institution by addressing the values earlier imprisoned in the aesthetic monad; and it designs to heighten it by effecting an authentic realization of the *promesse de bonheur* which previous art had been able only to mouth and never keep. I underscore this dialectical continuity between the bourgeois culture of aesthetic autonomy and the avant-garde in order to problematize the character of historical periodization in Bürger's account. Although he describes several institutionalizations of art (medieval sacred, courtly representational, bourgeois autonomous), it is only the transition from an autonomous to a postautonomous aesthetics within the context of a theory of the avant-garde to which he devotes extensive attention. One is consequently compelled to treat this historical rupture as a model for Bürger's general account of aesthetic discontinuity, which is based on descriptions of immanent completion. Following Marx's account of the development of the economic subsystem,[6] Bürger, insisting on the relative autonomy of the aesthetic dimension, describes the emergence of a program for autonomous art in German idealism and Weimar classicism and accounts for the subsequent history of bourgeois art as the consistent completion of that program, the progressive elimination of heterogenous elements from works of art which become increasingly self-referential and hermetic, ever more distant from concrete life practice. The completion of the program for autonomy in the art of the fin-de-siècle (symbolism, aestheticism) sets the stage for an attack on the bourgeois institution of art by the avant-garde, as if a credible attack were possible only once the immanent possibilities of the existent model are exhausted.

Despite the invocation of Marx, the character of this historical break is heavily indebted to recent developments in the history of science, especially Thomas Kuhn's understanding of a paradigm shift.[7] The suggestion that the bourgeois institution of art can be attacked only when it has immanently fulfilled its original project of autonomy forces Bürger to relegate competing aesthetic projects during the nineteenth century (the tendentiousness of the *Vormärz* poets, the explicit referentiality of realism and naturalism) to the secondary status of mere countertendencies. The engaged writing of the tradition from Rousseau to Heinrich Mann, which defined literary activity precisely in terms of life-practical consequences, is eclipsed by the alleged priority of the model of autonomy. Like Kuhn, Bürger describes the predominance of a single paradigm, which forces him to diminish the significance of alternative aesthetic conceptualizations. Yet the actual character of the aesthetic terrain within any circumscribed historical period depends on the conflictual simultaneity of a multiplicity of models and practices, dependent on each other for reciprocal definition and delimitation. The establishment of the bourgeois norm of autonomy relies on and produces the presence of nonautonomous alternatives in a contradictory dynamic: without reference to the agreeable and the sublime, the beautiful is devoid of meaning, and an ascription of a unitary hegemonic status of the latter remains necessarily trapped in the idealism of idealist aesthetics.

Thus rather than assert the priority of a single paradigm in the aesthetic subsystem, which can be displaced only once it is exhausted, it is crucial to recognize how the aesthetic norm of autonomy depends on the negativity of both denigrated sensual pleasure and the feared threat to bourgeois individuality inherent in the sublime. In addition to this contradictory nature of aesthetic culture within an institutional framework, marked by a simultaneity of heterogenous models competing with each other, the project of a normative autonomy is itself immanently contradictory. The autonomous work is, from the start, not only autonomous but also an object to be possessed; the idealist description of art also aims to make art a pure commodity. The subject of Schiller's "Spaziergang" (1795) separates himself from the life practice of the city only to praise economic productivity and the acquisitive individualism of a population designated as "delighting in property" (*"des Eigentums froh"*).[8] The rigorous separation of aesthetic form and practical reason enters a dialectic that generates a merely formalistic morality and an everyday practice emptied of substantive ethics.[9] The idealistic aesthetic exclusion of the good subjects the beautiful to a dialectical inversion and transforms autonomy into its opposite: in Adorno's words, "The Absolute turned into absolute horror." [10]

Bürger's central claim regarding the program of the historical avant-garde is certainly valid: the avant-garde constitutes itself in terms of a rejection of the aesthetic of autonomy that had attained a privileged (but by no means ubiquitous) status in the bourgeois culture of the nineteenth century. In fact one might push Bürger further on this point, for homologous rejections of idealist aesthetic are evident not only in the specifically avant-garde movements (dadaism, futurism, surrealism, constructivism) but also in the literary texts and theoretical reflections of authors who might be designated as "modernist" rather than "avant-garde": Thomas Mann, Ernst Jünger, Alfred Döblin, to mention only a few. [11] However, my critique of Bürger so far has been directed toward the formal grounding of this account in a version of a "paradigm shift," which implies the predominance of a single aesthetic model within an institutional phase and which forces him to ascribe an obviously counterfactual success to the model of aesthetic autonomy by the end of the nineteenth century.

Conversely, because the various avant-garde movements have not established the sort of hegemonic aesthetic normativity which Bürger projects in an excessively coherent manner onto pre-avant-garde culture, he must speak of a failure of the avant-garde. [12] Yet it is ultimately the idealist version of "paradigm" that forces him to view the contemporary plurality of aesthetic possibilites as a failure of the avant-garde. [13] Because of a noncontradictory description of institutionalization, multiple artistic models must be misunderstood as evidence of an unsuccessful attempt to establish a new paradigmatic identity. If however alterity is recognized as constitutive of identity, the polymorphous character of contemporary culture can be regarded as the legacy of the success of the avant-garde: a success however that is fully compatible with the progress of commodity society and therefore inimical to the explicit, social-revolutionary political goals of much of the historical avant-garde.

Modern high culture, the aesthetics of autonomy, emancipates art from the immediate control of church and state, while simultaneously differentiating this new domain of art from both popular culture and the experience of nature. [14] The presence of these foils, as domains of negativity against which art could define itself and from which it could draw substantive strength, was a crucial component in the construction of the bourgeois institution. Rather than describe the crisis of this institution in terms of the completion of a process of autonomization, one must register the erosion of the negative resources—popular traditions and nature—as a consequence of capitalist modernization. A commercial culture industry begins to expand in the second half of the nineteenth century and burgeons into the global hegemony of Hollywood, leveling local differences and genuine popular practices.[15] A modern mass culture emerges that lacks the traditionalist character of premodern popular culture. It is a mass-marketed culture, subject to public relations strategies and manipulative advertising techniques. Losing its former natural status, this artificial popular cultural dimension can no longer be viewed as exterior to art, just as nature, for an early phase of bourgeois society the alternative to culture, has become the universal object of industrial exploitation.[16] Thus the antinomic preconditions of bourgeois art, on which its definition and institutionalization depended, have been undermined by the progress of bourgeois economy, which therefore renders the identity of an autonomous bourgeois art increasingly labile.

In Weber's early work, especially the report on the agrarian question and the Freiburg Inaugural Address, a parallel argument is made in the political sphere: the establishment of the modern German nation depended on the availability of premodern resources—Prussian agriculture and the associated cultural traditionalism—which however were undermined by the progress of capitalism in the western regions of the Reich. Weber's solution, suggested at the conclusion of the dissection of the Protestant ethic, is a desperate invocation of prophetic innovation and charismatic leadership. The homologous solution in the aesthetic realm is a charismatic modernism, the attack by the intellectuals of the historical avant-garde on the categories of bourgeois culture and their program for an end to autonomy, the aestheticization of everyday life, and the liquidation of private individuality.

Unlike neoconservatives who attribute all the cultural crises of late capitalism to the nearly diabolical strength of avant-garde intellectuals, we must recognize how the commodification of popular culture and the exploitation of nature are consequences of an economic logic of the same capitalism which the neoconservatives are anxious to defend. Yet it cannot be denied that avant-gardism has contributed significantly to a profound reorganization of culture by integrating these previously excluded domains into the realm of art: in the case of popular tradition, consider the lineage from Kokoschka and folk art and the role of primitivism in cubist painting to the late-twentieth-century fascination with naive representation and tribal culture; similarly nature becomes an object of increasing aestheticization from the vision of landscape in Hofmannsthal's *The Fool and Death* to Christo's installations.[17] The construction of the bourgeois institution of art is no longer plausible once neither the contrast between high art and low art nor the difference between culture and nature can be maintained.

It is this universal aestheticization that renders an aesthetic theory still concerned with discrete works obsolete. Adorno's dictum that "today the only works which really count are those which are no longer works at all" has been transformed into a cynical platitude in the context of a false sublation of autonomy.[18] The avant-garde has contributed to a culture that regards everything as art, and this demolition of aesthetic hierarchy guarantees the continuity of heteronomy.[19] In a brief but suggestive passage, Bürger in fact points to this continuity between the avant-garde and a principle of commodity aesthetics: "Here too art becomes practical, but in the sense of domination."[20] Bürger draws a consequence that is reminiscent of Szabo's film: aesthetic avant-gardism, despite its emancipatory claims, is implicated in the construction of modernized systems of domination. The attack on the autonomous work collaborates with the erosion of the autonomous individual. This aspect of *Theory of the Avant-garde*, although apparently peripheral to Bürger's central concerns, sheds important light on the political character of postmodern culture.

Liberal culture thrived on the presence of external opposition; contemporary culture successfully integrates opposition and displays an aesthetics without a normative center. Its ostentatious eclecticism is often linked to a rhetoric of pluralism that allows its defenders to denounce the critical advocates of emancipation as totalitarian. Yet it is postmodernist eclecticism, the consequence of the avant-garde attack on bourgeois normativity, that precludes systemic criticism. The system can point to the artificial negativity of its internal opposition as proof of its own viability and the impossibility of an autonomous position outside the network of present practices. The cultural theory of postmodernism provides the affirmative descriptions of that which is merely given. Although it may carefully sketch power structures and practical strategies, its rejection of emancipatory autonomy precludes any systematic critical project. Once concepts of truth are treated solely as vehicles for the establishment of an exclusionary discourse and taste becomes only a ploy to establish social distinction, the utopian potential of the autonomous artwork is lost from sight.

Bürger's political agenda within the history of critical theory in *The Theory of the Avant-garde,* the historicization of the positions of Lukács and Adorno and the defense of a multiplicity of aesthetic models, can be read both as a response to the waning of the West German New Left and as a distant approach to the postmodernist fetishization of eclecticism. Yet because he restricts his argument to an ultimately still-autonomous aesthetic dimension and refrains from extensive reflections on the transformation of life practice, he insists on maintaining a theoretical discourse divorced from a cultural history of the present. However, his own emphasis on the avant-garde's intent to undertake a revolutionary transformation of everyday life sheds crucial light on postmodernist culture, characterized by the eradication of aesthetic autonomy, ubiquitous aestheticization, and collapse of liberal individuality that are features of contemporary capitalism. The superficially radical attack on the authority of high culture provides an alibi for social hierarchy within the postmodern condition; once wealth and poverty are declared to be equally valid cultural options, any egalitarian politics can be denounced as Jacobin terror. Artificial negativity permits social authority to thrive on its own opposition.[21] The spread of commodity relations into all social activity engenders a society of the spectacle, the bad legacy of dadaism, in which aesthetic consumerism becomes inescapable and every life practice is transformed into a life-style: music is technologically reproduced in commercial interiors as a self-evident marketing device; individual experience is reduced to narrative contingency; and public politics is displaced by public relations.[22] This manipulative aestheticization of everyday life may have always characterized aspects of bourgeois society, but, drawing on the legacy of the avant-garde, it acquires a predominant status, undermining earlier categories of politics, culture, and society.

The participation of the historical avant-garde in the emergence of a late-capitalist consumer society could be demonstrated with close examinations of particular cases, such as the role of surrealism in the modernization of the advertising industry, or that of architectural modernism in the production of the extraordinarily labile nuclear family and consumerist individuality.[23] On a more general level however such cases point to the social ramifications of aesthetic programs.

Bürger's periodization scheme for the various institutions of art certainly suggests a sociohistorical grounding for art (feudal, absolutist, bourgeois), yet his argumentative insistence on the relative autonomy of the aesthetic domain prevents him from entering into any elaborate discussion of the relationship between art and social structure. This was perhaps a necessary response to excessively reductionist accounts of base and superstructure, current in the reified leftism of the early seventies. Nevertheless only by thematizing such relationships in a manner which is a matter of neither structural homologies (Goldmann) nor crude determinism (Althusser) can contemporary critical theory begin to account for the specific character of consumer culture and the role of the historical avant-garde in its production.

CHAPTER FOUR

Writing for the Book Industry:
The Writer in Organized Capitalism

I

THE problem of the economic status of the author began to attract attention in German literary life during the second half of the eighteenth century. The Dessauer Gelehrtenbuchhandlung for example represented an early effort to establish an autonomous publishing house controlled by authors and therefore independent of the growing book trade. Similar issues were addressed both by Lessing in his proposal "Leben und leben lassen" (1772) and Wieland in his "Grundsätze, woraus das merkantilische Verhältnis zwischen Schriftsteller und Verleger bestimmt wird" (1791).[1] The increasingly commercial character of literary production and distribution, which contemporary authors eyed with suspicion but were perhaps prepared to accept as a necessary evil, was regarded affirmatively by representatives of the trade. Thus in 1802, Georg Joachim Göschen approached the issue with all the appropriate mercantile sobriety: "The book trade is a trade.—To trade means: to give another freely what one has for that which one wants to have and the other wants to give freely," so that the book dealer differs in no fundamental way from his professional colleagues, "the Canadian primitive, who gives fur and fish for nails and axes, the merchant with the treasures of both the Indies in his storehouses on the Thames, and the salesman who carries his whole stock on his back."[2]

The commercialization of structures of literary life obviously touched the basic self-understanding of the book trade at a time when production and distribution, i.e., publishing and retailing, were only beginning to separate; the first specialized retail bookstore in Germany was established by Friedrich Christoph Perthes in Hamburg in 1796.[3] The overall phenomenon as well as the differing reactions by authors and merchants can be understood as part of the transformation of German society in terms of the forms of early capitalist development. Several competing types of changes must be distinguished.

First, that authors began to regard the book trade as a threat to their literary independence reflected the emergence of an autonomous literary institution, which came into its own in the aesthetics of German idealism and the writings of the classic-romantic period.[4] In accordance with the basic structure of the commodity and the divergence of use value and exchange value, capitalist modernization induces an extensive social division of labor, i.e., the separation and specialization of previously identical or at least congruent realms of activity: religion, politics, economy, art. Thus one of the implications of a literary market is the gradual emancipation of literature from the exigencies of religion and politics which had prevailed in the presecularized baroque literature of the courtly absolutist period.

Second, once literature was liberated from explicit ties to the patrons of the social hierarchy, it could begin to present itself as the expression of general human interests. The anonymity of the literary market provided the foundation for the universalist claims of late eighteenth-century literature, in which the movement of bourgeois emancipation crystallized. Literature, which otherwise harbored an undeniable emancipatory potential, took on a classical ideological structure, presenting the particular as the universal, difference as equality. The insistence on the universal-human character of literary discourse and the denial of the specifically personal or class character of literary production mirrored the logic of the capitalist commodity,[5] especially the occlusion of concrete by abstract labor. It is hardly necessary to point out that the ideological content of literature in capitalism can vary widely, but its character as ideology remains a perennial feature of its social condition.

Third, the social status of the writer becomes a function of the capitalist mode of production. The writer is not only engaging in autonomous aesthetics and ideology but also earning a livelihood. Certainly authors, like everyone else, have always had to find a way to survive. However, a social history of literature necessarily differentiates between precapitalist forms of remuneration (patronage) and the characteristically capitalist dependence on the market and the publisher (especially in the form of royalties). In addition, it can be argued that capitalism places particular emphasis on the economy and (commodity) production, unlike earlier social forms. Finally, following Weber, one can distinguish between irregular and often unplanned profit-oriented economic activity in precapitalist contexts and, on the other hand, the consistent and rational pursuit of accumulation which comes increasingly to characterize the capitalist spirit.[6] Despite some countertendencies (including the promise of aesthetic autonomy), literary production becomes subject to the dictates of capitalist production, gradually after the middle of the eighteenth century and explosively in the late nineteenth century. In 1909, Hans Landsberg could sum up one hundred and fifty years of capitalism and literature with the same sobriety Göschen had earlier displayed: "The writer is an employee; the book publisher, the newspaper publisher, or the theater director, etc., with whom he constantly or occasionally is connected is his employer and entrepreneur."[7]

These three aspects of the capitalist transformation of literature reflect alternative although not mutually exclusive understandings of the problem posed by the sociology of literature: (1) the institutionalization of a specific logic of aesthetic autonomy; (2) the dialectic of aesthetic work and ideology; and (3) the instrumental reduction of literature within the capitalist mode of production.[8] Without suggesting a priority to the productivist approach, I will pursue this third element, because an examination of capitalist literary production—"writing for the book industry"—permits me to push the discussion in a specific direction. Against the eternally returning cultural conservative complaint that the purportedly low quality of popular literature merely reflects the desires of the masses, I will suggest that it was rather the experience of the book industry and its economic forms which led to the specific character of the maligned literature. No matter how literary production and consumption may be reciprocally determined, the nature of production has its own definite consequences: authors who understand themselves as employees dependent on publishing houses with precise marketing strategies will choose to write in certain ways. In other words, it is not the growth of the readership but the constraints on the writers, not democracy but capitalism which leads to Ganghofer and other proponents of pulp fiction. This concern led Adorno, by the way, to insist on his notion of a "culture industry" against the competing term of mass culture with its implication that the masses only got what they deserved.[9]

A second result of this focus on the experience of writing for the book industry, i.e., on a phenomenology of capitalist literary production, is to cast light on the problem of the avant-garde and modernism. Not only the authors of popular literature confronted and recognized the commodification of literary life; so did the participants in the various countercultural movements around the turn of the century.

The categories of capitalist production are comprehended and pre-served despite—and because of—the efforts to escape into aestheticist enclaves or alternative public spheres. The rejection of prevailing lit-erary life by figures as diverse as George and Brecht was based on the assumption of a developed capitalist context and remains impene-trable without reflection on the economic structure. Therefore when contemporary neoconservatives blame the emergence of an adversary culture on the malevolent influence of bohemian intellectuals, they disregard the intimate relationship between the literary advocates of alternative value systems and the capitalist mode of production which they, the conservatives, are so anxious to defend.[10]

II

The various thematizations of the relationship between authors and book trade during the eighteenth century corresponded to important changes in the traditional structures of literary life which had pre-vailed since Gutenberg's invention of printing from movable type around 1450 or at least since the early sixteenth century, when the system of exchange trade was introduced: at the annual Frankfurt book fair publishers traded their wares simply sheet for sheet, regard-less of the literary content. The system worked well in light of both the relative scarcity of currency caused by the religious wars and a homogeneous, predominantly scholarly readership interested above all in Latin texts and tied therefore to a European market. The differ-entiation of eighteenth-century literary production as well as the shift to a generally educated public attracted increasingly to German-language material led to significant changes, of which the transplan-tation of the book fair from Frankfurt to Leipzig was merely the outward symptom. The exchange trade gave way to a cash system, distribution *à la condition* was introduced which permitted the wide circulation of new titles, and the foundation was laid for the separa-tion of publishing and retail trade between which the rudimentary wholesale trade in Leipzig was mediating by 1800.[11]

These changes are confirmed by some interesting statistics. The early phase of the developing book industry witnessed both a quanti-tative increase and qualitative shifts in literary production. Ilsedore Rarisch points to a rise in total titles from 1,144 in 1740 to 2,569 in 1800, i.e., an increase of 140 percent.[12] The Latin component dropped radically in the same period from 27.7 percent to a negligible 3.4 percent. Not surprisingly, books concerned with theology and law gave way to belletristic and educational works, just as the intensive reading of a limited set of religious texts, especially the Bible, was replaced by the extensive reading of many secular texts. Specifically belletristic works which represented 5.8 percent of the annual production in 1740 rose to 21.4 percent in 1800, while works of religious edification dropped from 19.17 percent to 5.8 percent.[13] Thus secularization and the spread of the literary public went hand in hand, while the novel was quickly established as the literary genre par excellence, claiming in 1800 54.4 percent of the belletristic production and 11.7 percent of total book production.[14] Within this rise of the popular novel in the eighteenth century, marked by the repeated imitation of established themes, the spread of serialized production, and the pronounced emphasis on entertainment, Rarisch recognizes the roots of the industrialization and mass production of literature which later emerged fully in the course of the nineteenth century.[15]

It is not surprising that literary production was retarded by the turmoil of the Napoleonic Wars,[16] but a takeoff phase in economic development set in after 1830; annual production passed the 10,000-title mark in 1837 and reached a high point of 14,039 in 1843.[17] Certain technical innovations played a key role in this phase, especially the replacement of the iron stanhope press by Friedrich König's mechanical cylindrical press run on a steam engine, permitting quicker and more rationalized production (the new press was first adopted in 1814 by the *London Times*).[18] Consequently the period witnessed the first "speculation with mass production,"[19] such as the phenomenal success of Brockhaus' *Konversationslexikon*, the first edition of which appeared in 1809 with 2,000 copies; by 1823 (the year of Brockhaus' death) 32,000 had been sold. Especially during the period of economic expansion after 1830, the publisher appeared increasingly as an industrial entrepreneur, achieving a new sort of superiority over other participants in book production—printers, binders, retailers.[20] The quantitative production growth, the new predominance of the publisher, and the explicit emergence of speculative motives led to complaints regarding the commercialization and standardization within the *Literaturfabrik*, especially in the literature of the 1840s: vide Ernst Willkomm, *Eisen, Gold und Geist* (1843), Ernst Dronke, *Die Sclaven der Intelligenz* (1846), and Robert Prutz, *Das Engelchen* (1851).[21]

However, the increasingly bitter tensions between authors and publishers were not simply a function of the literary motifs of the *Vormärz*. Witness the case of the controversy between Karl Gutzkow and the Mannheim publisher Heinrich Hoff.[22] Eduard Jerrmann, theater director in Mannheim from 1836 to 1842, felt that he had been treated unfairly by the anonymous critic of the *Mannheimer Stadtpost*, a supplement to the *Rheinische Postillon* published by Hoff. An altercation ensued which reached an initial conclusion when Hoff rashly reduced the price of a brochure by Jerrmann which he had published from 36 to one single Kreuzer (corresponding today to a reduction from one Mark to 3 Pfennig)[23] and was thereby reportedly able to dump all six hundred copies one fine Sunday morning in August of 1838. Gutzkow, who in fact had previously maintained amicable ties to Hoff, came to Jerrmann's defense in the essay "Über Preisherabsetzungen im Buchhandel" published in Hoffmann and Campe's *Telegraph für Deutschland:*

> Nearly all book dealers in Germany certainly imagine that they can do whatever they please with a manuscript they have purchased, for example: that they need not even publish it! They treat the moral existence of a work as fully dependent on their whims and the honorarium they have paid, and they will be astonished to see us begin to challenge their right to depress the price of books. Of course, our laws which are so lax on this point do not restrain them; however we have now come far enough to integrate the more profound concepts of literary property rights into the law—concepts which regard an author's work as the expression of a free moral personality which must not be harmed except by the chances of criticism.[24]

Gutzkow opposed the unfettered capitalist entrepreneurship of Hoff by denouncing the venal perception of the literary work as a mere commodity and counterposing to it the work's ideal and moral value; when literary life undergoes industrialization and commercialization—so he suggests—literature is robbed of its true nature. Certainly Gutzkow protests sincerely and passionately against the power of the publishing industry, yet he does so by insisting that authentic literature and legitimate authors must stand outside the process of commodification. But, as will soon be shown, the growth of authors' organizations at the end of the century presupposed the recognition of the realities of the industrial structures as the prerequisite of contemporary literature. That recognition became possible only after the still relatively privileged status of the *Vormärz* author was lost.

After the violent conflicts of 1848, literary production was relatively low (around 8,700 titles annually).[25] Not until 1868 did it again reach the 10,000 mark, first passed in 1837, but then it shot up as part of the general economic expansion of the late nineteenth century: 1870 brought 10,108 titles, 1890, 18,875 titles, 1910, 31,281 titles.[26] Between 1875 and 1914 the number of periodicals (important for fiction authors as the financially lucrative place of publication for novellas and serialized novels) tripled,[27] as did, by the way, the number of bookstores. The *Adressbuch des deutschen Buchhandels*, not complete but certainly symptomatic, lists 4,614 establishments for 1875 and 12,650 for 1910.[28] The number of jobs directly related to the retail trade increased by a factor of 6 between 1875 and 1907, while the annual volume of the whole industry rose from 55 million Marks in 1875 to 500 million Marks in 1913.

In addition to the overall economic context, this growth depended on various other factors. Technical innovations in paper production, typesetting, and, above all, the rotation press were certainly important.[29] Changes in the legislative and administrative infrastructure also contributed: the rationalization of postal service including lowered rates, the laissez-faire restructuring of the commercial code, and the gradual strengthening and internationalization of copyright laws which transformed the book into a less risky object of speculation.[30] The dramatic turning point was the *Klassikerjahr* of 1867 when the "eternal publishing rights" for the classical authors lapsed and the general thirty-year copyright protection term was established. A flood of inexpensive, popular editions of classical literature followed: Cotta, which had produced a twelve-volume edition of Schiller in 1862 for nine Thalers, turned out a pocket-size edition in 1867, also in twelve volumes, for a mere two Thalers. This was still undercut however by the Leipzig publisher Payne whose one-Thaler Schiller edition was made available as a bonus to subscribers to his *Familien-Journal;* some 50,000 copies were sold.[31]

This period also witnessed the rise of the mammoth publishing houses Mosse, Ullstein, and Scherl, the last of which formed the basis of the Hugenberg empire of the Weimar Republic. Simultaneously the number of authors producing for this industry increased even more rapidly than the market could support, leading to a relative decline in income, as compared with the first half of the century. In 1893 Joseph

Kürschner described the growing "literary reserve army" of unemployed authors, trapped in a downward spiral of competition and proletarianization.[32] Theodor Fontane's contemporary estimation was not at all isolated:

> The situation of the author is miserable. Which country can claim priority in this impoverishment may be difficult to determine; yet it can always be said that Prussia-Germany has always been in the forefront and is making a successful effort to maintain this old prominence. Those who do business with literature and politics are growing rich, those who produce them either hunger or barely survive. This financial poverty leads to something even worse: the ink slave is born. Those who work for "freedom" are themselves unfree and are often worse off than the medieval serf.[33]

The dynamic of the capitalist book industry, with its basic opposition of publisher and author, entrepreneur and producer, not only impoverishes the writer but also robs him of his autonomy and thrusts him into a new form of servitude. Industrial expansion thus transformed both the social function and the self-understanding of the author, and we are led now to the question: in what specific ways did the capitalist restructuring of the institutions of literary life engender the production of a qualitatively new sort of literature?

III

With this brief and highly compressed account of the capitalization of literary production, I have been able only to scratch the surface of a multiplicity of phenomena regarding the conditions of production, the structure of the market, and the development of the productive forces themselves, especially the authors. In order to organize the empirical data which sociologically oriented research has amassed, it is useful to differentiate three basic types of transformations in literary life. While the following distinctions are in part artificial, they can serve as heuristic devices to explain important changes in the textual character of the literary product. Despite overlapping areas, one can conceptually separate: (1) the depersonalization and objectification (*Versachlichung*) of social relations in literary institutions; (2) the diversification of the literary public caused by market expansion; and (3) the desubjectification of writing as a social act within the industrial structure. Each tendency affects the literature itself in a particular manner and must be commented on separately.

The Depersonalization of Social Relations

In the present context, a full argument pertaining to a transition from *Gemeinschaft* to *Gesellschaft* within literary institutions cannot be made, since it would entail a thorough reconsideration of precapitalist formations.[34] Nevertheless in the limited period under investigation, one can recognize the key traits of this grand sociological theme: the loss of direct personal contact and the spread of abstract and formalized relations. The mechanization of production based on technological progress led to the loss of status and even disappearance of groups of laborers, for example the bookbinders, who in the early nineteenth century still could compete with the retail trade in the sale of standard items such as hymnals and calendars.[35] Other groups responded to modernization differently: the printers' strike in Leipzig in 1865 set the stage for the foundation of the Deutscher Buchdruckverband, the first union in the graphics industry and only the second—after the cigar workers—with a nationwide scope.[36] A similar shift from traditional social forms to the economic rationality of an increasingly organized capitalism is evident in the publishing houses as well. The patriarchal relations which prevailed in the cramped quarters of the older, often single-room firms, in which the few employees underscored their personal loyalty through codes of social deference, disappeared as the division of labor restructured the internal organization.[37] As late as the 1860s, the employees in the Friedrich A. Steinkopf firm in Stuttgart still lived in the publisher's own house. Traditional apprenticeship began to lose its legitimacy once the Book Dealers Academy was founded in 1852, and industry-wide standards displaced personal training.[38]

This process affected the intellectual dimension of publishing as well. The sort of human friendship which might link authors and publishers in the salon world of the early 1800s could not survive the economic rationality which privileged explicit contractual obligations;[39] Karl May's difficulties in the colportage industry seem largely to have resulted from a confusion of personal and professional dimensions.[40] As far as the retail trade is concerned, the formalization of social contact—as well as the quantitative growth in literary production—led to a decline in the importance of literary discussion among employees and an increased reliance on publishers' advertising, formal lists, and other external sources of information, notably the *Börsenblatt des deutschen Buchhandels,* established in 1834.[41] Despite a rise in the number of employees in bookstores, contact with the public became increasingly anonymous, commercial, and devoid of specifically literary content. The shift can be attributed in part to a basic economic calculation: the profits from the sale of an inexpensive Reclam volume could support less literary discussion than could the older elite editions.[42] Of course this single aspect cannot be separated from broader changes in everyday life, cultural values, and the character of literary reception.

An initial estimation of the consequences of this depersonalization process for literary production, i.e., for the internal textual structures, is provided by Conrad Alberti's attack on Paul Heyse of 1889. Instead of a desired authenticity, Alberti finds a merely formal and therefore empty entertainment in Heyse's novellas: "A big novella factory to satisfy the reading needs of intellectually lazy cultured plebeians, run along purely mercantile lines."[43] The critic complains that "Heyse is more a mathematician than a poet," because "his whole creativity depends on cool mathematical combinations, on the use of the principles of permutation and combination within narrative art."[44] Thus, Alberti suggests, the mercantile intention generates the arithmetic formality of textual production, which takes on a serialized character and therefore loses any aesthetic specificity. The commercialization of literary life induces a profound change in literary language, as Alberti underscores:

> The true novelist draws his creations either from the winged phantasy which carries him into the realm of dreams—E. T. A. Hoffmann, Poe—or from the sharp and perpetual observation of the real world around him in its constant changes—Zschocke, Kleist, Maupassant—or, if a genius, he can combine and integrate the two: Goethe, Balzac. Heyse, meanwhile, possesses neither drunken phantasy nor keen observation—he has nothing but the schematic mind of a merchant, sober calculation, and clichés.[45]

For Alberti, legitimate literature provides either expressive authenticity or social communication (in literary historical terms, it derives either from classic-romantic or Enlightenment-realist programs). It speaks a language of personal subjectivity or interpersonal norms, but Heyse's language offers neither. Just as it reduces its material to an object of commercial speculation, it objectifies its public as the passive consumer of merely instrumental enunciations.

I do not want to examine the legitimacy of Alberti's judgment on Heyse. As a paradigmatic description of the instrumental character of the industrially produced literary text, however, it sheds light on several issues. Language appears decoupled from both expression and discourse and becomes a merely external object for the professionalized writer;[46] a reification of syntax and stylized manipulation of form may have put Gustav Aschenbach's prose into textbooks, but they also cut off the sources of aesthetic creativity.[47] Furthermore, schematic structuring leads to an emphasis on an illusionist facticity in the narrative text. Neither irony nor allegory relativizes the one-dimensional images, the presentation of which takes on the character of an unquestionable report. Hence the frequent theme of inevitability and fatalism, tied to an elaborate ideology of destiny. The limitations imposed on literature by this reification of language and content provoked important protests, such as Hofmannstahl's Chandos Letter of 1902. In addition, the objectification of literary life transformed the book itself as an object. After industrialization turned the book into a commodity, the bibliophile movement around 1900 fetishized it as a sign of personal identity or social class. Interestingly this development emerged precisely in those circles where the cultural and noncapitalist function of literature was emphasized the most: the Insel group and Eugen Diederich's firm. Yet precisely the launching of bibliophile series (for example, the *Insel-Reihe*) indicates how the purportedly anticapitalist bibliophile cult itself rapidly became a marketing device.[48]

Diversification of the Literary Public

The capitalist transformation of literary life is inextricably bound to the expansion of the book market into previously peripheral sectors of the population. Phrased alternatively: ever wider circles are integrated as potential consumers. In fact, a popular book market existed for a long time outside of the regular trade; its stock was largely religious or practical (calendars), and it depended often on traveling salesmen for distribution.[49] The reorganization of the industry in the course of the nineteenth century tended to break down this distinction by establishing a unified market with a heterogeneous public.[50] The substance of old popular culture disappeared beneath the weight of an aggressively marketed bourgeois culture, suddenly available at popular prices, e.g., both the inexpensive classic editions after 1867 such as the *Deutsche National-Literatur,* edited by Joseph Kürschner, as well as the various series of novels like Engelhorn's *Allgemeine Romanbibliothek.*[51] Reclam's *Universalbibliothek* mixed the highbrow heritage with contemporary lowbrow hits and could therefore appeal to a mixed public.[52]

Yet the erosion of prices on which the expansion of the market depended soon met resistance from within the retail trade. In response to the threat posed by cut-rate, mail-order distributors especially in Berlin and Leipzig, the trade organization of the Börsenverein (est. 1825) approved the so-called Kröner reforms in 1887 which established set retail prices and prohibited markdowns.[53] This in turn provoked protests from consumer groups, especially Karl Bücher and the Akademischer Schutzverein which regarded the reforms as an effort to maintain artificially high prices in order to preserve an anachronistic economic sector.[54] If 1867 opended up the book market to previously excluded strata, 1887 tried to close it off again; the arguments for the reforms were marked both by the protectionist antiliberalism typical of the 1880s[55] and by a conservative anticapitalism which claimed for book dealers a heroic cultural role. Thus in a speech at the dedication of the Buchhändlerhaus in Leipzig in 1888, Adolf Kröner defended the new regulations against claims that they interfered in private affairs, and he called on the state to boycott any cut-rate dealers "in order to help protect our honorable and industrious retail estate. For it is of highest importance both for the state and our whole cultural life that the book trade not slip out of the hands of a professionally trained and solid retail trade and into the hands of an incalculable and constantly shifting merchant proletariat."[56] The book trade, which in fact defended its own profits with the reforms, rhetorically defended itself as unconcerned with profits. Its professed allegiance to culture as opposed to commerce turns out to be a loyalty to the state (Kröner's speech was delivered in the presence of King Albert of Saxony), a dynamic which came to the fore particularly in the work of Eugen Diederichs and the organization of young book dealers he inspired.[57]

In terms of the character of textual structures, the expansion of the market and the diversification of the public particularly affected the profile of the implied reader. Three types of solutions emerged: (1) an expressly esoteric writing defined by its purposeful rejection of the mass public (George); (2) an expressly exoteric writing in which an anti-elitist, protodemocratic stance could coexist with conformist or conservative ideological commitments (Courths-Mahler);[58] and (3) the characteristically early-twentieth-century efforts to write simultaneously for both publics, separate but equal (Thomas Mann, Hofmannsthal). On a fundamental level, the expansion of the market and the general commodification of literature transformed the status of the popular public. Once the objects of culture became primarily commodities, their recipients were transformed into consumers and therefore barred from participation in the Schillerian project of aesthetic education. Popular literature, now robbed of an older understanding of its social role, could not survive as mere entertainment (Lindau, Ebers) in a context where culture and nation were emphatically linked, and precisely that linkage marked the ethos of the book trade after the Kröner reforms.[59] Mass literature, uncomfortable as entertainment, consequently suffered from a legitimation deficit; if it could not carry out an aesthetic education, it would at least have to offer more than just distraction. Hence the susceptibility of much popular literature to conservative or reactionary ideologies. In Frenssen's *Jörn Uhl* (1910) or, later, in Grimm's *Volk ohne Raum* (1926), the appeal to a popular community (*Volksgemeinschaft*) corresponds to the presence of a real mass public—not as the masses per se but specifically as a mass of consumers.

The Desubjectification of Writing

Unlike the two areas already discussed—the depersonalization of literary relationships and the diversification of the public in the expanded market—this third and final feature affected the status of the author directly. Once capitalism renders the literary work a commodity, not only does the publisher become an entrepreneur and the readership become consumers; the author simultaneously becomes a commodity producer who therefore experiences the social distribution of his work as expropriation. In a letter to Theodor Storm dated August 12, 1881, Gottfried Keller recounted numerous incidents of publishers and editors grossly disregarding the wishes of authors, and he concluded with a pessimistic description of the current situation:

> The rage of publishers to print books appears to be growing into a passion to do it without the cooperation of the authors.

With the lapsing of the Schiller-Goethe privileges against re-
prints, they have tasted blood; every year the thirty-year protection term for this or that postclassic author comes to an end,
and the gang can pounce on it; so it makes sense that they are
beginning to scrape together books from living authors as well
without any costs or at most by feeding a couple of
compilers.[60]

Although the arduous struggle to establish a stable copyright system
and to prevent pirate editions was often waged in the name of authors'
rights, the results in fact benefited the publishers primarily, whose position vis-à-vis the author was consequently strengthened. Particularly
in the case of drama, authors were regularly compelled to sign over
their rights to theatrical agents as part of the price for production,
i.e., the spread of legal regulation could lead to a denial of rights to
the literary producers and basically served to organize the mode of
expropriation.[61]

In 1892, the naturalist Michael Georg Conrad commented on the
changed status of the author:

A publishing corporation is primarily an economic association
designed to exploit writerly labor in order to achieve the highest possible profit for the stockholders. The writer is proletar-
ianized, i.e., he is a supplier for the publisher and is respected
only to the extent that his work produces capitalist value.
Therefore the manuscript worker can be thrown out into the
streets and made breadless, as soon as his work load no longer
provides the expected profits for the publisher-entrepreneur.[62]

This recognition of structural conflicts of interest between authors and
publishers led to a series of writers' organizations; unlike the earlier
Leipziger Literaten-Verein (1842), concerned largely with problems
of censorship, or the predominantly conservative-nationalist Allgemeiner Deutscher Schriftsteller Verband (est. 1879), the new organizations rejected the traditional assumption that authors betrayed their
authentic calling if they began to worry about their financial status.
Thus Kürschner's battle cry in his *Deutsche Schriftsteller Zeitung*
(1885): "It is a harmful error of foggy idealists to claim that we would
become handworkers as soon as we undertook commercial calculations, sought legal protection for our labor, and openly examined the
conditions necessary for a profitable sale of our products. Precisely

the opposite is true!"[63] After the short-lived Deutscher Schriftsteller Verein of 1885, there followed the Kartell lyrischer Autoren in 1902, the Verband deutscher Bühnenschriftsteller in 1908, the Schutzverband deutscher Schriftsteller in 1909, and the Reichsverband der deutschen Presse in 1910. All were committed to a defense of the authors' economic interests; their establishment signaled the spreading awareness of the ambiguities of the relationship between the author-as-producer and the work-as-commodity in the capitalist context.

The intratextual consequences of the separation between author and work involve the problem of literary speech, or rather, the literary speaker, i.e., the narrator, whose profile grows increasingly ambiguous. The ideal speech situation—in which the writer engages as an autonomous subject in literary exchange among equal and homogeneous interlocutors—no longer provides a plausible, if counterfactual, norm. Instead, facing a diversified audience of cultural consumers, the writer experiences a hiatus between writer and text, between speaker and speech, and this distance engenders a desubjectification of the literary product which ceases to be the public expression of a private person. The consequent problem of the narrator, whose social status must be based on that of the author in capitalism, has several concurrent solutions: (1) the classical modernist model of the unreliable narrator who feigns subjectivity in an ironic effort to draw the reader into the hermeneutics of a pseudodiscourse (this possibility develops fully only after the period under consideration, e.g., in Hermann Broch's *Bergroman*); (2) the narrative claim to collective representation, both in avant-garde (expressionist) and political literature (Döblin), in which the authorial subject disappears in the fiction of epic intersubjectivity;[64] and (3) the popular literary narrator, an imitation of the omniscient bourgeois realist narrator. While realist omniscience was based on the author's subjective insight into the distance between the empirical world and a utopian ideal,[65] in capitalist narration that distance disappears and with it the grounding of subjectivity for the author (and for the reader as well; Lindau, Frenssen, Hermann).

In conclusion, I recall the introductory caveat that the problem of the writer in organized capitalism depends on a variety of tendencies. The increasing institutional specialization in the sphere of aesthetic values engenders bitter conflicts between the countercultural carriers of these values and the bourgeois world. Furthermore, the transition from laissez-faire to monopoly capitalism explains a plethora of ideological motifs—anti-individualism, leadership cult, belief in destiny, etc. Nevertheless the examination of the commodification of literary production enables one to account for basic shifts in the social character of language, the public, and the author, with specific consequences for the character of literary texts, the implied reader, and the narrator. Beyond these results, it should also be clear that capitalist literary production—the culture industry—is not simply a matter of the popular literature of mass distribution. Rather, in the age of organized capitalism, the categories of capitalist production are reproduced in all literature, since all texts, high and low, are caught in the same society of commodity exchange and reification.

CHAPTER FIVE

Modern Art and Desublimation

CLOSE to the beginning of "Death in Venice," Thomas Mann sets up a relationship between aesthetic production and social context that bears strongly on the parameters of twentieth-century cultural life. After introducing his central figure, the fictive writer Aschenbach, Mann goes on to offer some exposition which, as always with Mann, is much more than exposition, since it draws attention to one of the central philosophical questions of the text:

> It was a spring afternoon in that year of grace 19—, when Europe sat upon the anxious seat beneath a menace that hung over its head for months. Aschenbach had sought the open soon after tea. He was overwrought by a morning of hard, nerve-taxing work, work which had not ceased to exact his uttermost in the way of sustained concentration, conscientiousness, and tact.[1]

In the age of high imperialism, international tensions threaten to explode into war, and in the context of this political crisis, an aesthetic crisis ensues. To be sure, Aschenbach's writing problems are in no way an immediate reflection of international disputes, but the juxtaposition of the two crises in the opening lines of the text is significant, especially because when Aschenbach "sought the open soon after tea," he set out on a journey that leads eventually to Venice and the plague, "where horrid death" stalked the streets and "it seemed to him as though the moral law were fallen in ruins."[2] Aschenbach's narrative is embedded in the experience of social catastrophe, not the one intimated at first, but one equally devastating. Do Aschenbach's path and the specific character of his crisis as a writer derive in some way from the collective crisis? Or might it even be that the vicissitudes of art, the radical transformation in the character of aesthetic production recorded in the novella, contribute to the social catastrophe?

The ostensible argument of the novella sets up a parallel between the immanent contradictions of bourgeois Prussian society and its representative form of aesthetic production, both predicated on the viability of a Protestant ethic of repression and labor: Aschenbach's flight from work anticipates the crisis of the notion of aesthetic "work," while the shift of scene from German order, established by the force of Friderician arms, to Venetian lassitude emancipates previously sub-liminal forces that are quickly identified as a newly assertive death instinct. Because of this correlation between the social landscape and aesthetic form, the text can describe the genesis of modernism by pos-iting three aesthetic models: (1) Aschenbach's epigonic classicism; (2) the Dionysian imagination of the desublimated collective; and (3) the text itself carried by the tension between the fictive writer and the foregrounded narrator. The conventional work, dependent on the au-tonomous writer in whom repression and individuation coexist in a fragile balance, becomes obsolete in the face of the ecstatic crowd of the dream; Mann's modernism characteristically occupies the space between the two poles, dividing its loyalties and subjecting its own voice, the narrator, to parodic techniques. Yet the problem of the nar-rator is of less interest here than the description of the historical pro-cess; a dialectic emerges between the desublimation of art, no longer capable of effecting a repression of its own romantic-sensuous motor, its expressive content, and, on the other hand, an aestheticization of life. The writer who ceases to work on works engages in the ruses of real seduction, the self-debasing cosmetic escapades, and the peder-astic pursuit of beauty in vivo.

The decline of the individuated artist, the cipher of the formative principle and self-possession, corresponds to the aestheticization of life practice. In this sense, the account of "Death in Venice" corrobo-rates Peter Bürger's model of the avant-garde project. The sublation of life and art takes on the form of the renunciation of autonomous aesthetic production in order to realize beauty in sensual fulfillment. Of course Mann's pre–World War I evaluation of this project is char-acteristically pessimistic. By attempting to carry the sequestered values of traditional aesthetics outside the pale of the work, Aschenbach transgresses against the authenticity of aesthetic form, engendering a decay that forebodes the collapse of the moral order, i.e., the aesthetic crisis articulates and antedates the social catastrophe. Mann's own later accounts of a specifically modernist project beyond the precepts of inherited autonomy are less pejorative, just as his earlier conserva-tive pessimism could be contrasted readily with versions of the aes-theticization of life apotheosized by major figures of European mod-ernism as the guarantor of an epiphanic pleasure: "And she saw a long

Roman candle going up over the trees up, up, and, in the tense hush, they were all breathless with excitement as it went higher and higher and she had to lean back more and more to look up after it, high, high, almost out of sight, and her face was suffused with a divine, an entrancing blush from straining back."[3] For Joyce, the aesthetic impulse is not imprisoned in the work but becomes a constituent moment of erotic beauty in lived experience. For Mann in 1911, the aestheticization of life engenders a social collapse. Despite these antithetical judgments, in both Mann and Joyce the project of the historical avant-garde appears as the decoupling of utopian aesthetic ideals (beauty, sensuousness, freedom) from inherited poetological categories (the work, formal constraint) in order to transfer those ideals into social practice: social revolution via aesthetic innovation.[4]

Yet the apparently conservative judgment in "Death in Venice" regarding the revolt against form and convention ought not to be shrugged off too quickly. It is not adequate merely to relegate it to an early phase in Mann's career or to relativize it with reference to other proponents of the avant-garde project. For this essayistic novella poses foremost a question of contemporary relevance that can provide the discussion of postmodernism with a setting that extends beyond the limits of aesthetic debate: does there exist a subterranean relationship between the rejection of the aesthetic work, the desublimation of art, and the "menace" that now hangs over more than just Europe? Does the historical demise of autonomous art contribute to the virulence of social aggression, especially to recrudescent nationalism? Has the aestheticization of everyday life, the intended corollary to the avant-gardist attack on the institution of art, perhaps succeeded in transforming the life world, while setting off an unforeseen process leading less to collective utopias of beautiful harmony than to a barbarization no longer counteracted or harnessed by the values of a secure aesthetic institution? If modernism and the historical avant-garde have run their course, as the advocates of postmodernism claim, then it may be more productive to consider how the disappearance of traditional cultural forms contributes to the character of contemporary social life than to argue for this or that artistic ism as the heir to the canonic throne.

In order to clarify the sociological ramifications of the avant-gardist dual project of desublimation and aestheticization, it is crucial to point out a fundamental assumption in the current debate on modernism, shared by both the postmodernist and the critical theoretical camps. Both positions assert that the concepts of modernity and modernism which are at stake correspond to the cultural formations of humanism that have prevailed in the West since the Renaissance or at least the eighteenth century. Hence the apparent similarity of contemporary polemics to the confrontations between the Enlightenment and its romantic opposition, so often repeated during the past two centuries. The consequence of this epochal definition of modernity is the relative denigration of the aesthetic revolution at the end of the nineteenth and beginning of the twentieth century and the emergence of what is commonly known as "modern art" or "modernist literature" in contrast to the traditional and conventional forms of the preceding decades. On the one hand, Habermas incorporates this modern art into the larger notion of modernity by treating it as a consequence of the differentiation of an aesthetic sphere within a version of Western specificity derived from Weber.[5] On the other hand, critics like Jameson and Sussman push modernism back into the nineteenth century, by identifying either its purported values (subjectivity, individualism) or its rhetorical forms (bifurcation, sublation) with an inherited cultural legacy.[6] The two strategies pursue diametrically opposite goals: critical theory insists on the continuity of the epoch in order to demonstrate the relevance of the emancipatory contents of the Enlightenment, while the postmodernists subsume modernism in a Victorian (or Wilhelmine etc.) past in order to ground a decisionistic announcement of a new epistemic structure after "the end of man."[7] Given this implicit periodization, the radical aesthetic innovation of the early twentieth century tends to disappear. The lines that separate Joyce and Brecht from Dickens and Schiller, Picasso and Ernst from Ingres and Friedrich, Schoenberg and Stravinsky from Mozart and Schubert pale in significance once twentieth-century modernism is reduced to a mere phase within the larger notion of modernity.

For critical theory, this shift in attention from twentieth-century modernism to postmedieval modernity represents a profound conceptual break with its own origin in the early phase of Western Marxism, during which aesthetic discussion concentrated on the relationship between avant-gardist innovation and radical social transformation. The revolutionary optimism of Benjamin and Brecht hoped to harness the avant-garde immediately to political progress, while Horkheimer and Adorno viewed authentic art as the placeholder of a potential opposition to monopoly capitalism and the culture industry, i.e., in both cases, the contemporary aesthetic revolution was located within the terms of a profound social reorganization.

This particularity of the historical avant-garde, which has disappeared from Habermas' account, is maintained primarily within the work of Christa and Peter Bürger.[8] They present the avant-garde as a frontal assault on the bourgeois institution of art established in the age of German idealism and classic-romantic aesthetics, an assault in which the inherited dichotomy of "life and art" was to undergo a sublation whereby the postauratic work would lose its formal cohesion and work character through the incorporation of elements of life (collage), while social life would be transformed by an infusion of aesthetic values (a tendency apparent not only in the avant-garde movements per se but, with evident consequences, in the craft and industrial projects of William Morris, Josef Hoffmann, and, especially, the Bauhaus). This is the dual project alluded to above: desublimation and aestheticization, Aschenbach's renunciation of discipline and the pursuit of a sensuous immediacy.

While the Bürgers provide a convincing account of the transformed character of artistic objects in the wake of the historical avant-garde movements, i.e., the specificity of twentieth-century "modernism," their argument remains locked within the immanence of high cultural production. Neither do they relate the emergence of the avant-garde to extra-aesthetic developments (urbanization, industrialization, the First World War, or, more generally, the transition to monopoly capitalism and the transformation of the public sphere), or examine the social consequences of the avant-garde in the realm of "life," despite the pronounced revolutionary claims of the avant-gardists and modernists themselves. It will be helpful to recall these claims; three literary examples ought to suffice to demonstrate the pathos and ambivalence of the modernist project and to provide the foundation for an evaluation of the contemporary legacy of the aestheticization of everyday life.

Hermann Hesse was certainly not one of the most radical or sophisticated modernists, and his problematic reception during the sixties has compounded these shortcomings, but, for those who can stomach it, his *Steppenwolf* in fact provides an illuminating insight into the modernist project. Hesse's emphatic scrutinization of a paradigmatic psychological structure makes it clear that the aesthetic innovation of modernism is inextricably tied to a transformation of the individual within a social revolution. This revolution, furthermore, conjoins with hostility to the liberal nineteenth century, a feature of all versions of modernism with their privileging of the new and the young as the carrier of a *nuda veritas* against the *Lebenslüge* of the old world.[9] For Hesse this means a dual escape from the structures of inherited culture: an escape from a dichotomous individuality, oscillating between the bourgeois and the bohemian spheres, in the name of a decentered polyvalence as well as an escape from the reified forms of bourgeois art, where the great figures (Goethe and Mozart) are ensconced as marmorated heroes, while their authentic significance is obliterated. This critique of the past is however merely prologue to the project of an aestheticization of life and the production of a post-individuated community. Hesse describes "the mysterious merging of the personality in the mass, the mystic union of joy. . . . It was known, I knew, to every servant girl. . . . I had seen it in drunken recruits and sailors, and also in great artists in the enthusiasm, perhaps, of a musical festival; and not less in young soldiers going to war."[10]

After the attack on established bourgeois culture which is discussed in the initial sections of the novel, Hesse presents this account of the aestheticization of life, located, characteristically enough, at an artists' ball. It represents at least one version of the avant-gardist project, and its features point to some at least potential sociological consequences. First of all, the community is characterized by the obliteration of the distinction between high and low culture, i.e., great artists and servant girls, a theme carried out in the novel as the reconciliation of alternative musical forms, jazz and Mozart. Yet the legitimation of popular culture is apparently possible only through its elevation to a religious experience, i.e., the dance cannot be mere fun or entertainment but must, on the contrary, fulfill all the emphatic requirements of bourgeois art. Hesse's utopian redefinition of low culture therefore anticipates the left postmodernist position that claims to discover emancipatory yearnings in the products of the culture industry. Second, the community permits no individuality and certainly no privacy; all differences disappear in an ineluctable transparency that belies the claim to a mystery. The Dionysian revolt suddenly displays a totalitarian propensity which, in the case of Hesse's narrator, formerly an articulate antimilitarist, forces an identification with fanatic recruits. Not only must his personal history be denied, it is overpowered by a death instinct, hostile to all particularity and intimately tied to the process of desublimation. This restructuring of individuality leads, third, to a universal eroticization, the apparent ubiquity of pleasure beyond all taboos, in which however pleasure is perpetually denied because of the nonspecificity of any union. The corollary to the attack on the traditional aesthetic form is a duplicitous instinctual emancipation which in fact subjugates eros to the capitalist logic of serial commodities; the partners at the ball are thrust on the narrator, one after another, by a force beyond his comprehension, let alone under his control. This is the secret of the supposed mystery: the capitulation of the individual during the transition to monopoly capitalism.[11]

The social consequences intended by Hesse's modernist desublimation of art are clearly problematic, to say the least. Yet just as Mann's conservative appraisal could be balanced by Joyce's enthusiasm, the regression inherent in Hesse's Dionysian crowd has to be contrasted with an alternative version of the postindividual community inspired by a leftist project. Benjamin's argument in "The Work of Art in the Age of Mechanical Reproduction" is well known: the deauraticization of art carried out by technological innovation and social modernization potentially replaces the fragmented and passively contemplative recipient with a critical audience. It is important to point out that this account of the democratizing function of the cinema postdates Benjamin's similar defense of a modernist literary project: a new way of writing, which breaks with the inherited forms of bourgeois aesthetics, produces a new, postbourgeois public. Like Lukács, Benjamin uses the term "epic" to designate the literature of a nonindividuated community, but while Lukács ascribes the epic to the "integrated civilization" of the distant past in Homeric Greece, Benjamin identifies an epic potential in contemporary culture.[12] Consider, for example, the following passage from his 1930 review of Döblin's *Berlin Alexanderplatz:*

> For the epic, being is an ocean. There is nothing more epic than the ocean. One can of course treat the ocean in very different ways. For example, lie on the beach, listen to the surf, and collect the shells it washes ashore. That is what the epic author does. One can also travel the ocean. With many goals and none at all. One can take an ocean voyage, and then, out there, with no land in sight, only sea and sky, wander aimlessly. That is what the author of the novel does. He is truly lonely and mute. Epic man is only at rest. In the epic, the people rests after the day's labor; it listens, dreams, and collects. The novelist has separated himself from the people and its activity. The birth chamber of the novel is the isolated individual who can no longer discuss his most important concerns in an exemplary

manner, who is confused and oblivious to advice. In the presentation of human existence, the novel pushes incommensurability to an extreme. One can feel the difference between the novel and the true epic by thinking of the works of Homer and Dante. Oral tradition, the material of the epic, has a makeup different from the substance of a novel. The novel differs from all other forms of prose—the fairy tale, the legend, the saying, the funny story—in that it neither derives from nor enters into an oral tradition. It differs most clearly however from the narration of epic prose. Nothing contributes more to the dangerous silencing of the human spirit, nothing stifles the soul of narration more thoroughly than the shameless expansion that the reading of novels has undergone in all of our lives.[13]

In his literary criticism from the end of the Weimar Republic, Benjamin develops a modernist program that can be designated as "epic leftism" which puts him at odds with the representatives of various forms of tendentious literature and the emerging socialist realism. For Benjamin, epic literature operates less through the advocacy of any particular message than through a reception process that overcomes individuation in order to invoke a democratic collective: "It is a matter of life or death for the new epic to liquidate this privacy from which the novel derives its legitimacy."[14]

One need not belabor the startling conjunction of a program to liquidate privacy and the Stalinization of European communism. Benjamin's program converges with Hesse's rejection of individuality as the corollary to the deautonomization of art. It evidently lacks, however, the romantic, instinctual coloration of the Dionysian crowd. Benjamin's community is linked instead to the possibility of knowledge. It can learn and listen; the epic is its own speech; and while the individual of the novel remains hopelessly lost in incommensurable particularity, the epic collective can reflect on its experiences "in an exemplary manner." This cogitational character of epic leftism corresponds to the familiar intention of Brecht's epic theater: criticism and ratiocination rather than emotional identification and catharsis.

Yet despite this critical characterization of the community intended by the modernist project of epic leftism, the rhetorical designations employed by Benjamin indicate other, highly ambivalent features as well. It is an image of sedentary indolence, an archaic and organic collective that is not only democratic but also potentially national:

both epithets are legitimate corollaries to the German term *Volk*. While Hesse links modernist deautonomization to an imitation of military groupings, Benjamin's epic stands in a subliminal relationship to a national identity. It would be wrong to argue that every critique of bourgeois aesthetics necessarily instigates a nationalist mobilization, but this process seems to be at least a potential tendency even within the leftist version of modernism.

This is not the place to enter into an examination of those dubious arguments regarding the progressive potential of a leftist nationalism in the twentieth century,[15] nor can one impute an intentional nationalism to Benjamin and his allies; on the contrary, their work is marked by an unmistakably internationalist allegiance. The point is rather this: while epic leftism offers a modernist program with claims to emancipate a critical audience, the realization of those claims is extraordinarily difficult to demonstrate, and the real historical result of the leftist attack on bourgeois forms may have been to amplify the general modernist dismantling of traditional culture with unintended consequences, including the unleashing of collective nationalist impulses. Given the continuity of a heteronomous social organization, the public produced by a postauratic art form (despite the claims of Benjamin and Brecht) may end up more a national folk than a democratic folk.

Deautonomization, which generated Hesse's dance crowd and Benjamin's ambivalent folk, has related but different ramifications in the fascist version of the critique of bourgeois aesthetics formulated by Ernst Jünger. Despite his own highbrow predilections, a central theme in his writings from the twenties and thirties addresses the alleged obsolescence of the forms of bourgeois culture, key categories of which however are projected onto the battlefield or the organization of the totalitarian state. While the autonomous work of art, for example, is rejected as part of an anachronistic prewar bourgeoisie, its features recur as the beauty of the battlefield or the perfection of the military machinery: "Today we are writing poems of steel, and we are fighting for power in battles that unfold with the precision of machines. There is a beauty in it which we can already sense: in these battles on land, on sea, and in the air in which the hot will of our blood controls itself and finds expression in the mastery of the technical miracle machines of power."[16] This is what Benjamin would call the "aestheticization of politics," with reference to a quotation from Marinetti, and Jünger's proximity to the Italian model of a fascist futurism is evident.[17]

Yet war does not only replace the artwork by usurping its categories; it also transforms them radically, for the aesthetic experience, an erstwhile constituent of the bourgeois public sphere, now no longer permits any individuation. The hostility to differentiation that marked Hesse's serial eroticism becomes a heroic denigration of individual suffering:

> All goals are transitory, flux alone is eternal, and it constantly produces wonderful and pitiless spectacles. Only few are granted the opportunity to lose themselves in their sublime purposelessness, as with artworks or the starry heaven. But whoever perceives in this war solely the negation, solely his own suffering, and not the affirmation, the greater movement, has experienced it all as a slave. He has had not an inner, but only an outer experience.[18]

The continuity with traditional bourgeois culture is unmistakable: the purposelessness of art, reception as contemplation, the beauty of nature, the dichotomy of outer and inner (body and soul), and especially the elitist class distinctions as the underpinnings of cultural activity. Yet now differentiation, the imperative expression of "individual suffering," which had always been denied to the "slave," is withheld from the members of the elite as well. The passage marks a revolutionary transformation in bourgeois culture where the invocation of interiority, an "inner experience" of the battle, is mobilized against atavistic claims to a privacy that is liquidated in the heroic collective.

Jünger's account describes a process that is fundamentally homologous to the transformations outlined by Hesse and Benjamin: the modernist rejection of inherited bourgeois aesthetic forms is implicated in a dismantling of bourgeois subjectivity and the corollary production of a charismatic community that breaks radically with the individualism and legal rationality of the liberal period. This shared paradigm holds despite obvious differences among the political intentions: Hesse's romantic pacifism, Benjamin's maverick communism, and Jünger's emphatic militarism. Similar differences can be located in the competing aesthetic programs. Yet despite the relevance of both Hesse's insistence on the convergence of high and low culture and Benjamin's attention to the cinema, one finds in Jünger's reflections particularly trenchant observations for our contemporary situation. After linking the art of the bourgeois era to the cult of genius in which the work ultimately represents an "autobiographical document" of the great figure, he underscores the contemporary "decline of the individual and his inherited values not only on the battlefield, not only in politics, but in art as well."[19] The "worker," who is never individuated, replaces the soldier as Jünger's point of reference in the early thirties.[20] Art consequently no longer expresses subjectivity, demonstrating instead the exigencies of total planning and the absence of any separate spheres for private endeavors:

> For the same power that the art of politics represents in the exercise of authority is revealed by art in its formative activity. Art must demonstrate how, from a lofty vantage point, life is understood as totality. [Art] is nothing separate, nothing that possesses validity in itself or because of itself. There is on the contrary no realm of life that could not be regarded as material for art.[21]

For two centuries innovative aesthetic production had claimed for itself the right to treat previously proscribed material, e.g., the breakdown of class barriers in the drama of the eighteenth century and later on the naturalist stage, as well as quotidian motifs in nineteenth-century painting, both tendencies generally considered to be progressive attacks on academic classicism. Jünger appropriates this movement and radicalizes it: because art can address everything, nothing can escape the universal process of aestheticization.

The modernist attack on autonomous art and individual privacy consequently points toward two consequences. The first is a generic shift toward types of aesthetic products which were disprivileged within liberal culture because of their essential incompatibility with prevailing notions of privacy: Jünger mentions sculpture, drama, and architecture, all public forms (unlike the novels disdained by Benjamin). Their corollaries in contemporary culture are the installation, performance art, and architectural postmodernism. Second, once the aesthetic principle escapes the strictures of the autonomous work, it invades the previously extra-aesthetic life world and becomes a formative force that transforms the contemporary individual into a constant recipient, not only in museums or at concerts but in all spheres of daily activity.

If one can speak today of a postmodern situation, then it is only in terms of the vicissitudes of the modernist project. Modernism has aged, the avant-garde has become obsolete, to the extent that the early-twentieth-century faith in the revolutionary power of the artist and the work has dissolved, in part because the utopian social transformation promised by so many avant-gardists has not taken place.

The *promesse de bonheur* has lost its credibility. On the other hand, modernism has succeeded, albeit in an unforeseen manner, in its dual program of dismantling the autonomous work and aestheticizing everyday life, and this success defines the substance of the postmodern situation. The avant-garde derived its pathos from the fact that the bourgeois aesthetic assumptions that were the object of its protest were still very powerful. The same tradition which was under attack provided the antitraditionalists with their strength. Today that tradition has disappeared, thanks in part to the historical labor of the avant-garde, and there is no longer a foil against which an effective repetition of modernist protest can define itself. No longer committed to traditional aesthetic forms, today's public will no longer be outraged, and it is this obsolescence of shock, a central category of the avant-garde, that explains the resounding inconsequentiality of contemporary aesthetic production.

Given the waning of the avant-garde in the wake of its own success, important changes in the character of artworks take place. This distance from the legacy of the historical avant-garde can be discussed in terms of formal technique, the objectivity of works, and their relationship to history. One predominant strand of modernism moved along a trajectory of rationalization toward an increasing abstraction fundamentally hostile to the representational arts of the nineteenth century: cubism, de Stijl, constructivism, leading eventually to minimalism, conceptual art, and superrealist painting (understood as concerned less with its putative content than with an analysis of the relationship between painting and its ubiquitous technical competitor, photography). Parallel developments include the abstract descriptions in Kafka, the language crisis in Musil, and the self-referentiality of literature and film. Yet, while an aesthetics of abstraction thrived on a critique of a retreating representationalism, more recent works display a sudden revival of figurative painting (neo-expressionism) and referential literature (new subjectivity). Representationalism and the denigration of form set the stage for the new popularity of naive painters and the rediscovery of artists such as Frida Kahlo and Grant Wood. The return to representation in fact implies a devaluation of formal-technical matters, i.e., the medial self-reflection that was a hallmark of modernism. This explains the technical incompetence that sometimes characterizes recent painting (a feature which is of course also a consequence of the heightened commodification of aesthetic production in the context of a vigorous art market).

While neofigurative painting and new subjectivist literature present their disdain for formal considerations as a protest against an academic modernism (and therefore in fact continue to participate in a discourse of formal reflection), the content of the expression regularly limits itself to a nebulous emotional rage. The public display of the purportedly personal denies any distance between the public and private through a decisionistic declaration of a universal libidinal impulse, as in the sexual projections of Christian Attersee's paintings. Neo-expressionism as the unmediated revelation of instinctual force can therefore be viewed as the uncritical mirroring of the repressive desublimation of everyday life under the aegis of aestheticization.[22] This conservative authoritarian implication of the antimodernist return to figurativism corresponds to the historical conjunction of the postmodern discourse and the neoconservative politics of the late seventies, both of which railed against abstraction and called for the reinstitution of legible, i.e., representational, systems.

While the avant-garde defined itself through the attack on the autonomous work, it still maintained for its own works a claim to objectivity and enclosure, at least as negative moments. Adorno captures this contradictory, i.e., transitional, stage in the paradoxical formulation that "today the only works which really count are those which are no longer works at all."[23] In Picasso's collages or the political photomontages of Heartfield, elements of everyday life are integrated directly into the work, implicitly exploding its autonomy, while the objectivity guaranteed by the frame retains a labile legitimacy, derived from the object of attack, the premodernist organic totality. This receding totality finally disappears in the hegemonic forms of contemporary aesthetic production: the negative space of video art and the ephemerality of performances. Installations similarly radicalize the avant-gardist critique of self-enclosed objectivity and tend toward a multidimensional aestheticization of the environment, as in Thomas Lanigan-Schmidt's *Childhood Memories,* while others still operate within a late abstractionist discourse of formal coherence, e.g., Bruce Naumann's *Dream Passage.*

The success of the avant-gardist critique of self-enclosed objectivity implies an obsolescence of this critique; what follows is not necessarily a return to the traditional work form (parallel to the return to representation) but rather a transformed function of the open work which ceases to carry a protest potential vis-à-vis a traditional standard of closure. This leads first to a decided enervation, particularly evident if one considers the history of the poster, a popular form related to the avant-garde, from the fin-de-siècle through the revolutionary twenties to a late renaissance in 1968. The decline of the poster as an artistic genre in recent years is perhaps the clearest indication of depoliticization and a new transformation of the public sphere. It has been replaced by the non-self-enclosed form par excellence, mail art (correspondence art) as graphic epistolary communication among the members of a marginalized neobohemia. A similar weakening is evident in the transition from the political drama of the avant-garde, epic theater, and even its latter-day offspring, the living theater, forms which interlocked with political subcultures and demonstrations, to contemporary performances; this postmodern popular theater oscillates between marginalization and a breathtaking commercialization, as in the case of Laurie Anderson.

In addition to this diminutive character of the nonobjective work, an expansive tendency is equally characteristic of recent cultural life. In place of individual aesthetic objects, major events with aesthetic claims or aestheticizing intentions increasingly occupy the place reserved for art in traditional bourgeois culture. These range from forms of drama as archaic as they are hypertrophic (Hermann Nitzsch's orgone-mystery theater in Prinzendorf) and state-sponsored spectacle (André Heller's fireworks in Lisbon and Berlin), to imperiously grand museum shows (King Tut, China, Alexander, the Vatican); their grandeur tends to dwarf the significance of any individual work, which in turn corresponds to their ultimate goal. For they are designed less to display particular aesthetic objects than, through their very size and substance, to celebrate power. This celebration can provide the mediation for specific political programs (e.g., in Sino-American relations); in general, however, the international character of the exhibitions indicates a universal function: the relegitimation of authority through aesthetic representation. The range of aestheticizing productions can be traced further through media events like the 1984 Olympics (conservative insofar as it still pretended to sequester aesthetics in the accompanying arts festival) and the political spectacles of the party conventions. The false sublation of art and life culminates when, in the age of mechanical reproduction, the most advanced technical means available are employed to aestheticize political discourse fully, an aestheticization that is exposed by the nomination of an actor as best suited to carry on the bluff. The deautonomization of art and the aestheticization of life become indistinguishable.[24]

In addition to their formal technique and objectivity, the relationship to history of recent artistic works is indicative of the transition from modernist protest to postmodern ornamentalism. The modernist work locates itself along a diachronic axis through an immanent critique of tradition, thereby describing an emphatic present counterposed to a rejected past: vide the versions of the Mona Lisa by Duchamp and Dali. The modernist present continues history by producing the new, while simultaneously rejecting history as the nineteenth-century narrative of development. This contradiction, which echoes the self-contradictory character of the avant-gardist work, is played out in *The Trial* as the tension between the rationalized time of the office world and the organic time of the single year of Josef K.'s life in which the events unroll. A similar tension is evident between the developmental narrative and the stasis of montage in *Doctor Faustus,* a corollary to the dialectic of myth and history in Adorno's essay on natural history.[25]

The historicity of the modernist work disappears in postmodernism which, no longer defining its present against a rejected past, exists in a temporal void in which any notion of historico-philosophical progress, any promise of hope, becomes meaningless. In contrast to the prototypes by the avant-gardists Duchamp and Dali, Warhol's *Twelve Mona Lisas* has no critical edge because of the obsolescence of the diachronic tension. With the end of history, the aesthetic category of the new loses its relevance; instead the aesthetic debris of the past (which is no longer a past opposed to the present) reappears as immediately accessible in the historicist eclecticism of postmodernist architectural referentiality. A similar tendency is evident in the proliferation of references to traditional works and the allegorical and mythological languages of earlier eras in works by figures as diverse as Sandro Chia, Gerard Garouste, and Vettor Pisani. If Arnulf Rainer's *Grünwald Variations* displays some exceptional force, it is undoubtedly due to the continued comprehensibility of the Christological reference in the "overpainting" of images from the Isenheim altar. Otherwise the mythic lexemes are addressed to a public no longer familiar with the encompassing narratives, nor is such familiarity even expected.

The striking tendency for neofigurativism to turn quickly to myth despite the absence of a correspondingly literate public indicates that the communicative character of artworks is not at all the real issue. Instead, neoclassical mythic images are meant to be recognizable simply as contentless signs of culture and can be displayed as such by a public eager to distinguish itself through the possession of an art that leaves no doubt as to its artistic character. This instrumentalization of artworks in a semiotic display of class identity was certainly a pronounced tendency in the late nineteenth century as well, when however it was still relativized by the claims of autonomous aesthetics; the philistine misappropriation of art could be condemned in terms of the hegemonic aesthetic values. Today those values have been eroded, and philistinism can flourish without fear of condemnation; hence the conspicuous consumption of neoclassical imagery, a style which has repeatedly been used for the conservative representation of power.

While contemporary aesthetic production has finally escaped the limitations demanded by the formal sublimation of the traditional work (and its avant-gardist counterpart), the bourgeois separation of life and art too gives way to a massive aestheticization of everyday life. The aesthetic impulse, which has marched out of the museums and into the streets, casts an inescapable spell, transfiguring both slum and suburb. This encompassing universality still echoes the universal-human claims of classical aesthetics, but while the older notion of beauty was ultimately compatible with a utopia of freedom, the contemporary aestheticization of life turns out to be a prime guarantor of order. Art becomes the extension of politics, as the system of domination modernizes its mechanisms of control; not even the most Argus-eyed cop-on-the-block could compete with the omnipresence of music, the most romantic of arts. Stores, markets, shopping centers, bars, restaurants, and airplanes are alive with the sound of Muzak, and tunes regularly drone out over loudspeakers in public parks and pools, from hypertrophic radios at the beach and in the city, and even in the relative privacy of the telephone, when one is placed "on hold."

The behaviorist thesis that the musical supermarket stimulates the consumer's will to buy is a crudely mechanistic trivialization of a profound restructuring of the public sphere. The ubiquity of Muzak tends to obliterate communication and to break down individual resistance, constructing instead the beautiful illusion of a unanimous collective. Yet because it is a false collective in which no one is ever at home, it constantly collapses in a sadomasochistic antinomy: on the one hand, the autistic pseudoprivacy of the Walkman, on the other, the megalomaniacal self-assertion of the ghetto blaster. The former apparently creates a self-enclosed passivity, while the latter imposes itself aggressively on its surroundings, and each of these gestures stands in an inverse relationship to the social status of the group associated with the respective technical device: the poorest sound the loudest. This contradiction indicates how, even in the context of the aestheticization of daily life, the postauratic work still operates with a vestige of autonomous aesthetics: the nonidentity of appearance and reality. The power of the music does not reflect the power of the recipient—the reverse is rather the case—and the corresponding principle of illusion is located at the intersection of aesthetic resources and political control.

Yet the hypothesis that the intonation of society acts as a vehicle for illusion is only an external explanation. The destruction of the public sphere through musical blockage is not only manipulation but also the desublimation of a desire for isolated passivity, speechlessness, and silence which are demanded of the recipient precisely by the overwhelming volume of the music. The deadening roar of the underclass radios conjoins with the catatonia of the Walkman victims in a mimesis of death. The secret of the libidinal economy is revealed in the locus of postmodern sociability, the dating bar, in which the decentered individual moves relentlessly from union to union, while the electronic noise guarantees the obsolescence of language and the pointlessness of communication. The specific constellation of sexual desire and deathly silence, eros and thanatos, indicates a new logic. Live performance has survived only in nostalgic enclaves—Dixieland in New Orleans or high school bands at football games. Elsewhere music exists mainly as technical reproduction. In this form, as dead labor, it envelops the contemporary listener who, still alive, pursues death through imitation in a revised political economy. As passive as the absent producers, he fully understands the violence of the productive system, and even when it is directed against himself, precisely that violence fascinates his instinctual aggression. The aestheticization of life appeals to a death desire that redefines artistic consumption; the exponential violence in the mass media and in spectacular crimes reflects a fundamental revision of the political-instinctual foundation of social organization. For the collapse of the ethic of worldly asceticism contributed to the end of autonomy aesthetics (Aschenbach's work); the subsequent aestheticization of everyday life, however, transforms experience in ways that uncover a considerable potential for aggression.

The architectural counterpart to the abstraction of music is the concrete organization of space in definitively solid forms: shopping centers, airports, housing developments, convention halls, and the other accessories of city planning that overwhelm and overpower their inhabitants. The modernist relationship between the body and its spatial environment was determined by the discovery of sensuous plasticity (Rodin, Isadora Duncan) as a gesture against Victorian repression, and by the dissolution of the oppressive nineteenth-century architectural shells that were replaced by the transparency of glass in order to flood the new interiors with the light of natural truth (Bruno Taut). In contrast, postmodern antisubjectivity denies the presence of the body, while arbitrarily erecting concrete structures that compress space, channel movement, and decisionistically affirm their own power as epistemic paradigms. The borderline between the two models separates the still-modernist Hancock Building in Boston, dissolving into the sky and reflecting on the history of its local environment, from the Portland Building in Portland, Oregon, with its historicist façade signifying nothing, its reassuring coloration, and its oppressively cozy lobby. After the escape of the work of art from the rationalization of form, the aestheticization of everyday life imposes form on the recipient as victim, and this formative imperative draws from the same authoritarian source as does the revival of a neoclassical language in painting. The new architecture does not open a public space; instead it encloses it in a carapacial covering designed to ensure order. Its stable solidity, historicist timelessness, and dark opacity all reveal its tomblike character, providing an appropriate setting for the desublimation of thanatos.

This tendency to aestheticize space in terms of a deathlike order extends as well to the reorganization of the body, which mirrors its new environment. As buildings take on an antimodernist solidity and the power of mausoleums, bodybuilding produces a muscular shell; beneath the ostensible intent to improve one's health lies an imitation of rigor mortis, the mimesis of death in the aestheticization of flesh, the symbol of which is the cult of weight training with its icons, Schwarzenegger and Stallone. Like the mythic references in painting and the formal imperative of architecture, the contemporary veneration of the body and athletics draws on a neoclassical, Hellenistic language; beauty and appearance are central categories in the new sports, but so are aggression and competition. The belligerent content in the martial arts and weight training is blatant, while even the apparently innocuous jogging culture is surrounded by an aura of violence. The new athlete has trained his body to imitate machines, not to overcome them like John Henry. Competitiveness and survivalism abound; because he can run like hell, he looks forward to an imminent catastrophe, be it cancerous, ecological, or nuclear, from which he alone, like Bunyan's Christian, will escape. Conversely it is this expectation of catastrophe, a fixation on death, that fuels the health cult as the inversion of the latent content. Just as the Victorian repression of sex communicated with a distorted erotic desire, the contemporary insistence on health and the hysterical fear of disease point toward a deeper desire, as the joggers get ready for boot camp. Of course, the discourse of physical fitness has long been driven by a militarist concern for national preparedness.

In addition to the aestheticization of the formerly public sphere via Muzak, architecture, and sports, a more encompassing aestheticization with particularly destructive consequences for the private sphere takes place through the process of commodification. The illusion of commodity aesthetics was always inherent in the capitalist relationship between use value and exchange value. However, in the pre-Taylorist phase of the nineteenth century, the market mechanism remained largely external to some traditional formations, such as peasant and working-class culture, religious and regional heritages, and family loyalties. These identities, which could provide the individual with at least partial protection from commodification, become exhausted during the long transitional period from 1905 to 1968. With the demise during the seventies of the last generation that had known a noncommodified culture, i.e., one not organized in terms of a consumerist ethic, the stage was set for the final invasion of the remaining private sphere by the logic of commodities, accelerated by the delegitimation of traditional gender roles and the crisis of the nuclear family.

The atomistic individual, denied any inherited mechanism of self-identification, finds a helping hand in the world of commerce which proceeds to organize private lives in aesthetic terms: the life-style as the new colonial dumping ground for industrial overproduction. The atomized life that has been denied an authentic social context (family, community) becomes the object of commodified aestheticization. One consequence is the internal diversification of department stores where the multiplicity of tastes and tendencies quickly outdoes the touted polyphony of any postmodern novel. Yet the process of life-stylization applies not only to the department store set; it refers as well to the universal disappearance of an outside to art. There is no preaesthetic dimension to social activity, since social order has become dependent on aesthetic organization. Similarly nature, which art once imitated, has become secondary to art; any given piece of coastline, any single craggy peak cannot measure up to the standards set by the nature photographers and the Sierra Club calendars.

The double tendency examined so far—the desublimation of art in the wake of the avant-garde attack on the work and the extensive aestheticization of everyday life as a central strategy of capitalist progress—points to the historicity of the classical positions of critical theory. Adorno's account is based on the two assumptions that, first, culture (both high and low) represented a separate sphere of activity distinguishable from the rest of society, especially the realm of production, and, second, that a distinction between high and low culture was still tenable. Neither of these claims remains fully plausible today. Adorno's modernist aesthetics has been robbed of much of their relevance for the contemporary situation by a multifaceted transformation of cultural organization: the denigration of technique, the accelerated commodification of artistic production, the destabilization of the institutional discourse, and the loss of faith in the objectivity of the artwork. High art has rapidly integrated culture-industrial forms in its works (Lichtenstein, Warhol) as well as in its mechanisms of distribution (televised concerts, mass marketing of subscriptions).

Critical theory today means understanding the transformed character of the culture industry in the wake of the avant-garde. For Horkheimer and Adorno, the culture industry provided normative role models to integrate the masses into a conformist homogeneity through the identification with indistinguishable stars. Today the culture industry flaunts the outrageous and abnormal, the violent and the tabooed, although in the end it is all just good clean fun, so Michael Jackson can be received at the White House. In contrast to the golden age of Hollywood with its unwrinkled uniformity, contemporary commercial culture generates an artificial alterity: as entertainment, as a show of pluralism, and as an effort to counteract the deadly sameness that advanced capitalism constantly produces. This internal diversification of the culture industry corresponds to an external flexibility; no longer directed largely toward white America (as was the case at the time of the writing of the seminal analysis in *Dialectic of Enlightenment*), it has penetrated the black subculture and quickly coopted indigenous cultural forms: rap music, break dance. Historically the culture industry has sapped the energies of black culture since the days of minstrel shows; today the industry is assimilating that culture in a manner that may put an end to its autonomous character. Simultaneously the culture industry continues to succeed in foreign markets, with the ability to penetrate into the socialist East and to coopt the productive talents of any potential competitors (Caribbean music, German film). The first line of defense of American world power is culture, not the cruise missiles.

The historical avant-garde, despite its revolutionary gestures, still depended on features of nineteenth-century cultural life that have since disappeared in the course of social modernization: the public's faith in the objectivity of art; the hermeneutically competent recipient; an acceptance of the work as the locus of an aesthetic otherness. The personality type of bourgeois culture (who alone was the object of dadaist shock), the associated structure of the public sphere, and the institutional credibility of the work no longer support the modernist revolt, and this defines postmodernity as a new version of the end-of-art thesis. This does not mean that poems and paintings will soon become scarce, but it does mean that they lose their emphatic character as "works," that the public ceases to treat them with the reverence still common two decades ago as potential sources of values, and that the inherited generic identities quickly give way to hybrid forms.

It is precisely this desublimation of works of art, no longer subjected to formal rationalization and increasingly expressive, that corresponds to the aestheticization of everyday life which too initiates a desublimation that revises the fundamental instinctual economy by agitating a death instinct that takes the aestheticized form of an aggressive collective. The renunciation of control and rigor leads Aschenbach to his encounter with the new community:

> He craved with all his soul to join the ring that formed about
> the obscene symbol of the godhead, which they were unveiling
> and elevating, monstrous and wooden, while from full throats
> they yelled their rallying cry. Foam dripped from their lips, they
> drove each other on with lewd gesturings and beckoning hands.
> They laughed, they howled, they thrust their pointed staves
> into each other's flesh and licked the blood as it ran down. But
> now the dreamer was in them and of them, the stranger god
> was his own.[26]

The end of autonomous art as a vehicle of truth, which is the substance of postmodernism, engenders the violence of the desublimated collective held together only by myth. Mann's Dionysian cult as an alternative to classical art therefore anticipates the contemporary predilection for mythic material: Christa Wolf, Michael Ende, Michel Tournier, J. R. R. Tolkien, as well as that wing of "spiritual feminism" that dabbles in the purportedly prepatriarchal mythology of the distant past in order to cement a subcultural community.[27] The West German national revolutionary Henning Eichberg argues for the political revitalization of Germanic mythology, and Joseph Beuys, engaged for the Green party, invokes the magic numinosity of the German oak.[28]

These final examples point toward the potential social consequences of the postmodernist end of art. The avant-gardist attack on the autonomous work finally succeeds in delegitimizing the aesthetic institution, while the desired aestheticization of quotidian experience stimulates a latent aggression no longer held in check by traditional cultural mechanisms. From modernism to nationalism to war? If one considers Marinetti as a model, the thesis can appear plausible, and the "menace" that hangs over international politics turns out to have very much to do with Aschenbach's seeking "the open soon after tea." Three mechanisms in particular mediate the passage from cultural transformation to the aggressive nationalist collective. First, after the disappearance of high art as a credible source of values, the propagandistic potential of the culture industry grows rapidly, abetted by the full aestheticization of everyday life. The propagandistic mobilization of nationalist identity is nothing new, as the role of Hollywood during the Second World War makes clear. Yet the relationship between cultural propaganda and nationalism has undergone an important change. The antifascist film redirected libidinal energy from erotic fulfillment (Bogart's self-denial in *Casablanca*) to substantial values of solidarity, i.e., nationalism operated with alibis like the defense of civilization, democracy, or culture. The new nationalist propaganda, which emerged clearly during the 1984 Olympics, is linked to no such values. Instead an unmediated narcissistic egoism, fully oblivious to the competitors (which is why the absence of the Russians made no difference), celebrates itself, as it directs a blind aggression toward any otherness it might encounter. The new nationalist mobilization has no pathos of values, and it no longer depends on a traditional bourgeois oedipal socialization leading from family to the state. On the contrary, the propaganda is informal and unpretentious—aggression in shirtsleeves, unmediated selfishness turning into absolute misanthropy. The increasingly violent character of culture-industrial manipulation is evident not only in the blood lust of films like *Friday the Thirteenth* and

Halloween but in the murderous sociability portrayed in daytime soap operas or prime-time series ("Dallas," "Dynasty") in contrast with which the television figures of the fifties and sixties seem endearing in their naively humanistic values.

This transformation of culture-industrial nationalism depends on a second mechanism: a revised libidinal economy in the wake of the counterculture. If the counterculture represented a late stage in the modernist demontage of Victorian repression, it was also itself a vehicle for the aestheticization of everyday life, since its hedonist critique of the Protestant ethic eventually contributed to an acceleration of consumerism and the colonialism of life-styles. Despite this unintended consequence, it argued that a breakdown of traditional structures and prohibitions would have desirable political results; "Make love, not war" means that the spread of the sexual revolution would undermine discipline and block military belligerence. The argument assumes a traditional model of authoritarianism in which excessive instinctual denial produces the potentially violent personality. It is a liberal argument insofar as it posits a fundamentally good human nature and treats the discontents of civilization as unnecessary deformities caused by reformable social structures. The later Freud, however, located a different tendency: the natural potential for violence and aggression that is kept in check only by a displacement of erotic force. Freud's thesis sheds an important light on the changed character of nationalist aggression after the counterculture. For the new nationalism is fully compatible with a nonascetic, post-sixties life-style. It does not depend on restrictive high schools, macho football coaches, fifties fathers and limited petting; it thrives instead on the culture of selfhood, jogging narcissism, multiple divorces, and the absence of sexual prohibitions. The instinctual desublimation unleashes innate aggression in the personal self that is transferred to the national self, where it takes on the character of a global threat.

This appears at first to be paradoxical. The hedonist project, that stretches from the emphatic eroticism of modernist art and literature to its social realization in the counterculture, does not lead to the authentic increase in pleasure or the genuine hedonism that the neoconservatives complain of. The emancipation of eros has been shortcircuited as the "sexual revolution," the main benefits of which have accrued to the culture industry. Its main consequence has been the delegitimation of the institution of marriage and a heightened experience of social atomization. Traditional pleasure probably had to do with a victory over aggression in the exceptional moment of a clandestine union when individuals escaped the hostile logic of competitive individuality. The attack on erotic restriction has backfired, resulting in the restriction of eros to universal competitiveness and a weakening of the structures with which eros held thanatos in check. The modernist promise of unlimited pleasure (Hesse's ball) has been realized as a constantly increasing aggressive potential.

This magnification of aggression as it becomes nationalized can be explained with reference to a third mechanism. The dual process of cultural transformation—the aestheticization of life and the desublimation of art—carried an inherent violence which, after the completion of the process, is assumed by the new nationalism. The aestheticization of life depended on this violence because an organic resistance to consumerism (for example, within the family) had to be overcome; the concretization of that violence took the form of generational conflicts with extraordinarily destructive outcomes. In addition, because consumerism and the counterculture insisted on the model of a basically harmonious instinctual nature, they directed a repressive force toward instinctual aggression to the extent that authentic conflicts and differences were denied (vide the suppression of particularity in Hesse's Dionysian crowd). An economy that wavers between cult of self and visions of unmediated solidarity fails to articulate genuine tensions which are suppressed and consequently nourished by the violence of their own suppression.

Yet aggression accrues as well from the modernist process itself, i.e., the critique of autonomous art. Avant-garde iconoclasm, the hostility toward traditional modes of representation, reveals a basic antipathy toward beauty, pleasure, and rest. The attack on the institution of art is not only a consequence of the specific character of the turn of the century; it simultaneously represents the remobilization of a self-destructive hatred endemic to modernity in the larger epochal sense. The derision directed toward bourgeois art, the contempt for contemplative satisfaction, and the hostility to peace that characterize the historical avant-garde all echo elements familiar from Savonarola's autos-da-fé and the Puritans' polemics against the theater. Paradoxically the artistic movement that accompanies the aestheticization of life is implicated in a profound denial of pleasure, inherent in all anti-aesthetic gestures. This hostility to pleasure, in turn, engenders increased violence in the nationalist collective. Despite the ideology of hedonism and the demise of restrictive codes, the instinctual desublimation remains repressive, as pleasure is constantly promised and always withheld. The logical response to this frustration is aggression, misdirected however against irrelevant outsiders: the accumulated marital crises of 1984 fuel the invasion of Grenada.

Yet the antimimetic program cannot be reduced to this one anti-aesthetic element. Modernism was above all an effort to break the spell of the enchanted work and light up the world with the glow of Joyce's roman candles, not Savonarola's Florentine bonfires. The utopian desublimation of art, the promise of the early-twentieth-century avant-gardists, can still be articulated as a desideratum, no matter how its social ramifications have been deformed by commodity aesthetics and the culture industry. If the avant-garde has failed to reach the envisioned emancipation precisely because of the coopted success of its dual strategy, then criticism ought at least to preserve that vision as a standard with which to measure the culture that contemporary society declares successful. The modernist utopia, which was concretized in the aesthetic theory of the Frankfurt School, can—despite its obsolescence—be preserved and renewed in a critical appraisal of both the aestheticized society and the potentials for new artistic production.

After the completion of the avant-garde project, works of art have lost their privileged status and are no longer a safe harbor for the utopian image of a successful civilization, but the principle of aestheticization expands throughout society as a crucial medium of manipulation. In turn however social contradictions are transferred directly into the aesthetic sphere. Critical theory always insisted that society recurred within the autonomous work, inscribed in the constellation of aesthetic categories. The congruence of society and art remains valid today, but in a new sense. The work of art which once appeared to be the final enclave of truth and resistance has been dismantled, and the end of the work means the end of art, understood in terms of the traditional bourgeois institution. Yet the aestheticization of everyday life as a crucial mechanism of control suggests the ubiquity of the signs of political power. As aesthetic manipulation expands into all facets of social activity, manipulation can be confronted from any point within aestheticized society. In the wake of the deautonomization of art, culture may potentially undergo a politicization that will transform it into the primary terrain for social conflict and reveal the fundamental weaknesses in a cultural defense of the heteronomous order. The "aestheticization of politics" and life, which won out over

the "politicization of aesthetics," does not generate a monolithic stability. The conflation of art and politics may certainly operate as deception to the extent that issues of substance are hidden by a charade
of signs. However, this distinction between rhetoric and power is
hardly new. The point is that in the wake of the aestheticization of
everyday life, political power is dependent on a thoroughly transformed language and may become more labile. It is therefore crucial
to ask where new points of tension emerge along with new structural
deficiencies.

First, while aesthetic culture might seem to provide a natural legitimation for a system of commodity aesthetics, all aesthetic claims
have in fact been wounded by the avant-gardist attack on art. The
collapse of objective notions of beauty, the lack of credible experts in
(high or low) cultural matters, and the constant destruction of the
auratic claims of culture-industrial figures add up to an immanently
labile mechanism of manipulation. Bourgeois aesthetic taste was remarkably stable during the nineteenth century, if contrasted with the
speed of technological innovation. Today the velocity with which the
fashions of the aestheticized life world are transformed is a function
of revolutionary capitalism, and the perpetuity of change robs the social order of the signs of traditional legitimation. Not long ago, the
domestic interior was dominated by inherited objects, laden with family memories; today they have been liquidated or return solely in the
weak form of commodified antiques. While this transformation is undoubtedly a symptom of social amnesia and dehistoricization, it also
implies an extraordinarily flexible present that can engender either an
easily malleable victim for manipulation or a potential subject that
might finally free itself from the nightmares of the past.[29] The disappearance of history in postmodernity is clearly not by itself a radical
project. The point is rather that a new political terrain is emerging.
Traditional signs of authority tend to lose their effectiveness, which
leads to anti-authoritarian opportunities. Such possibilities must however necessarily compete with nontraditional signs of authority as well
as with the erosion of subjectivity, no longer able to constitute itself
through a critique of tradition.

Second, the aestheticization of everyday life tends to erode its own
credibility by never fulfilling its promises. Neither the shining temptation of consumer goods nor the irresistible aura of the culture star
anticipates the perpetual experience of disappointment on the part of
the consumer or spectator; the sensuous gratification promised by the

aestheticized object is never adequate. This dynamic is related to the exaggerated self-esteem of the narcissist who can never be satisfied by his environment. The resulting aggression need not necessarily become an object of manipulation in the new nationalist collective. On the contrary, the more illusion becomes the predominant characteristic of commodity production and marketing, the more susceptible does the system become to criticism from consumer groups. The limit to capitalist abstraction is the concrete use value demanded of the product. This points to various forms of politicization: regulation of advertising, heightened safety standards, and—more radically—a desertion from the dictated life-style of consumerism. The limits to these strategies are equally obvious: eventual conflicts with producers (unions), the shift in the economy from concrete goods to abstract services, and the pending alliance between anticonsumerism from below and austerity measures from above.

Third, the transference of social conflict into the cultural sphere due to the aestheticization of everyday life implies that societal contradictions will take on a visible concreteness. The tendency of the bourgeois public sphere to subject politics to a process of abstraction and restriction, both in a temporal sense (election year) and a geographical sense (the parliament as the sole forum of debate), gives way to the immediate presence of the signs of social membership. If image has replaced substance in the new social spectacle, then any struggle over images becomes a struggle for power.[30] The ideological conflict between the major parties is overshadowed by the competition between alternative strategies of self-representation and display: the classic simplicity of Republican unanimity or the gothic diversity of Democratic pluralism. Political commentators direct their attention nearly exclusively to image production and ignore substantive difference. While sensuous appearance displaces conceptual debate as the primary medium of national politics, the same principle of aesthetic concretization forces the subcultural opposition to a similar localization of its concerns: instead of a general critique of, for example, nuclear power, campaigns against single plants. The aestheticization of everyday life promises an escape from the abstract universality of traditional politics and a recognition of the primacy of particularity, a category previously reserved for works of art. It could therefore potentially engender a reinvigoration of political conflict. However, it is unlikely to generate emancipatory political values from within; while it may successfully mobilize aestheticized crowds, they will have difficulty escaping the tide of collective aggression that has emerged from the process of cultural transformation.

By shifting social conflict into the cultural sphere, aestheticization initiates at least these three new sorts of political developments: the iconoclastic delegitimation of the signs of authority; the expressionist critique of (commodity) illusion; and the sensuous concretization of practice. Similarly the other aspect of the dual strategy of the avant-garde—the attack on autonomous art—may open up possibilities for contemporary artistic innovation that ought not to be surrendered prematurely to the culture industry. To the extent that innovation continues to generate qualitatively new works, it is first of all crucial to provide a critical defense of their authenticity as exceptions to the rule of commodification. Critical theory's traditional insistence on aesthetic autonomy retains its relevance, despite the leveling of the difference between high and low culture and the dissolution of the work. In fact, these factors make a defense of authenticity all the more urgent, even if such a defense no longer credibly represents a full strategic opposition to the administered society. In the complex landscape of contemporary artistic production, it is necessary to differentiate and locate the singular works which continue to shelter utopian alternatives; this critical project amounts to a theoretically conservative allegiance to genuine innovation against regressive forms of progress.

Outside the magic circle of genuine works, the art market, instead of fulfilling the promises of the avant-garde, has made nonautonomous artistic production its watchword. A reversal of this situation would entail an emancipatory reauraticization of art, which may in fact be evident already in the most extreme stages of art's self-alienation: the radicality of minimalist formalism and the postmodernist scrutiny of traditional contents. Is it possible to imagine an art that participates in society neither as commodity nor as ornament nor as an engaged exponent of politics but as the placeholder of a radical otherness which is therefore utopian? A genuine retrieval of aura, which would necessitate a reversal of the trajectory of bourgeois culture, might counteract the perpetually heightening aggressive potential and articulate a project of community. Contemporary aesthetic theory faces the task of articulating an account of reauraticization that neither capitulates to the culture industry by designating its schmaltz as utopian nor demands a civilizational regression by linking aura exclusively to rebarbarization. To overcome the extirpation of culture by reinvoking Weber's new prophets is neither theoretically honest nor politically desirable.[31] The problem remains however that the charisma of community has disappeared, while false collectives constantly generate self-destructive aggression, mobilized by a plethora of would-be charismatic leaders.

Finally, a reauraticization of art that would escape the force of the culture industry cannot return to the traditional elitism of the liberal bourgeois period. In fact, it was precisely that elitism that provoked a populist hostility which avenged itself through the victorious culture industry: the Marx Brothers at the opera. The same dynamic determined the demise of the political avant-garde and epic leftism: the Leninst elitism of the twenties was liquidated by the pseudopopularity of socialist realism in the thirties (Lukács contra Brecht). Clearly the future of art depends on an escape from both elitist conspicuous consumption (the culture vulture as recipient) and mass manipulation (putative realism and naive art). The alternative for authentic art would be authentic democratization, the necessary corollary to the theory of reauraticization. If art is to resist the aggression of a self-destructive society, then it has to reject any heteronomous institutionalization that appropriates the aesthetic object as a weapon against the excluded social groups. The bourgeois reification of culture transformed the aesthetic utopia into a sign of class privilege in order to wage a domestic war: the work of art as the mechanism of barbarism. To escape the logic of violence, art would have to renounce its elitist elevation, which was always an abuse. Because the hidden agenda of elitism was commodification, which reduced art to a fully secular object of investment, a retrieval of aura today can only mean a renunciation of privilege and the construction of a democratic culture. It is a tendency already anticipated by subcultural transformations where works of art become increasingly accessible and the notion of the artist, stripped of much of its romantic pathos, is turned into a universal potential, "an art *per du* with humanity."[32] A reconciliation of the isolated artist and the aesthetic public—the antinomic poles of the classical modernist project—could emancipate the sense of the citizen. For now however the false reconciliation of postmodernity has only aestheticized the lackluster forms of capitalist relations.

Written Right Across Their Faces: Leni Riefenstahl, Ernst Jünger, and Fascist Modernism

IF the will triumphs, who loses? Leni Riefenstahl's cinematic account of the 1934 Nazi party convention at Nuremberg is one of the few aesthetic monuments of German fascism that have attracted serious critical scrutiny. In scene after scene one finds evidence of the ideological self-understanding of National Socialism: Hitler's descent from the clouds, the cathartic applause welcoming the charismatic leader, the visions of the medieval city, the unified folk including contingents of peasants in their traditional costumes, the rough-and-tumble life in the encampment, the mass chorus of the Work Front, the demonstration of the Hitler Youth, the celebratory display of banners, torchlight processions, and a sound track that mixes Wagnerian strains with patriotic songs and martial anthems. The list could be extended, and each item could be decoded and explained within the constellation of the right-wing populism, the *völkisch* ideology, on which German fascism thrived. That sort of investigation can have a compelling explanatory value in regard to the political content of the film. However, for a moment I should like to eschew the ideology-critical stance and investigate the rhetorical grounding of Riefenstahl's *énonciation,* an investigation which can shed light on a politics prior to ideological contents, i.e., the politics of fascist representation. It is this rhetorical politics that will concern me later when I turn to Ernst Jünger's construction of a fascist modernism, and it is the examination of rhetoric which may allow me to answer the question posed initially: if the will triumphs, who loses?

Triumph of the Will begins, like most films, with script, with words on the screen, but this opening gesture takes on particular importance within fascist rhetoric. Elsewhere titles name the individual work, give credit to individual artists, and, perhaps, locate the precise historical setting. Here, by way of contrast, the writing on the silver wall invokes history—or historiography, the writing of history—in order to introduce the agent of its supersession: in the cloudy heavens emerges an airplane, the paradigmatic modernist vehicle, bearing the body of the divine leader, the guarantor of national resurrection, whose arrival on earth signifies the miraculous incarnation of the will triumphant. Henceforth history is overcome, and the jubilant folk rejoices in a redeemed present provided by the presence in flesh and blood of the visible savior. The point is not that Hitler lands in Nuremberg; the point is that Hitler lands in Nuremberg and is seen. "*Wir wollen unsren Führer sehen* [We want to see our leader]," cries the crowd, and the film, *Triumph of the Will,* defines itself as the proper medium of a fascist privileging of sight and visual representation. The will triumphs when it becomes visually evident, and it triumphs over the alternative representational option, cited at the commencement of the film—writing and an associated culture of verbal literacy. When the will triumphs as image, it is script that is defeated: the verbal titles of the cinematic preface, henceforth displaced by Riefenstahl's shots; the written signatures of the "November traitors"; the Versailles Treaty, denigrated as just so much paper; and the volumes that disappeared in the conflagrations of May 1933.

Triumph of the Will defines a fascist rhetoric as the displacement of verbal by visual representation: the power of the image renders scripture obsolete. This contention may be tentatively, although not conclusively, confirmed by two pieces of evidence. I draw the first from the folklore of fascism, the infinitely repeated vernacular attribution of Hitler's success to the unique power of his eyes that allegedly fastened his interlocutors and fascinated the captivated masses, as if the force of fascist rhetoric depended less on words than on the energy of vision (vide the parallel claim that no one ever "read" *Mein Kampf*). I return to the film for the second piece of evidence, the self-effacing signature of the director. After Hitler's triumphal arrival and the evening demonstrations outside his window, the cinematic narrative proceeds to the next morning, crack of dawn in Nuremberg—sleeping streets, the city walls, the ancient bridges—and for a brief moment one catches a glimpse of the shadow cast by the photographic apparatus. Note: not a glimpse of the apparatus itself (technology is excluded) but its shadow projected onto the wall as a metaphor of the cinematic screen. The signature announces the age of the film and the priority of visual representation as the rhetorical practice of fascism. Hitler turns out to be precisely the enigma described by the subtitle of Hans-Jürgen Syberberg's cinematic investigation of National Socialism: "a film from Germany."

Much more could be said about the specifically rhetorical problems posed by *Triumph of the Will*, especially with regard to the status of speech in the film: the political speeches at the convention, Hitler's several addresses, and the text of the mass chorus. Briefly, I would argue that the verbal character of speech in the film is always secondary to the visual spectacle and the image of the present speaker, and that speech in the film therefore differs fundamentally from the initial script, the writing whose author is necessarily absent. A considerably more difficult problem involves the role of radio and loudspeakers in National Socialist Germany, an obvious case of disembodied speech, on which the power of the regime indisputably depended. I cannot pursue this matter now and want to conclude these introductory remarks, having used Riefenstahl's film in order to isolate a crucial conflict between visual and verbal representation, in particular the insistence on the priority of image over writing as a stratagem of fascist power. I call this a crucial conflict because it turns out to be the central rhetorical principle in Ernst Jünger's formulation of fascist modernism as described in his 1932 volume *The Worker* that bears the telling subtitle *Herrschaft und Gestalt,* which I render inadequately as *Domination and Form.* For it is visual form that will, in Jünger's modernist account, displace an obsolete culture of bourgeois writing and guarantee the authority of fascist domination.

Jünger's proximity to the problematic isolated in Riefenstahl's film is evident in the first paragraph of the 1932 preface. I will cite it now and then comment on its rhetorical self-positioning, its claims regarding competing modes of representation, rather than on its ideological contents, i.e., the significance of terminology such as "worker."

> It is the plan of this book to make the *Gestalt* of the worker visible, beyond all theories, all parties, and all prejudices—to make it visible as an effective mass, which has already intervened in history and imperiously determines the forms of a transformed world. Because this is a matter less of new thoughts or a new system than of a new reality, everything depends on the sharpness of the description, which demands eyes capable of a complete and unclouded vision.[1]

It is nearly unnecessary to underscore Jünger's insistence on the urgency of visual representation. The project of his book amounts to a making visible (*sichtbar zu machen*) of a form (*Gestalt*); this in turn leads to a presentation that demands eyes (*die Augen voraussetzt*) with an unclouded vision (*denen die volle und unbefangene Sehkraft gegeben ist*). The desiderata of sight and form, the image of images, pervade the text which consequently defines its rhetorical mode as *descriptio*—to be understood less in terms of the etymology pointing toward writing than as a project of visualization to be carried out by a descriptivist writing. Imagistic vision is then set in contrast to an alternative constellation of theories, parties, and prejudices, a domain of ideas, defined as mere ideas, i.e., separate from reality. The descriptive representation of *Gestalt* has powerful practical consequences (*die bereits mächtig in die Geschichte eingegriffen*), as opposed to the ultimately powerless ephemera of "new thoughts or a new system." "System"—a standard Nazi pejorative for the Weimar Republic; Jünger is suggesting in 1932 that a new order of power, structure, and form will replace an anachronistic amalgam of empty theories, political parties, and effete idealism. This paraphrase points out the underlying diachronic presumption, the transition from a bourgeois age of subjective interiority, the site of literary culture, to a postindividualism of visible power. This transition is central to Jünger's political ideology, his hostility to democracy, and his totalitarian preferences. It is moreover central to his aesthetics; the disparagement of a powerless culture of idealism and the advocacy of artistic formation (*Gestaltung*) with life-practical ramifications are homologous to the terms of the modernist attack on the bourgeois institution of autonomous art as Peter Bürger has presented it in his *Theory of the Avant-garde*.

In *The Worker*, Jünger undertakes myriad permutations of these themes, but the overriding concern remains the *Gestalt*, the visual form or structure: "The *Gestalt* contains the whole that encompasses more than the sum of its parts and which an anatomical age could never achieve." Here Jünger borrows from a reactionary strain in German romanticism running through Wagner and Langbehn that denounced the analytical intellect and the individuation of bourgeois society; in the *Gestalt*, Jünger discovers the synthetic power. "It is the sign of an imminent epoch that one will again see, feel, and act in the thrall of *Gestalten*." Again Jünger declares an epochal transformation and emphasizes the practical ramifications of the *Gestalt*. "In politics too everything depends on bringing into battle *Gestalten* and not concepts, ideas, or mere illusions."[2] The force of the *Gestalt* is set in contrast to the forms of subjective consciousness, denounced for their irrelevance. Thus the *Gestalt* is capable of totalization, it is practical, and it is therefore superior to the verbiage and concepts of autonomous culture. The visual *Gestalt* displaces the terms of writing. The fascist *Gestalt* displaces the bourgeois who was never a *Gestalt* but only an individual, a mere part, in an "anatomical," which is to say analytic or atomistic, age. It is finally the heroic *Gestalt,* the will incarnate, plain for all who have eyes to see, whom Riefenstahl brings to Nuremberg, to wipe away the writing and everything that writing represents.

Before proceeding with my discussion of *The Worker* and the particular character of the descriptive rhetoric of fascist representation, I want to explore some aesthetic and aesthetic-historical aspects of the problem of fascism and modernism. Fascism and modernism—that is a touchy combination. Postwar criticism, at least in the West, was eager to exclude literature complicitous in fascism from serious discussion. A conservative humanism attempted to escape the political turbulence of the twentieth century by turning its gaze toward the values of an unimpeachable occidental tradition with which one could hope to overcome the political catastrophes of the present. The same exclusionary move could of course be repeated on the left, for example, Sartre's reading Céline out of the French literary tradition. A further case that makes the issue clear: the efforts by the defenders of Ezra Pound to separate his poetic from his political imagination in order to canonize the former while relegating the latter to the domain of insanity, as if modernist innovation were necessarily separate from or even opposed to fascist totalitarianism. Meanwhile, during the first postwar decade in the East, when the Lukácsian paradigm held sway (before the Hungarian Revolution of 1956), an association of modernism and decadence tended to lead to a collapsing *tout court* of modernism and fascism. That may overstate the case and do the critic Lukács some injustice, but it certainly corresponds to widespread political judgments associated with the aesthetics of socialist realism in that period. Classical critical theory, anxious to develop a general account of fascism, did little better in formulating a specific account of fascist aesthetics, although it provides a wealth of insights and comes close to an answer in the exchange on surrealism.

Recent critical work has begun to move beyond both the absolute separation of fascism and modernism and the thorough identification of fascism and modernism. Several preliminary points can be made. First, against efforts to prohibit a thematization of fascism within literary criticism, one notes that a considerable number of authors, whose works are irrefutably embedded in modernism, were drawn to various models of fascism: Marinetti, Céline, Maurras, Pound, Lewis, Hamsun, Benn, and Jünger. Second, against (socialist realist) efforts to collapse fascism and modernism, one notes the plethora of clearly modernist authors to whom it is patently absurd to ascribe an association with fascism: Brecht, Kafka, Mann, Döblin, Proust, Sartre, Joyce, and Woolf. Therefore if one were to endeavor to set the poetics of the modernist authors attracted to fascism in some resonance with their political proclivities, then the resulting model (or models) would not be adequate as accounts of modernism in general. A fascist modernism would have to be distinguished from competing versions which, being also modernist, are likely to display certain affinities or homologies, but which will be clearly distinct variations of the modernist problematic. Finally, the aesthetic profile of fascist, leftist, or liberal modernism ought to highlight aesthetic features and not concentrate on the political deeds of the historical individuals. Writers near political movements may alway tend to be eccentric figures, outside of the inner circle of institutionalized political power. The proper question for literary critical inquiry has to do with the extent to which the political imagination of the author or the text (which may be extraordinarily eccentric when measured against the standard of the established political power) contributes to the construction of an aesthetic project and, in particular, one that can be labeled characteristically modernist.

In order to describe three competing models of modernist aesthetics—all of which are initiated by political motivations—I begin by limiting the term to its normal usage, in accordance with the connotation of the term "modern art," i.e., the radical aesthetic innovation that commences around 1900. Whether the proper dating begins somewhat earlier (with Heine and Baudelaire) or later (the generation of 1914) is less important than distinguishing this sense of the "modern" from the larger usage of a postmedieval modernity suggested by the German term *Neuzeit*. In his *Theory of Communicative Action*, Habermas works with this second, epochal model and, drawing on Weber and one strand in Adorno's thought, describes the differentiation of a particular aesthetic value sphere undergoing a linear progress of autonomization. More sensitive to the vagaries of aesthetic representation in the twentieth century, Bürger insists on a rupture in the trajectory of autonomization produced by the historical avant-garde movements. In this context, I cannot even attempt a critique of Bürger's analysis of that rupture (see Chapter 3, above) and cite him only in regard to his insistence on the distinction between an aesthetic culture of the eighteenth and nineteenth centuries, and, on the other hand, one of the avant-garde and modernism (I will also bracket a discussion of the exaggerated distinctions between modernism and the avant-garde).

These reflections on the theoretical construction of a category of modernism indicate the need for a nonmodernist foil, a countermodel of bourgeois culture against which one indeed finds all the aesthetic innovators of the early twentieth century railing: the art of the Victorian or the Wilhelmine establishment, which they regarded as just so much philistinism, historicism, sentimentalism, ornamentalism, and so forth. The key features of that countermodel include: (1) developmental teleology, especially in the linear narratives of the *Bildungsroman* as well as in the bourgeois drama; (2) a thematics of identity construction for the bourgeois subject undergoing the development; (3) an aesthetics of fictionality guaranteeing an autonomy, i.e., a separation of the work of art from immediate life-practical concerns. It is this third point which Bürger underscores, singling it out as the object of attack by the historical avant-garde movements in their effort to sublate art and life practice. That attack also leads, I contend, to a revision of the other aspects of the model—teleology and subjectivity—and all three aspects are lodged in an ostentatious antibourgeois gesturing that often induced an explicit politicization, particularly in the context of the First World War and its aftermath. The moment of modernism was marked by the belief in the confluence of aesthetic and political change. The optimistic and perhaps self-serving assumption of modernist writers was that literary innovation stood in some easy correspondence with political innovation. Hence the political motivation behind the competing modernist models.

Modernism was constituted by what it perceived to be the bourgeois aesthetics of autonomy, i.e., teleology, identity, and fictionality. I identify three ideal types of German modernist aesthetics—fascist modernism, epic leftism, and liberal modernism—and each proposes homologous alternatives to the terms of autonomy aesthetics. I can sketch out these relationships now only in a highly schematic fashion and will cite examples only as a shorthand for the necessary extended discussions. In place of bourgeois teleology, fascist modernism operates with iteration, a perpetual repetition of the same, suggesting the eternal return of a cyclical history. In place of identity construction, it offers the spectacle, unnuanced and unquestioned, the authoritative presence of Jünger's aestheticized battlefields. In place of fictionality, it denounces escapism and claims for its texts a curious pseudodocumentary status. Hence Dinter footnotes his *völkisch* novels with alleged proofs, and Jünger prefers the memoir; he does not turn to the novel form until the mid-thirties, when, as in the case of Benn and Heidegger, a disappointment with the reality of the fascist revolution began to induce minor revisions of the positions he had held earlier.

Epic leftism replaces development with static examples of false consciousness (Döblin's Biberkopf); identity with dialectical constellations (Brecht); and fictionality with an operative aesthetics of documentary literature (Ottwalt). For liberal modernism, the corresponding features are seriality (Mann's *Doctor Faustus*); ambivalence (Broch's *Bergroman*); and the objectivity afforded by essayism (Musil). This map is of course only a map and would need extensive elaboration. I mention it here in order to locate a fascist aesthetics within the modernist field next to alternative versions of German modernism. This is a necessary task within this discussion, since Jünger himself underscores only the diachronic component—fascist aesthetics as a critique of an obsolete autonomy aesthetics—and does not recognize simultaneous but alternative critiques of the same autonomy aesthetics. Nevertheless this map has in fact only placed modernism as a catalogue of aesthetic categories. It has not yet led us much closer to the answer to the question which I began to examine before regarding the rhetoric of fascism: is there a specifically fascist politics of representation? Now I add an additional question: how does fascist representation subvert its own claims? Do immanent contradictions erode the flaunted stability of fascism? To find the answers, it is necessary to return to *The Worker* and to investigate a rhetorical micropractice in Jünger's text.

In the second part of *The Worker*, sections 58–67 bear the title "Art as the Formation [*Gestaltung*] of the World of Work." Since the whole book is devoted to the project of producing form as visually evident, the question of representation is not at all restricted to these passages. Everywhere the grand theme is the imposition of contours and the description of surface structures. There is no longer any inside and outside; there is no longer any above and below but only a ubiquitous constellation of power as form. Therefore the whole book enters a plea for the projection of the categories of art onto everyday life, an "aestheticization of politics," to use Benjamin's designation of fascism. In sections 58–67, Jünger consequently does not articulate a separate aesthetics, describing instead the separation of an aesthetic realm as itself anachronistic. Autonomous art is an expression of the obsolete bourgeois worldview, i.e., in place of an explicit aesthetic theory, Jünger provides a fascist version of the end-of-art theorem.

For Jünger, bourgeois conceptions of aesthetic autonomy are corollaries to the modern, i.e., postmedieval (*neuzeitliche*), constructions of individuality. Despite the fragmentation of the universalist claims of the Catholic church and a sweeping process of secularization, bourgeois individuality remains grounded in the tradition of the Christian soul. The constitutive categories of the autonomous personality recur in the autonomous work of art as the discourse of the individual genius: "The history of art appears here above all as the history of the personality, and the work itself as an autobiographical document."[3] As the bourgeois individual loses legitimacy—Jünger counterposes him to the soldier in his war memoirs of the twenties and to the worker in 1932—so does the bourgeois understanding of art. In the era of total mobilization, autonomy in no field can be tolerated. To the extent that bourgeois culture still plays a role, it merely provides an escapist refuge for a privileged few, while impeding the urgently necessary decisions in the ongoing state of emergency. Jünger has nothing but contempt for the manner in which the Weimar state draped itself with signs of culture—the portraits of writers and artists on stamps and currency—as compensation for its inability to master the political crisis. "It [culture] is a kind of opium that masks the danger and produces a deceptive sense of order. This is an intolerable luxury now when we should not be talking about traditions but creating them."[4] Bourgeois autonomy has run its course and can no longer claim the allegiance of the generation of the trenches: "Our fathers perhaps still had the time to concern themselves with the ideals of an objective science or an art that exists for itself. We however find ourselves clearly in a situation in which not this or that but the totality of our life is in question"[5]—thus the fascist version of the modernist hostility to the culture of the philistine nineteenth century. In place of philistinism and autonomy aesthetics, Jünger advocates a postautonomous, postmodern culture that structures life experience within an overriding *Gestalt* of authority. He identifies public practices likely to organize the masses and abolish private identity: film, architecture, urban planning, *Landschaftsgestaltung*—practices which are inimical to the victims of fascist modernism: subjectivity, privacy, and writing.

I turn now to a passage which I consider particularly important, not only because it again repeats the critique of autonomy aesthetics—such repetition corresponds to the iterative aspect of fascist modernism—but because it does so with a phrase that will allow me to unravel the textual web and explore the politics of fascist representation. Jünger first identifies a "parasitic art world [*schmarotzender Artistentum*]" which, like standard bourgeois art, sets itself apart from life practice but which, in addition, has lost the genuine values of earlier generations. Clearly the object of attack is contemporary innovative art which, for Jünger, is not only bourgeois (which would be bad enough) but epigonic as well.

Jünger then proceeds to associate these "parasitic" artists with the advocates of an aesthetics of autonomy. Recall that for Jünger, the insistence on the autonomous status of art represents an impediment to resolving the political emergency. He therefore accuses the proponents of autonomy of treason with a remarkable turn of phrase: "Therefore in Germany one meets this art world with dead certainty [*tödlicher Sicherheit*] in close connection with all those forces on whom a hidden or overt treasonous character is written right across their faces [*denen ein verhüllter oder unverhüllter verräterischer Charakter ins Gesicht geschrieben ist*]."[6] Why does the accomplished stylist Jünger choose this phrasing? Whose faces does he envision and what is written in them? And what does this figure of speech tell us about the status of writing in fascist rhetoric?

Let me first complete the recapitulation of the passage in order to indicate the importance of the matter for the history of fascism and the status of literature within it. Jünger goes on to predict, or better, to look forward to the wrathful retribution these treasonous aesthetes will soon meet:

> Fortunately one finds in our youth a growing attention to these sorts of connections; and one begins to understand that in this domain even just the use of abstract thought is tantamount to a treasonous activity. A new sort of Dominican zeal has the nerve to regret the end of the persecution of heretics—but have patience, such persecutions are in preparation already, and nothing will hold them back, as soon as one has recognized that for us a factual finding of heresy is called for on the grounds of the belief in the dualism of the world and its systems.[7]

Clearly Jünger is not, as he has recently claimed in retrospect, merely describing an objective historical process but rather applauding the impending initiation of a new inquisition in order to purge Germany of the heresy of dualism, i.e., the claim that autonomous dimensions of human activity might operate outside the structure of power. The general heresy exists in several versions; he speaks of materialist and spiritualist positions which appear to be mutually exclusive. He must be referring to Marxist materialism and conservative idealism, the twin opponents of fascism which the Nazis would name with the crude alliteration of *"Rotfront und Reaktion."* Despite their apparent antagonisms, Jünger insists that both have a fundamental hostility to the survival of the German Reich: November treason in art. Both are implicated in an ultimately bourgeois discourse of an emancipatory narrative; both propagate the ennervating nihilism of dialectical thought, shattering the totality into an endless series of antinomies; and both are blind to the *Gestalt* of *Herrschaft.*

The passage and especially the description of opponents with treason written right across their faces immediately suggest several points. Recall that their crime involves the advocacy of autonomy, i.e., the separation of art and, more broadly, all representational practices of culture from life practice. Jünger's image denounces that belief by reducing the distance between writing and the body to nil. The body of the text is transformed into the body as the text, as if Jünger were already preparing to tattoo the victims of the emerging Dominican zeal. Jünger metes out a punishment fit for the crime: the proponents of bourgeois idealism learn about the materiality of language by being branded in their flesh, across their faces, with script.

In addition to this corporealization of writing, homologous to the appearance of *Gestalt* and the incarnation of the will in the body of the leader, the passage betrays a simultaneous hostility to particular identity. The victims are guilty not simply of treason but of having treason written in their faces, which has rendered them identifiable. Because they emerge as particular, they are fair game for particular persecution. Jünger does not like their faces because he does not like faces, i.e., the representation of an individual personality, at all, especially those which are constituted by writing. The persecution to which he looks forward anticipates the book burnings of 1933, which can be considered not only as political demonstrations but as literary acts, the fascist realization of the generally modernist posture of iconoclasm toward a literary culture deemed traditional.

Beyond these explicit ramifications of Jünger's figure of the inscribed physiognomy, the passage is implicated in fundamental aspects of fascist representation. I want to isolate three points and comment on each of them: (1) the moment of recognition and the priority of vision (sight and the faces); (2) the perception of particular identity through a characteristic marking (writing as scar); and (3) the antipathy toward a symbolic order and the imaginary desire to escape writing.

Throughout Jünger's oeuvre, a series of descriptions defines the dimension of sight and its counterpart, physiognomy, in both negative and positive versions. The sentimental bourgeois, with sight clouded by emotion, is out of place in the age of total warfare, for "it is not the time to read your *Werther* with tearful eyes." [8] Eyes trapped in the darkness of bourgeois interiority cannot provide the clarity of vision demanded at the outset of *The Worker*. Moreover it is writing—a founding text of German bourgeois culture, *Werther*—that leaves its traces on the cheeks, traces that mark the individual as such, while they simultaneously distort his vision.

The positive *Doppelgänger* of the lachrymose bourgeois stares out from under the *Stahlhelm*, a physiognomy devoid of literacy or emotions but toughened by modern warfare into a callous clarity:

> [The face] has become more metallic, its surface is galvanized, the bone structure is evident, and the traits are clear and tense. The gaze is steady and fixed, trained on objects moving at high velocities. It is the face of a race that has begun to develop in the peculiar demands of a new landscape, where one is represented neither as a person nor as an individual but as a type. [9]

The right-wing critique of bourgeois individuality could not be more explicit; it announces the end of interiority and the emancipation of vision. The new man has an unimpaired sight, just as the contours of his face take on the sharp and clear lines of *Gestalt*. Ambiguity disappears. The face of the hawk-eyed soldier is the diametrical opposite of the image of a spectacled intellectual; it is a rigid mask without nuance. [10]

Jünger's moment of recognition privileges the clear image of the soldier and then underscores the point by attributing to that soldier a clarity of vision. Conversely the bourgeois, who cannot see through his tears, is embedded in a literary culture of writing. Hence the treason of those whose faces are marked by writing: they disrupt the image with the mendacity of their words. Jünger's fascist modernism promises to liberate the imaginary from the Jacobin tyranny of the symbolic order. It draws on a long-standing reactionary tradition, a Wagnerian formulation of which can help us identify Jünger's traitors. Polemicizing against the actor Josef Kainz, Wagner writes, "One's impression is as though the Saviour had been cut out of a painting of the Crucifixion, and replaced by a Jewish demagogue." [11] It is not Christ but Christ's image that concerns Wagner, but the point is moot since Christ as the visible incarnation is image and is threatened by the Jews who represent language as the people of the book. Based on the Old Testament prohibition of graven images, the aporetic construction of Wagnerian anti-Semitism contrasts the visible *Gestalt* with an alternative defined as verbal and hence inimical to visual appearance. Wagner's logic is perversely consistent when he continues: "A race whose general appearance we cannot consider suitable for aesthetic purposes is by the same token incapable of any artistic presentation of its nature." Because their God is invisible, Wagner denounces the visible appearance of Jews and considers them a threat to any representative images. Wagner's anti-Semitism recurs in Jünger as the contrasting physiognomies and the agonistic confrontation of *Gestalt* and writing. Figures with writing in their faces are Jews: "And thou shalt bind them for a sign upon thy hand, and they shall be for frontlets between thine eyes" (Deut. 6.8). The phylacteries, the sign of treason, become the mark of Cain by which the fascist modernist recognizes the enemy. The French racial anthropologist and fascist collaborator Georges Montandon entitles a pamphlet *Comment reconnaître le Juif?* Jünger's answer must be: by signs of writing.

Signs of writing in the face mar the image and make it particular. The scar produces identity, be it the wound received by Rotpeter in Kafka's "Report to an Academy" or the tattoo, the significance of which is expressed in an advertisement: "Who you are / What you stand for / On your skin / If you like—forever." [12] Scarring the face in the ritual dual, the *Bestimmungsmensur,* a key element in German student culture, survived despite an imperial prohibition of genuine duels in 1883, various papal encyclicals, and the agitation of the Deutsche Antiduell-Liga, founded in 1902; if the social function of the *Schmiss* was to serve as the sign of an elite, its expressed purpose involved the preservation of individual honor and the strengthening of the participant's personality. [13] Jünger could recognize treason "written right across their faces" because that writing, the scar, produced individual identity which was anathema, as we have seen, for fascist modernism.

This connection is confirmed by the discussion of the scar of Odysseus in the first chapter (written in 1942) of Erich Auerbach's *Mimesis* (1946). When Odysseus returns to Ithaca, the servant Eurykleia, who had nursed him as a child, recognizes him by a scar on his thigh, as if the marking on the body were the locus of the personal identity that Jünger detests. Auerbach describes how Homer interrupts the narrative at the moment of recognition in order to recount how young Odysseus, visiting his grandfather Autolykos, received the scar. The wound marks the body and marks the rite of passage from a preliterate infancy to a symbolic maturity associated with writing and language. This suggestion goes beyond Auerbach but is compatible with his argument that the interpolated incident does not heighten suspense; instead it testifies to the mimetic impulse in the Homeric text to encompass the world with language and to omit nothing from the verse. The scar on the body which grants Odysseus identity and personal language also generates the expansive agility of poetic language.

Auerbach juxtaposes the story of Odysseus' return and the sacrifice of Isaac in order to contrast Homeric and biblical narration. However, critics have pointed out the fundamental similarity, the thematic concern with the production of male identity in barely hidden practices of ritual scarring.[14] When Jünger denounces the marked bodies of his opponents, he participates in a sublimated anti-Semitism by articulating a displaced critique of circumcision. His critique of identity is a fascist critique of *male* identity. Patriarchal culture depends on the symbolic order of law and language; fascist antipatriarchy, which is always implicitly an attack on the patriarch as Jew, is an attack on the practices of writing in order to resurrect the imaginary as *Gestalt*, the visible body without stigmata, descending from the clouds over Nuremberg.

"Written right across their faces"—the scar in the face is a longstanding topos of the writer. It is because of a scar of irresolution that Montaigne, in his essay "Of Presumption," chooses a private life of writing and abjures the courtly public where kings are represented in portraits.[15] The writer Jünger abhors that bourgeois privacy and casts constant aspersions on "the desks of Europe" where the culture of literacy takes place.[16] The fascist modernist denounces identities constituted by language, while expressing a desire for the image freed from verbal mediation. Of course both this denunciation and this desire are themselves lodged in language. Jünger's prose searches for the *Gestalt*, which is outside of language, by means of language. Its descriptive *parole* is committed to the abolition of *langue*. Similarly Jünger hopes to be able to recognize the new postbourgeois type who, by definition, can have no identifying features. This slippery rhetorical situation can be analyzed through the tropic parameters of ekphrasis.

The ekphrasis was the primary technical option in the speech of praise (epideixis or panegyric) which, during the Roman Empire, overshadowed the other two objects of classical rhetoric, judicial and deliberative speech. It profoundly influenced the poetry of late antiquity and the Middle Ages.[17] For Curtius, ekphrasis is above all laudatory description, accounts of beautiful persons and landscapes, leading to the topos of the *locus amoenus,* in the tradition of which the sensuous spectacles of Jünger's battlefields have to be placed. However, as a description of beautiful objects, ekphrasis has a somewhat more precise usage, which Leo Spitzer articulates with reference to the definition of the trope provided by Théophile Gautier, "'une transposition d'art,' the reproduction through the medium of words of sensuously perceptible *objets d'art* (ut pictura poesis)."[18] Classical examples include the descriptions of the ornamental shields of Achilles (*Iliad* 18.478ff.) and Aeneas (*Aeneid* 8.626ff.) and of various cups, garments, and sculptures. The term is occasionally extended to include descriptions of poetic renderings, e.g., the interpolated narrations included in the *Metamorphoses,* although this usage certainly goes beyond the limits suggested by Spitzer.[19] In either the limited or this extended sense, ekphrasis has to do with the verbal representation of aesthetic representation. It functions either to interrupt the course of the narrative (like the account of Odysseus' scar which is ekphrastic only if one accepts my suggestion that the scar is an instance of writing or aesthetic marking) or as an allegorical interlude; Achilles' shield reproduces the cosmos, and Aeneas' shield predicts the future: "Its images of Roman history chart the course of destiny in which the hero must play his inevitable role and illumine the similarity between his own deeds of violence and those of his descendents."[20] The proximity to Jünger's military fatalism is evident.

However, the connection between this aspect of classical rhetoric and fascist modernism is not merely thematic. Jünger's descriptivism and his fascination with the visible *Gestalt* are ekphrastic in a new and revealing manner. The authors of antiquity devote special attention at particular moments to works of art, as if art were already a relatively autonomous sphere, separate (no matter how integrated) from the rest of the narrative, to which the author would return at the conclusion of the aesthetic description. For Homer the whole world and all its details can of course be mastered by poetic representation, and Auerbach could therefore contrast the detail of the Homeric text with the sparse abstraction of the biblical epic. This does not mean that the Homeric cosmos is always fully aestheticized in advance or that the work of art is indistinguishable from other dimensions of human activity. Yet this is precisely the case for fascist modernism where the aporias of bourgeois autonomy are sublated through a universal aestheticization. The writer approaches a cosmos which is only art, and he can only recount its aestheticized *Gestalt*. Ekphrasis becomes the sole option of a literature that takes the classical admonition to an extreme: *ut pictura poesis*.

I have tried to demonstrate the ekphrastic character of Jünger's rhetorical stance not only to identify the continuity of certain topoi—from Achilles' shield to the *Stahlhelm*, from *locus amoenus* to Langemarck—but to investigate the politics of representation in fascist modernism. Ekphrasis necessarily implies a double dialectic: it invokes as present a missing object, and it appropriates speech to produce a visual image. Each of these points is worthy of consideration with reference to Jünger's writing.

Ekphrasis conveys the desire for an absent object which Jünger attempts to redeem as *Gestalt*. Just as the *Gestalt* of Hitler that arrives in Riefenstahl's Nuremberg is the vehicle of national resurrection, a regenerative aesthetics pervades much of European fascist ideology: the object which is missing has to be retrieved from death. Jünger's writing constitutes an extended project to overcome the mass death of the First World War. In *The Worker* he asks: "What kinds of minds are these that do not know that no mind can be deeper or wiser than that of any of the soldiers who fell on the Somme or in Flanders?"[21] Jünger, the intellectual, is prepared to sacrifice intellectual identity in order to revivify the anonymous cadavers of the war. Ekphrastic writing becomes an exchange, a sacrifice or atonement as payment for the absent bodies. Because bullets have robbed them of their subjectivity, Jünger makes a career of denying his own and repressing his pain. This self-denial and repression account for the banality of his contributions to the recent controversy around his receipt of the Goethe Award, which betray a fundamental inability to give serious consideration to the consequences of his fascist advocacy. As with Arendt's Eichmann, Jünger's mental blockage is due to the trauma of the trenches. He is marked by the guilt of the survivor who cannot account for his having escaped death. When asked by an interviewer if he was sad to have survived 1914, he objects only to the coarse phrasing and adds that he "agrees with the ancient Greeks: those who fall in war are honored by men and gods. That would have been a good ending." [22] He refers to his refusal to flee into a bomb shelter during a British air raid on Paris in 1944 (the incident is described in *Strahlungen*) as a "toast with death [*ein Bruderschaftstrinken mit dem Tode*]." Similarly when critics complain that he did not resist the Nazis adamantly enough after 1933, his testy response that opposition would have led to execution in a camp has all the earmarks of a classical psychoanalytic denial: as if he knew he should have acted differently and had met his death long ago.

His ekphrastic rhetoric expresses therefore both a desire for the absent object and a desire for the absence of the author. Jünger simultaneously undertakes resurrection and enacts his own death. In this gruesome exchange, the idealized physiognomy of the new man is the *facies hippocratica:* for Benjamin a critical tool to pursue the mortification of the artwork with an eye to redemption, for Jünger a prescription for an aestheticization of life that produces a death mask without transcendence.

Jünger's version of the death of the author can be treated as one item in the history of the response of German intellectuals to the catastrophes of war and holocaust. It is also implicated in the second dialectic of ekphrasis, the effort to appropriate language in order to surpass it with image. This tension is characteristic of the trope in general but comes to the fore in the ekphrastic rhetoric of fascist modernism. It corresponds to the displacement of writing by image in *Triumph of the Will* and to the emphatic prescription of *The Worker* where "it is a matter no longer of a change of styles [i.e., modes of literary expression] but rather of the becoming visible of another *Gestalt* [*das Sichtbarwerden einer anderen Gestalt*]." [23] Fascism as the aestheticization of politics transforms the world into a visual object— the spectacular landscapes of industry and war—and this renders writing solely descriptive only to proceed to the denigration of writing as not visual. The author's hatred for identities constituted by the presence of writing in their faces is also a self-hatred of the author as writer. His is a writing trying to escape writing. In fascist modernism, the imaginary rebels against the symbolic order of language where the author, dependent on language, is necessarily at home. This writing is literature at the moment of the auto-da-fé, always about to go up in flames along with the identity of the writer. If Jünger's military thematics recall Virgil's account of Aeneas' shield, his self-subverting writing is closer to the Ovidian version of ekphrasis, the perpetual destruction of the second-order narrators in the *Metamorphoses:* Jünger's decimation of his own subjectivity repeats the slaying of Marsyas, a myth whose content is the death wish of the descriptive poet, fleeing language.

Fleeing language, the fascist rhetorician also flees time. The classical ekphrasis interrupted the linear progress of the surrounding narrative, drawing attention to a particular *locus* apparently impervious to the vagaries of temporality. In fascist modernism, ekphrastic representation resonates with the antiteleological bias which all versions of modernism share in their rejection of traditional bourgeois culture. I want to conclude with a remark on the organization of time associated with autonomy aesthetics and its critique at the moment of the modern.

Horkheimer and Adorno's account of Odysseus and the Sirens in the first chapter of *Dialectic of Enlightenment* describes the moment of birth of bourgeois aesthetic culture. It is a process of autonomization, insofar as the local myth, still embedded in primitive religious cult, is subjected to the force of enlightenment secularization and robbed of its apotropaic power: the song of the Sirens becomes the song of art. Henceforth art has no life-practical consequences, although the nonoperative character is experienced in different manners by the opposed classes in heteronomous society. Art is simply denied the slaves whose ears are plugged with wax, while the bourgeois adventurer can partake of aesthetic expression only at the price of binding his hands to the mast. This cultural autonomization is located meanwhile within the context of a victory over space: Odysseus, the first hero in the age of discovery, navigates unknown seas and subdues them, while his body, which is separated from art, also escapes danger. Mastering the globe, he lives to tell the tale, and this is the birth of history, the victory over the lyric entreaties of forgetfulness, which allows the constructions of narratives of teleological practice.

Because historical memory and aesthetic autonomy are consanguinous, the modernist attack on autonomy aesthetics begins to pull apart the intricacies of the Odyssean nexus. The distance between body and text is radically reduced, and experience undergoes a respatialization: Odysseus could traverse every dangerous terrain, while Jünger's hero remains in the field of battle with no personal past or individual future. The optimistic linear progress of temporality is frozen, but each version of modernism records the end of history in a different way. Liberal modernism, as a rhetoric of irony, critiques structures of representation and explores the immobility of the present. Epic leftism, with its anticipatory hopes of radical revolution, operates as prolepsis and explodes the continuum of history. The ekphrasis of fascist modernism asserts the immutable presence of *Gestalt* and exalts the luminous positivity of visible power that will shine for a thousand years, uncorrupted by the infectious nihilism of writing. It glows with the light of the image: "The fully enlightened earth radiates in the sign of disaster triumphant."[24]

CHAPTER SEVEN

The Routinization of Charismatic Modernism and the Problem of Postmodernity

LONG before Thomas Mann leads Gustav von Aschenbach—whom I understand as a paradigmatic representative of authorship in the bourgeois nineteenth century—to his death in Venice, symptoms crop up indicating that all is not well in hegemonic literary life. The novella begins with an account of a frustrating writer's block; Aschenbach perceives his highly regulated routines to be increasingly restrictive; and the description of his background suggests a considerable degree of repression as the basis of the successful authorial personality. More important, Aschenbach's writing itself registers its integration into the system of cultural and political authority in Wilhelmine Germany. The narrator describes this model prose in the following manner:

> With time an official note, something almost expository, crept into Gustave Aschenbach's method. His later style gave up the old sheer audacities, the fresh and subtle nuances—it became fixed and exemplary, conservative, formal, even formulated. Like Louis XIV—or as tradition has it of him—Aschenbach, as he went on in years, banished from his style every common word. It was at this time that the school authorities adopted selections from his works into their text-books.[1]

This account is not yet particularly critical of Aschenbach. On the contrary, the narrator admires his ability to give expression to values of order, form, and stability and only later begins to distance himself from Aschenbach when the writer loses himself in his Venetian escapades, exploring instinctual and aesthetic material inimical to established society.[2]

All this raises numerous crucial issues which I mention now only to bracket them: the changing judgment of the narrator; the specific character of Aschenbach's crisis; and especially the question whether the real prose of Thomas Mann's "Death in Venice" somehow represents an alternative to the described prose of the fictional Aschenbach.

Instead of pursuing these problems, I want to use the above passage in order to introduce the problem of bureaucracy and culture. For although the narrator may, at this point, admire Aschenbach's success and, in particular, his appropriation by the cultural bureaucrats in the educational system, it is also evident that Mann includes this detail so as to point subtly to the ambiguity of the relationship between bureaucratic administration and cultural production. At least for the mind of an early twentieth-century modernist, it is not surprising that a writer whose works are applauded by bureaucrats may find his productive creativity stifled and may even be headed for a rather dramatic sort of breakdown.

The notion that bureaucracy and aesthetic culture stand in an antithetical relationship to one another is by no means universal. In some premodern societies, the continuity of literary life was one of the regular concerns of members of the governmental or ecclesiastical bureaucracy. Yet it is equally certain that to the extent that the process of occidental modernization has been characterized by a separation of value spheres, the impingement of political authority on aesthetic autonomy is immediately understood to be a transgression against the fundamental organization of modern culture. An American president's praise for a popular film or—to cite a more egregious and less exceptional case—the ongoing practice of censorship in Soviet-style societies wounds the autonomy of culture and can be condemned from the standpoint of an ideal, that is to say never fully realized and completed modernity.

This liberal line of thought, which presents the problem of bureaucracy and culture in terms of an insistence on the freedom of culture from political control, is both compelling and timely. It leads to a civil libertarian stance which no progressive political program can afford to surrender. Yet as an analysis of the relationship between bureaucracy and culture, it does not go far enough, neither in the late twentieth century nor even in 1913, the year of publication of "Death in Venice." Aschenbach's problem is certainly not censorship; he has no difficulty getting published. He does however have a problem writing, and, as this farsighted text suggests, that problem derives from a specific organization of the life world, an ethic of rationalized production that increasingly precludes the free reign of spontaneity. The paradigmatic author of the bourgeois nineteenth century is also a "specialist without spirit, a sensualist without heart."[3] Trapped in an iron cage of capitalist productivism, he watches his literary powers dry up, until he discovers a strange god—Weber would say "new prophets"—in the Dionysian dream that marks the end of Wilhelmine culture as well as the origin of aesthetic modernism.

Again I emphasize that an analysis of the problem of bureaucracy and culture cannot afford to omit a thematization of efforts by political bureaucracies to administer culture in order to control it. A parallel problem concerns the control over aesthetic production exercised in terms of rationalized economic interests by bureaucratized culture industries. Yet the broader issue which I should like to address has to do with the transformation of aesthetic culture in the context of an everyday life increasingly shaped by bureaucracies of various sorts. The commonly held assumption that innovative aesthetic activity is or ought to be a carrier of an antibureaucratic potential must be scrutinized: Is aesthetic culture truly a genuinely oppositional alternative to bureaucratic administration? Or is the modernist attack on the premodernist culture of the nineteenth century somehow compatible with bureaucracy? Or polemically: Does the avant-gardist attack on the traditional institution of art lead successfully to an aestheticization of everyday life, generating a life world that is particularly susceptible to bureaucratic control? I therefore link the problem of bureaucracy and culture to a reevaluation of modernism and its relationship to postmodernity. This discussion in turn raises questions about the changing status of literary intellectuals in the course of the twentieth century and their attitudes toward hegemonic power.

Aesthetic modernism, which I associate with the historical avant-garde, at least claimed to represent a powerful alternative to a purportedly desiccated culture of the nineteenth-century bourgeoisie. Aesthetic innovation promised to lead to profound social transformations, often described in explicitly emancipatory terms. The modernist vision of a cultural rejuvenation generated a specifically charismatic authority, and indeed one finds Weber himself, the seminal theoretician of bureaucracy and charisma, occasionally describing modernist literary figures like Stefan George as charismatic leaders.[4] Charismatic modernism emerges however not simply as a critique of denigrated literary practices—although these are thematized as well—but as a critique of an everyday life that is experienced by intellectuals as repressively constraining.

Modernism protested against the aesthetic as well as the quotidian activities of the nineteenth-century bourgeoisie. Initially organized around principles of individual subjectivity, Enlightenment cognition, legal rationality, and aesthetic autonomy, this culture appeared increasingly unable to realize its own emancipatory goals, inherited from revolutionary traditions, and became susceptible to thoroughgoing critiques. Modernist antiliberalism was regularly directed at the failures of a progressivist liberal project, and led in turn either to a rejection of that project (fascist modernism) or to its radicalization on the left. Yet for all modernisms, the reified forms of the nineteenth-century background became the initial object of polemical rejection.

Before examining this phenomenon with specific reference to aesthetic culture and literary intellectuals, I want to point out a particularly convincing piece of evidence provided by Weber in a letter to his mother which he wrote during a trip through England, Scotland, and Ireland in the summer of 1895. Weber describes an empty English countryside; the enclosure acts, urban industrialization, and capitalist modernization have led to the erosion of rural society: "only here and there a castle in a park separated from a few tenant dwellings and a single barn, and occasionally a church from the thirteenth or fourteenth century among a dozen workers' huts rather than, as in the past, fifty to sixty peasant homes—too big for its congregation, like a suit on a consumptive." [5] In the back of his mind is certainly the study of the East Elbian latifundia which he had recently prepared for the Verein für Sozialpolitik. His contention that the capitalist transformation of Prussian agriculture would undermine traditional social structures seemed to be confirmed by the underpopulation he encountered in England. This future shock and the subsequent sociological generalizations which anticipate D. H. Lawrence's mournful complaints regarding the passing away of Merry Old England lead into an account of a seemingly trivial event. Weber writes:

> By the way, even in Great Britain the world is just a village; can
> you believe that we met acquaintances from Berlin here? On
> the steamer to Loch Katrine I suddenly saw, among the faces of
> those pushing to board with their sharp English mouths,
> Gierke's Germanic face of a bard. We traveled together to Loch
> Lomond where our ways parted. Meeting compatriots is odd:
> we are otherwise so acclimatized that we have adopted the general whispering tone, pretend not to see the people sitting to
> our right and left, and only when asked do we give short and
> very polite answers. We always eat a little less than we would
> like, open our mouths as little as possible, and even when the

stomach is audibly growling, we just splash around with our
spoon in the soup, as if we were not at all interested in the
slop. But as soon as Germans were nearby, such a laughter
arose among us when we were just waiting for the coach that
all the English hurried over to see the barbarians, and I heard
someone on the coach say "Merry Germany." And before our
departure we had a lunch that the waiters won't soon forget.
G. started a meal like in the Teutoburger Forest, and I kept up.
The confused waiters brought, as everything kept disappearing,
ultimately superhuman quantities of roast beef, salmon, etc.,
probably fearing that we would otherwise start eating the
guests. Three of them stood around our table, staring horrified
at the destruction of their wares, and they were visibly relieved
when the steamer tooted and put an end to the meal.

The alternative characterizations of English and German mannerisms
have less to do with simplistic national stereotypes (as significant as
they may have been for Weber) than with models of cultural-historical
practices. The same process of modernization that has unfolded in
England and destroyed traditional agrarian culture leads to the restrictive codes of behavior in polite society. Against this modern present,
Weber mobilizes images of immediate physical experience (the growling stomachs) and an archaic past (barbarians, Merry Germany, and
the Teutoburger Forest). The encounter with the everyday life of capitalist society, whose rationalization becomes particularly obvious to
Weber in the foreign setting and on the eve of his nervous breakdown,
leads him to conclusions not uncommon around 1900. He constructs
the image of an idealized past in which fuller social relations prevailed, as well as an authentic aesthetic culture: note how the calcu-
lating sharp English mouths contrast with the poetic face of the bard
(*Bardengesicht*) of his German friend. This is certainly a typically
modernist antimodernism, a yearning for a precapitalist past, that follows logically after the account of the English countryside. Yet it is
also more: it is a yearning not essentially for pastness but for a genuine
community of pleasure, loyalty, and freedom, a charismatic community not encumbered with the restrictions of bourgeois civility.

In the same year—1895—that Weber traveled to England, Henry
Adams visited France and made his first extensive study of Gothic
architecture, leading in 1904 to the publication of *Mont Saint Michel
and Chartres*. Weber and Adams have a good deal in common. Both

academics are concerned with cultural history and especially the construction of their respective national identities. Furthermore both speculate on the cultural consequences of capitalist modernization, and both, in typically modernist fashion, elaborate charismatic alternatives to the reified culture of the late nineteenth century. This modernist turn is perhaps even more striking in the case of Adams, given his specific cultural context and his own youthful attraction to the Puritan revolutionary legacies of eighteenth-century New England. Yet the scandal is there, a scandal at least from the standpoint of Boston Unitarianism, for the description of the cathedral at Chartres is nothing less than a prayer to the Virgin, a celebration of an aestheticized religion of magical wealth and medieval pageantry fully foreign to the severity of the whitewashed churches of Lexington and Concord:

> Her great ceremonies were as splendid as her rank of Queen in
> Heaven and on Earth required; and as her procession wound
> its way along the aisles, through the crowd of her subjects, up
> to the high altar, it was impossible then, and not altogether
> easy now, to resist the rapture of her radiant presence. Many a
> young person, and now and then one who is not in first youth,
> witnessing the sight in the religious atmosphere of such a
> church as this, without a suspicion of susceptibility, has sud-
> denly seen what Paul saw on the road to Damascus, and has
> fallen on his face with the crowd, groveling at the foot of the
> Cross, which, for the first time in his life, he feels.[6]

Like Weber with his Teutoburger Forest, Adams too appeals to images of archaic experience, medieval religion, in order to construct an alternative to the disappointments of capitalist rationality. In his prose he repeatedly includes derisive jabs at practical Americans whose venal concerns make them immune to the forces that are fueling his own conversion.

Adams' articulation of an archaic charisma in opposition to the legal rationality of the nineteenth century is particularly interesting because later, in his autobiography, he recounts an experience which indicates the specific relevance of this new experiential dimension to the twentieth century. Furthermore, the setting is a decidedly modern one, the Hall of Machines at the Paris Exposition of 1900, and the chapter is symptomatically entitled "The Dynamo and the Virgin." I quote:

But to Adams [he writes of himself in the third person] the dynamo became a symbol of infinity. As he grew accustomed to
the great gallery of machines, he began to feel the forty-foot
dynamos as a moral force, much as the early Christians felt the
Cross. The planet itself seemed less impressive, in its old-
fashioned, deliberate, annual or daily revolution, than this huge
wheel, revolving within arm's-length at some vertiginous speed,
and barely murmuring,—scarcely humming an audible warn-
ing to stand a hair's breadth further for respect of power, while
it would not wake the baby lying close against its frame. Before
the end, one began to pray to it; inherited instinct taught the
natural expression of man before silent and infinite force.
Among the thousand symbols of ultimate energy, the dynamo
was not so human as some, but it was the most expressive.[7]

At Chartres, five years earlier, Adams had mobilized the past against
the present; in Paris he discovers the future. What past and future
share are the experience of a mystical force that transcends what appear to be the limits of an individualist rationality and an ability to
produce a community that is not organized in terms of market exchange. Be it the splendor of the Virgin or the radiance of electricity,
a power emerges that seems irresistible, while promising to put an end
to the greed, corruption, and decadence which, for Adams, had characterized American culture in recent decades.

Two points must be made now before proceeding. Weber and
Adams articulate models of a new cultural legitimacy that share a
good deal with the modernist programs that would prevail during the
early twentieth century. In addition to the ambivalence of an idealized
traditionalism side by side with highly modern material, one notes—
for Adams—the enthusiasm for technology that anticipates motifs of
constructivism and futurism (Marinetti); the insistence on sensuous
immediacy, aesthetics, and experiential irrationality hostile to the
logic of conceptual thought; the valorization of collective identities;
the antipathy to established bourgeois culture; and especially the predominance of a rhetoric of religious grace (Adams' Virgin and Weber's
new prophets). One can consequently borrow from Weber's own categories and speak of a charismatic legitimacy of modernism, opposed
to the legal rationality of post-Enlightenment aesthetic culture. The
charismatic character of modernism has varied manifestations, but it
nevertheless links together features as diverse as the divine voices at

the conclusion of Eliot's *The Waste Land,* Lawrence's phallic mysticism, the revolutionary pretenses of the surrealists, Kurt Hiller's activism, and the ambivalent collectivism at the end of Döblin's *Berlin Alexanderplatz.*

From this perspective, modernist culture seems to have an adversarial character, to the extent that it protests and attempts to overcome the Protestant ethic of the capitalist nineteenth century. Clearly this designation takes modernism on its own terms, for it perpetually staged itself as a culture of opposition. Although the subsequent partisan allegiances led to extraordinarily divergent commitments (Pound's fascism, Brecht's maverick Marxism, Mann's militant humanism with welfare-statist coloration), the aesthetic critique of bourgeois society was generally intended as part of a radical social transformation; hence the sympathy of many aesthetic avant-gardists for revolutionary politics. This is of course the basis of the neoconservative attack on the adversarial culture of modernism as the cause of the erosion of traditional values, as if other, social—and not aesthetic—factors did not contribute to the contemporary legitimation deficits of the political and economic systems.

Yet an alternative evaluation of the historical consequences of modernism is possible, the applicability of which to Henry Adams has been worked out in detail by Jackson Lears.[8] Peter Bürger describes the project of the avant-garde as an effort to overcome the bourgeois separation of life and art in order to emancipate the values previously sequestered in aesthetic works—beauty and autonomy—and transfuse them into life.[9] Adams is a modernist insofar as his account of Gothic architecture does not restrict itself to aesthetic connoisseurship but endeavors to produce an aesthetic life-style by describing an everyday life (initially of the Middle Ages) that has the character of a work of art. The same totalizing aesthetic religion is then modernized through an association with electricity. In place of rationality, he invokes experience; in place of calculation, feeling; in place of practical utility, works of art. In addition to the bureaucratized political parties, Weber, in a striking parallel to Adams, calls for the charismatic president. In place of industrial urbanization, Lawrences insists on eros, as much as does his antagonist Eliot. And instead of exemplary prose for school texts, Aschenbach finds love, death, and Dionysus in a Venice that sounds curiously like Adams' Chartres and Weber's Teutoburger Forest.

All these modernist gestures stage themselves as oppositional.

Yet—this is the alternative evaluation—it can be argued that they in fact contribute to the transition from the liberal industrial capitalism of the nineteenth century to the consumer societies and bureaucratized administrations of the present. For example, the vitalist emphasis on experience as opposed to individual rationality, presented initially as an emancipatory strategy, has at least two unforeseen consequences. Within the context of wide-ranging economic and social transformations, it paves the way for patterns of increased commodity consumption, no longer inhibited by the asceticism of an earlier acquisitive individualism—Weber's sharp English mouths, that have long since turned into acquiescent smiles in the wake of the modernist critique. Second, although modernism attacks nineteenth-century individuality in the name of some desirable collective social forms—and the examples of such attacks are legion—it fails to achieve that collective; the force of aesthetic innovation is not powerful enough to institute the intended social transformation, which is to say an unintended social transformation is enacted instead. This discrediting of rational individuality and inherited bourgeois social forms, one of the major cultural tasks of historical modernism, creates a social vacuum into which the administrative bureaucracy can expand. Despite the anticapitalist and generally antibureaucratic strains within the avant-garde, i.e., despite its own claims and the vernacular understanding of a fundamental opposition between bureaucracy and culture, its aesthetic revolutionism turns out to have itself contributed significantly to bureaucratic power.

Modernism and the avant-garde are not alone responsible for the disappearance of liberal bourgeois society; that sort of claim is made by neoconservatives who, ignoring other changes in social organizations, economic structures, and political authority, are eager to blame intellectuals for a misleadership that allegedly generates a crisis of authority.[10] But modernism and the avant-garde certainly may have accelerated the process of social transformation, leading to the typical twentieth-century forms of administration. I want to flesh out this claim—that modernist culture contributes to bureaucratic expansion—first by way of an analogy between two simultaneous early twentieth-century phenomena, the aesthetic avant-garde and the political avant-garde, i.e., Leninism. That the latter, despite its radical opposition to the czarist state bureaucracy, ends up generating an extremely bureaucratic organization is indisputable. My argument has nothing to do with the political loyalties of the aesthetic avant-garde or with the aesthetic predilections of the political avant-garde. Instead I claim that both phenomena operate in parallel vanguardist manners that are susceptible to processes of bureaucratization.

Vanguardism, aesthetic and political, in the early twentieth century displays three crucial features that influence the reorganization of everyday life. (1) The invocation of crisis: both vanguardist phenomena claim that established culture and society thrive on mechanisms that threaten to engender catastrophes. The dadaists blame the First World War on bourgeois philistinism, while the Leninists blame it on the bourgeois economy. On occasion, other crises are thematized. In any case, the result is the absolute priorization of the particular vanguardist program: unless art or the economy is revolutionized, Armageddon may follow. (2) Cadre leadership: the aesthetic avant-gardists present themselves as a small group opposed to the masses of philistines; the Leninists are counterposed to the merely trade-unionist masses of workers. In both cases, the subaltern masses are described as venally materialist, while the self-appointed leaders (closet bureaucrats?) present themselves as carriers of ideas, values, or theory. (3) Life commitment: aesthetic bohemianism is not restricted to the genuine loci of aesthetic production (studios, theaters, writing desks) but entails a life-style replete with fashions, demeanors, and places of sociability (coffee houses, communes). The Leninist cadre member, subject to a perpetual party discipline, is constantly in the service of the revolutionary project (not unlike the *Beamte* in the German civil service). Because aesthetic and political vanguardism are full-time occupations, the elitist exclusivity is heightened; most of the denigrated masses cannot participate, while the vanguardist stages an exemplary life-style in which one value sphere (aesthetic or political) displaces a plurality of competing interests.

By invoking an imminent crisis of extreme urgency, vanguardism generates a motive for bureaucratic administration. By legitimating the notion of a leadership cadre ontologically superior to the majority of the population, vanguardism produces the bureaucratic actors. And by insisting on the need to regulate all features of everyday life—the ineluctability of life-styles—vanguardism describes the space in which bureaucratic control can operate.

In this context, the analogy between aesthetic and political avant-garde serves solely as a heuristic device that leads to the recognition of an at least latent tendency toward a legitimation of bureaucracy in the culture of charismatic modernism. To understand the success of modernism in the West, however, it is crucial to hold onto both its adversarial promise, which could appeal to bona fide emancipatory instincts in the recipients, and its affirmative function in the modernization of forms of authority and the transition to the social structures of advanced capitalism. This double character of modernism is in turn subject to a historical dynamic that has rendered the oppositional claims of aesthetic innovation increasingly untenable. The "obsolescence of the avant-garde" can mean only that the culture of charismatic modernism has undergone a process of routinization leading to its integration into its erstwhile opponent, the bureaucratic administration of everyday life.[11]

This general process depends on several interrelated phenomena that await extensive study from the perspectives of various disciplinary orientations. The cultured middle-class public, the *Bildungsbürgertum,* against which historical modernism directed much of its rage has ceased to function as a hegemonic carrier of taste.[12] The force of the classical avant-gardist devices of shock and estrangement declines proportionately. Meanwhile the residual popular culture from which modernism derived some of its forms has been displaced by industrially produced entertainment and the mass marketing of consumer goods.[13] Every discotheque in the West promises an "experience" as overwhelming as Adams' encounters at Chartres (in fact the descriptions of Chartres, the excitement of dadaist provocations, and Aschenbach's dream—the modernist accounts of overpowering moments of sensuous aesthetic events that displace the ratiocinative character of earlier liberal bourgeois culture—provide the blueprint for contemporary mass entertainment). These transformations of both "high" and "low" culture reshape the terrain on which the avant-garde can pursue its provocational strategies and therefore contribute to the erosion of the adversarial claims.

In addition, not only the aesthetic works of early twentieth-century modernism but even contemporary works characterized by formal innovation have been integrated into the standard programs of university study. At the turn of the century, academic literature departments were still devoted largely to classical philology and rhetoric or the elaboration of national literary identities, with particular emphasis on medieval material. Precisely these areas have been marginalized by a revised canon emphasizing modernism; the burgeoning of Kafka research after the Second World War is a particularly salient case in point. Furthermore, despite the undoubtedly legitimate complaints of productive artists regarding a perpetual dearth of funds, one is struck by the extent to which governmental agencies and, especially, established foundations subsidize contemporary aesthetic culture. The role of foundations in the establishment of a hegemonic modernist taste remains an especially crucial research problem. Finally the expansion of the publishing and culture industries not only creates numerous managerial positions but also ensures access to a mass market. Weber's charismatic artist George published his *Blätter für die Kunst* for an extremely circumscribed audience, and Adams' study of Chartres first appeared in a private edition of one hundred copies; the integration of aesthetic innovation into mainstream taste makes that sort of esotericism obsolete.

Because of this multifaceted integration of aesthetic culture, the adversarial claims that marked the modernist self-understanding of artists and literary intellectuals hardly continue to seem convincing. Against this background, the debate on postmodernity arises, once the charismatic legitimacy of modernism has been routinized and appropriated by hegemonic institutions. The ambivalence of postmodernity, the simultaneity of radical gestures and a conformist celebration of social power, exposes the contradictory double character inherent in the historical avant-garde, while at the same time echoing the rhetoric of neoconservatism, with its attack on bureaucracy in the name of the state. The contemporary cultural situation is defined, at least in part, by a critique of authority designed to stabilize authority. Culture, as the purported antagonist of bureaucracy, becomes bureaucracy's best alibi, as two examples from two very different realms of aesthetic practice can demonstrate.

One of the influential new literary-critical modes, *Rezeptionsästhetik* or reader-response theory, appears particularly well suited to call into question the legitimacy of traditional interpretations and, by extension, the authority of all established critical judgments. Precisely this relativistic potential has led conservative critics to denounce it in the name of the determinate meanings of texts. Yet as Stanley Fish, one of the leading reader-response advocates, repeatedly insists, the result of the theory is not a dissolution of critical or textual authority but a recognition of the constant "authority of interpretive communities," i.e., established university critics. Because "interpreters act as extensions of an institutional community, solipsism and relativism are removed as fears because they are not possible modes of being. That is to say, the condition required for someone to be a solipsist or relativist, the condition of being independent of institutional assumptions and free to originate one's own purposes and goals, could never be realized, and therefore there is no point in trying to guard against it." [14] No interpretation is permanent, but every interpretation must respond to established norms (because an autonomy outside of established norms is inconceivable); scholarship consequently loses any cognitive importance—it is not concerned with knowledge as an approximation of truth—and becomes a matter of performative capacity designed to persuade the intra-institutional interlocutors in the interpretive game.

Fish's antitraditionalism turns into a cynical defense of established criticism simply as established. The authority that once adhered to innovative modernism is transferred to the critical guardians of culture within the academic literary institutions. This same dialectic turns up again, unexpectedly enough, in the current film to which I before referred obliquely as the object of presidential approval in the United States, Sylvester Stallone's *Rambo*. It is not necessary to pursue an extensive discussion of the plot or the ideological ramifications in the context of a recrudescent nationalism. [15] Suffice it to point out that, in addition to Rambo's victories over scores of Vietnamese and Russian soldiers (all poor shots), the film enacts a struggle between the soldier-hero and the military bureaucrat; for it was after all the military bureaucrats who tied the hands of the front soldiers who, left on their own, would have won the war in Vietnam. It is this antistatist and antibureaucratic aspect that generates suspense in the film; the other, more evident conflict between the American hero and the communist hordes is tediously one-dimensional. Rambo promises to "get" the bureaucrat who betrayed him, and the viewer is invited to look forward to the fulfillment of the promise. Yet at the film's conclusion, when Rambo can in fact "get" his antagonist, he refuses to do so. The film mobilizes a nationalist belligerence, fueled in part by antibureaucratic resentment, and the war fever to which the film contributes will provide ample opportunities for the maligned military bureaucracy to reassert the "authority of military communities," if I may adjust Fish's phrase appropriately. The literary critic and the fictional soldier are caught in the mendacious logic of artificial negativity: the attack on entrenched powers relegitimizes the power structure which is never genuinely called into question.

The film not only demonstrates the relegitimation of bureaucracy via a coarse critique of bureaucracy. It also displays the vicissitudes of the counterculture of the sixties, which in many ways was heir to the adversarial culture of modernism. Rambo is endowed with all the emblemata of a hippie: his hair is long and he wears a headband; he distrusts technology as much as artificial food; he fights on the battlefield without any cumbersome ideological apparatus; and he declares that he does it all only for love, for apparently love is all one ever really needs. Stallone transforms the counterculture hero into a contra, and this inversion is implicated in the dialectic of aesthetic culture and bureaucratic authority.

As the duplicity of the aesthetic cultural opposition to bureaucracy becomes increasingly evident after the institutionalization of modernism, certain consequences follow for literary intellectuals. All of them are hallmarks of the postmodernist position. The implausibility of the adversarial stance leads to a phenomenon that has been addressed as the "disappearance of the author." In terms of public life, this means the gradual retreat of authors from regular intervention in political debates. In Germany a continuity exists between the politicization of literature in the Weimar Republic and the activist stance adopted by authors during the sixties. With the death of Heinrich Böll that tradition may have come to an end. This is to say not that all authors or literary texts lose political significance, but that the role of a major author as a public "conscience of the nation" no longer seems desirable or credible. A similar conclusion may have been marked in France by Foucault's death.

One formal corollary to the disappearance of the author is the critique of narrative. Early twentieth-century modernism made various attempts to reinvigorate the narrative, e.g., Lukács's *Theory of the Novel* or Benjamin's elaborations on the problem of *erzählen*. Postmodernist taste is marked by considerable suspicion of narrative literature and, especially, film, which is denounced as authoritarian and/or patriarchal.[16]

The critique of narrative merges with the valorization of deconstructive readings, the insistence on the self-subversion of meanings and on the impossibility of consensual communication. Literary life is consequently asked to surrender its historical role as a medium of cognition and critique of social experience. This critical paradigm shift is lodged, it is true, in a collection of radical gestures, but at the same time all discussions of emancipation are prohibited as vestiges of an anachronistic Western metaphysics.

The termination of the cognitive function of aesthetic culture is one consequence of modernist iconoclasm. It also deprives the administrative bureaucracies of one of their erstwhile checks and balances. Meanwhile, the successful completion of the modernist attack on traditional culture renders modernism obsolete, or at least puts an end to a heroic phase, which survives only in the studied heteromorphism of institutionalized culture. Finally, the experiential models of historical modernism have generated the patterns of mass marketing and consumerist behavior. The surrealist interludes in television advertising, the cruel theater of music videos, the ubiquity of Muzak, and the proliferation of life-styles add up to a seamless aestheticization of everyday life.

Yet precisely this ubiquitous aestheticization of everyday life is the point at which considerations of a potential opposition to bureaucratic control can begin. Not that "culture" is to be again invoked as the emancipatory alternative on the grounds that the aesthetic experience is opposed to bureaucratic regulation. The aestheticization of everyday life has both distributed culture and secularized it, robbing it of its pomposity—Adams' Chartres—while making it universally accessible. In addition to the forms dictated by university mandarins and official museums, institutionalized neo-avant-gardes and pop stars, culture gradually takes on the form of an endless collection of signs of identity and authority that may be available for political formation outside of and against the bureaucracy. Such an aesthetic of the everyday would have to take the form of a parodic inversion of consumerist material, without itself falling into the trap of consumerism or allowing the bureaucracy to neutralize it in characteristic fashion: coopting culture by labeling it as culture and therefore fair game for control.

However, that sort of solution, a radical aesthetic of the everyday, is probably no solution at all. At best it could lead to the marginalized practices of an anarcho-situationism or the neocounterculture of the German alternative movement. To the extent that they are not repressed or coopted by state bureaucracies, these solutions easily fall prey to the subculture apparatchiks, Leninist and otherwise, who are always ready to turn spontaneity into organization. Is there then no way out of the alliance of bureaucracy and culture? Or can one describe sorts of cultural practice that would operate outside of bureaucratic administration? An answer cannot do without a reconsideration of the history of bourgeois aesthetic formations.

The significance and legacy of cultural modernism can best be understood if it is located in relation to both the premodernist culture of the nineteenth century and to the issues grouped today around the theme of postmodernism. These three cultural programs—the premodernism of bourgeois realism, etc., the modernism or avant-gardism of the first half of the twentieth century, and contemporary postmodernism—correspond to three distinct political-economic formations: first, laissez-faire capitalism in which market exchange organizes social interaction relatively independently of political intervention on the part of the liberal state; second, modern administered societies, marked by Keynesian and other forms of economic regulation carried out by an expansive bureaucratic apparatus; third, deregulated economies in which the welfare state is dismantled and the role of governmental activism in civil society is generally diminished.

The relationships between the three cultural programs and the corresponding political-economic formations are complex and multifold, as has been underscored in recent attempts to provide political evaluations of modernism and postmodernism.[17] A thorough discussion would have to examine issues of social composition, e.g., the entrepreneurial bourgeoisie and the vicissitudes of the nineteenth-century salon; structural homologies between social organization and aesthetic features, e.g., the demise of the individualist genre par excellence, the *Bildungsroman,* in the collectivism of the welfare state;[18] functional connections between aesthetic programs and social transformation, e.g., the process by which the aesthetic avant-garde attacks the nineteenth-century bourgeoisie and thereby contributes to the emergence of bureaucratic administrations or—to cite another example in which the relationship is reversed and social transformation generates an alternative aesthetic program—the delegitimation of Eurocentric cultural traditions in the wake of decolonization as the precondition for the stylistic exoticism and historical eclecticism of postmodern art.

Obviously these points of intersection between cultural programs and political-economic formations by no means exhaust the issues at stake. I present them in order to outline a full project in which social composition, structural homologies, and functionality would have to be addressed for premodernist, modernist, and postmodernist culture. In addition, by setting these three cultural phases in relation to three stages of capitalist modernization—liberal market capitalism, welfare-state bureaucracy, and the contemporary critique of the administrative state—one can begin to discuss contemporary culture in a way that is not trapped in the logic of an obsolete avant-gardism or tied to anachronistic projects of engagement. Nor should this discussion be satisfied with transporting the categories of bureaucratic administration into aesthetics by insisting on a new canon organized around the objects of welfare-state control (minorities and women), just as it must clearly avoid the traditionalism-by-fiat advocated by the neoconservatives; for what traditionalism is legitimate after the thorough destruction of tradition?

Neoconservative and neoliberal critiques of the welfare state as well as—on the left—the attacks on the state bureaucracy emanating from the new social movements share crucial motifs, no matter how their respective political values may vary. All valorize a deflation of the state and a deregulation of different areas of civil society, and this chorus of opposition testifies to real processes that have eroded the legitimacy of the model of administrative expansion. This rejection of bureaucracy has even made its way thematically into the cultural sphere—recall the examples from academic criticism and popular film.

Both the neoconservatives and the new social movements have, in addition to their critiques of the state, their respective cultural programs. These however are less interesting than the repetition of the antibureaucratic discourse of deregulation in the postmodernist cultural programs in terms like polyphony, heteroglossia, the mixture of high and low forms, eclecticism, etc. No matter how postmodernist works may differ from the traditionalist canon advocated by neoconservatives, these same postmodern works in fact reproduce neoconservative values, beginning with their shared hostility to the revolutionary experimentalism of historical modernism.

The aesthetic-cultural corollary to the contemporary crisis of welfare-state capitalism can lead, as I have tried to suggest, to the authoritarian cynicism of literary criticism, the culture-industrial duplicity of war films, or the confluence of neoconservativism and postmodernism. Can it lead elsewhere as well? Is there a progressive answer to the question of culture *after* bureaucratic capitalism? Modernist art, despite and because of its adversarial claims, found its home in the enclaves of museums; by suppressing any adversarial claims, postmodern art thrives on a reinvigorated art market, as if the deregulation of culture could only mean a return to market exchange and an intensified commodification of art. Can the critique of the welfare state be appropriated with an emancipatory intent and lead to other solutions?

After administrative capitalism, a deregulation of culture could imply a breakup of culture-industrial monopolies; a decentralization of cultural production, including the invigoration of regional and local arenas; and broadened popular access to cultural institutions. This program remains problematic to the extent that no substantive agents of popular cultural identity—postmodern corollaries to premodern communities—are available. The insistence with which Afro-American literary critics sometimes speak of tradition can be seen as one response to this situation.

In addition, to the extent that bureaucratic capitalism and the aestheticization of everyday life (meaning both the culture industry and commodity aesthetics) have gone hand in hand, a critique of bureaucracy could imply a vernacular deaestheticization as a corollary to deregulation: community control of public advertising; workplace and consumer control of aesthetic settings; authentic public debates on matters of urban development and architecture. Finally, postmodernist insistence on mixing high and low forms (which corresponds to neoconservative anti-intellectualism) has regularly led to the integration of popular material into the art market as commodified material (e.g., graffiti art). Alternatively, popular forms could be relegitimized outside of the culture industry and outside of the market.

This last case makes the crux of the question clear. Affirmative versions of the critique of the bureaucratic state advocate a return to the market principle. Not only are the terms of postmodernism structurally homologous to this neoconservatism; postmodern aesthetics corresponds directly to this program, insofar as it emerges simultaneously with large-scale corporate investment in art. Yet postmodernism and neoconservatism resonate with the new social movements and their utopian vision of a postbureaucratic society. If a critical alternative to the conservative critique of bureaucracy is to develop, then it must articulate its own alternative to the state and to the market as well. An aesthetic corollary to that critical politics would have to describe cultural practices outside the state and its buttresses—the museums, universities, and the culture industry—and outside the market too. If it is difficult to imagine a place for culture in local communities or civil society, then we have another piece of evidence indicating the degree to which our experience and thinking are still caught in the categories of bureaucratic culture.

CHAPTER EIGHT

Myth and Modernity in *Der Park*

THESEUS, the Duke of Athens, begins *A Midsummer Night's Dream* with a recognizably modern gesture, the designation of the moment of the present as an isolated instant in a continuum of time:

> Now, fair Hippolyta, our nuptial hour
> Draws on apace. Four happy days bring in
> Another moon; but O, methinks, how slow
> This old moon wanes! She lingers my desires,
> Like to a stepdame or a dowager,
> Long withering out a young man's revenue.[1]

Theseus is evidently anxious to wed Hippolyta and, as the concluding metaphor suggests, to consummate the marriage. The initial temporality of the drama is marked by an anticipation that constructs the present as a moment of incompleteness oriented toward a closure that will be achieved by the end of the play. By deferring pleasure into the future, the text describes a current disorder and promises that the dramatic action will somehow lead to a teleological conclusion.

The significance of this promise is magnified when that initial disorder—a foregrounded absence of completeness—multiplies. It is by no means only Theseus and Hippolyta who first meet the audience in a state of unsatisfactory separation. The Athenian lovers, Lysander, Hermia, Demetrius, and Helena, are trapped in a chain of amorous confusion that has set the generations against each other and produced conflicts that can only be described as a crisis of the patriarchal order. Meanwhile the royalty of the fairy world, Oberon and Titania, are at odds, accusing each other of multiple infidelities, while they quarrel over a ward of Titania, a "changeling boy," the daughter of an Indian "votress" of the queen, about whom I will have more to say later (2.2.123). Finally, the motley collection of artisans, Quince the carpenter, Bottom the weaver, and their companions, double the problematic of separation, for they look forward to the completion of a project, the presentation of a play at the wedding of the Duke, and that play will represent the fate of the separated lovers Pyramus and Thisbe.

136

Aristocracy, citizenry, fairies, and artisans: the four levels are marked by homologous crises, and the drama promises (and on one level seems to provide) an ultimate conclusion. The temporal premise is specifically modern insofar as a stable order of cyclical permanence is relegated to a traditionalist past that is quickly sinking out of sight. The dramatic action appears to constitute a version of history in which suffering—here, above all, as the denial of love and pleasure— is overcome and an order is achieved in which personal happiness and social cohesion cease to be mutually exclusive: a free association of individuals. It is not hard to recognize that trajectory as an early version of an Enlightenment narrative of emancipation and progressivist optimism.

On closer examination, however, one must note how the crisis of the present, with which the play commences, is transformed into the final closure only with the help of some extraordinary legerdemain. Oberon has forcibly extorted the disputed boy from Titania, and the confusion of the youths has been first exacerbated and then quelled by Puck's supernatural interventions. Time has passed, which allows both for the ducal marriage and the performance of the artisans, the play within the play. It is therefore not at all genuine Enlightenment progress but time, magic, and power which have overcome the opening confusion and permitted the play to come to an end.

Yet the end, which ought to be the promised end to the history which began with the crisis of the opening, is hardly as conclusive as its powerful rhetorical setting would suggest. In his final blessing, Oberon wants to close off the future, but his speech indicates only that the present continues to face an open future of crisis and danger:

> So shall all the couples three
> Ever true in loving be;
> And the blots of Nature's hand
> Shall not in their issue stand.
> Never mole, harelip, nor scar,
> Nor mark prodigious, such as are
> Despised in nativity,
> Shall upon their children be.
>
> (5.5.396–403)

Although the happy resolution of the conflicts seems to be conclusive, Oberon's final words themselves demonstrate the impossibility of finality and the continued threat of blots and markings. To the extent that the problem of the scar has to do with diacritical marks, the verses point to an incipient crisis of representation that is not resolved by the play. I will return to this matter below. The verses also indicate a suppression of nature, i.e., the teleological trajectory of progress which constitutes the manifest meaning of the text depends on a latent denial of nature—rather odd in a passage having to do with human reproduction—and a denial of human mortality. In order to announce the end of the play, Oberon excludes the end of life and is forced to resort to the same command with which Theseus began: "Awake the pert and nimble spirit of mirth, / Turn melancholy forth to funerals; / The pale companion is not for our pomp" (1.1.13–15). The pursuit of happiness apparently demands the occlusion of death and the repression of the past. Similarly Theseus wants to forget his own past and how he conquered his fiancée: "Hippolyta, I wooed thee with my sword, / And won thy love doing thee injuries; / But I will wed thee in another key" (1.1.16–18). The present as the moment of crisis exists less in anticipation of a future which will be achieved through a history of action than as an erasure of a history of violence, melancholy, and material oppression. It is an obligatory amnesia that refuses difference in order to represent harmony and identity. Individual fulfillment, romantic love, is incompatible with the order of nature, indeed, with any order at all, probably even with the order of marriage that is constantly threatened by nature. "My soul consents not to give sovereignty," announces Hermia, ostensibly rejecting patriarchal authority but in fact revealing the desire to separate the spirit from the mythic power of the earth, a power however from which it cannot escape, despite the optimism of progress (1.1.82). It may successfully dislodge itself from traditionalist "sovereignty," but, at least in *A Midsummer Night's Dream,* it does not achieve a "sovereignty" of its own.

I have begun this chapter with these brief comments on the Shakespearean text because of the extensive references to it in *Der Park* by Botho Strauss (1983). In addition to direct citations, the contemporary play maintains some crucial elements: Oberon and Titania reappear, as do the four confused lovers, wandering now through the desolate landscape of the affluent Federal Republic. Puck is transformed into the artist Cyprian, and the Indian changeling returns as "the black boy," still hotly disputed. Shakespeare's epithalamium is echoed in the final scene, Titania's silver wedding anniversary. However, the aristocratic sovereigns, Theseus and Hippolyta, have disappeared in twentieth-century democracy. Gone too is the play within the play, although some of the minor figures might be regarded as corollaries to Bottom and his crew.

All this is of course more than external embellishment. On the contrary, the relationship to *A Midsummer Night's Dream* is central to the project of *Der Park*. In the preface, Strauss insists that "the plot of this new play is held and moved, elevated and fooled by the spirit of Shakespeare's *Midsummer Night's Dream*." Perpetually referring to the older text, the play nevertheless draws fundamentally different conclusions: "Yet changes take place and topple the humans, the spirits, and the plot—*A Midsummer Night's Dream* goes on, and no one stayed awake to bring that good antidote that could free everyone from their errors." [2]

Shakespeare's Oberon was able to manipulate the mortals, control Titania, and restore the appearance of an order, no matter how problematic its constitution. Strauss's Oberon fails, and the concluding celebration, the silver wedding anniversary, is a party where nearly none of the invited guests arrive. *Der Park* is therefore certainly not a mere adaptation of Shakespeare, a contemporary rewrite of a popular classic. It insists instead on a dialectical relationship to the past, measuring the misery of the Federal Republic against the Elizabethan utopia, while at the same time suggesting that the contemporary misery is a consequence of the flawed project of enlightened modernity announced by the older drama. Put bluntly, Shakespeare is both standard and culprit for a work whose intertextuality provides it with the character of a "sundial of history." [3]

The historicity of *A Midsummer Night's Dream* was determined by the opening exchange: Theseus' "Now," and Hippolyta's reply that the few days remaining before their marriage would pass quickly. Strauss echoes that exchange and comments on it as well, as *Der Park* begins with a parallel thematization of temporality. Georg enters and approaches Helen with a simple "*Guten Abend. Wie geht's?*" She answers with an even simpler "*Ach. Tach. Na ja. Geht so*" (9). Recall that Theseus and Hippolyta, although not yet married, were already disagreeing: his anxiety about time was countered by her assurance that they would soon wed. Georg and Helen, who, like their Athenian antecedents, will soon enjoy nuptial bliss, are even further from an auspicious consensus: his "*Abend*" is her "*Tach.*" They cannot even agree on the time of day, and this confusing lack of sense is repeated in her contentless speech, where the temporal "*Tach*"—instead of the standard German "*Tag*"—rhymes with the exclamatory "*Ach*," an echo that is underscored by the cadence of the subsequent double syllables, "*Na ja. Geht so.*" The extreme reduction of language and the exclusion of expressive differentiation are reminiscent of Beckett. Helen's speech becomes noise, dialogic communication loses any substance, and a future-oriented project of temporality, such as had been provided by Theseus' speech, is missing. History, as a subjective pursuit of enlightenment and human happiness, is absent in *Der Park,* or, measured against *A Midsummer Night's Dream,* it is present only as absent.

With this negative judgment on the constellation of consensual communication, history, and emancipation, *Der Park* appears to draw close to theoreticians of postmodernity such as Lyotard, with his insistence on the obsolescence of the metanarratives of knowledge and politics. Neither of course partakes of a naive Enlightenment optimism; yet while postmodernity claims to identify an epochal transformation that relegates the discourse of emancipation to the past, *Der Park* investigates the self-subversion of emancipation through an analysis of the dialectic of enlightenment. Lyotard rejects an Enlightenment that allegedly succeeds as enlightenment only by means of a Jacobin totalitarianism he imputes to Habermas;[4] *Der Park* critiques a flawed Enlightenment that constantly prevents itself from achieving its own goals.

Consider another altercation among lovers, the counterparts to Georg and Helen: Wolf and Helma. She recalls how he used to possess a linguistic facility to command physical nature, i.e., human speech as the medium of enlightenment: "You used to be able to explain the constellations to me. You knew where Sirius was in Canis Major and why it is important. Today? You've forgotten everything. Do you ever still look up at the starry canopy?" (42). The strangely archaic "*Sternenzelt*" stands out from the predominant rhetorical level—especially in the mouth of the naive and unsophisticated Helma—as an allusion to the verse from Schiller's Ode to Joy which is crucial in Beethoven's setting: "*Überm Sternenzelt muss ein lieber Vater wohnen.*" Wolf has lost interest in both scientific cognition and practical reason, and Helma can continue to berate him for his historical amnesia: "You used to wax eloquent over the French Revolution. Now you wouldn't even know when it took place. Or even if it ever did" (43). He no longer speaks with her because he lacks language, and without language he lacks narration and history. Elsewhere we learn that he in fact once studied history but gave it up in order to take over his father's driving school. The compromise with the reality principle, a bad reconciliation with an oppressive nature, entails a surrendering of his youthful ideals; he confuses Danton and Desmoulins, and can remember only that the battles in Paris took place "back then [*Annodunnemals*]" (44). Patriarchal authority, challenged by Hermia at the outset of the Shakespearean text, is restored by Wolf, who trades the French Revolution for his bourgeois patrimony. His solution is reminiscent of that of Theseus: he relegates violence to a past that is to be forgotten.

> *Helma:* Once you were able to bring the French Revolution so close, as if it had taken place yesterday.
> *Wolf:* It is a distortion to suggest that the Great French Revolution took place yesterday. It didn't take place yesterday. (44)

Historical consciousness and narrative talent, once linked to the political practices of the generation of 1968 to which all the figures belong, are transformed into a pedantic and incapacitating historicism. Pushing the revolution back behind "yesterday," Wolf guarantees the stability of the present, while attempting to disguise his betrayal of his ideals by labeling the Revolution "great." Far from following Lyotard in his conservative applause for the obsolescence of the metanarratives of emancipation, *Der Park* demonstrates the desiccation of language and personal experience in the wake of the crumbling of emancipatory ideals, as the metanarrators make their peace with a present whose crises they frantically deny.

Both the initial dialogue and the history lesson manqué suggest a crippled historical consciousness. The present is marked by a confusion more excruciating than the one with which *A Midsummer Night's Dream* begins, but it is no longer experienced as a crisis, and the plausibility of a goal-oriented human action is consequently eroded. Oberon and Titania appear in order to overcome this listlessness that enervates all desire and extirpates the erotic power necessary for social cohesion and creative activity. Thus Oberon:

> Humans know nothing about pleasure. They know nothing about the force with which creatures are drawn to each other on other planets. . . . Their sense of pleasure is as distant from ours as is this newt from a dragon. In fact recently it appears to be dwindling even more and will disappear altogether, if we don't incite their drives. (15)

The reassertion of desire as a solution to the sorry flaccidity of contemporary culture depends no longer on the magic ointments of Puck but on a reenchantment by aesthetic appearance: in the second scene

Oberon and Titania expose themselves to Helma, as if the sight of the body could revive a desire that might ignite action and history. Oberon makes clear the connection between eros and temporality with his comment: "The instant is injected [*Der Augenblick ist eingeimpft*]" (15). Only the erotic vision of the body reveals the urgency of the moment of the present, a logic embedded in the double meaning of "*Augenblick*" referring to both sight and time. The rediscovery of temporality furthermore grounds the dramatic opposition of subject and object in an encounter of recognition. It is that dialectic of modernity that Oberon and Titania hope to reinitiate. They will fail, and *Der Park* investigates the consequences for art, politics, and representation.

The text itself undertakes a homologous project. Like Titania and Oberon who expose themselves in the park, *Der Park* exposes the body of the Shakespearean text in order to arouse a tired cultural audience. The author of *Gross und Klein* gives vent to his frustration with the public in a hidden self-reference, spoken by the artist Helen: "Sometimes they don't like my timing, sometimes I'm too big, sometimes too small, it all depends, there's always something wrong. Oh, what the fuck, I'm not such a dumb little cutie that they can always boss around" (10). Against the never-ending pickiness of small-minded critics, *Der Park* tries to invoke the redemptive potential of art by displaying the range of its strength and its expressive modalities. It recapitulates the development of modernist drama by mustering stylistic elements as varied as a naturalist use of language, Wedekind's allegories, Sternheim's satire of the *juste milieu*, Artaud's theater of cruelty, Brecht's appropriation of classics, and features of absurdist theater (this aspect could be described as "postmodern" in the sense of stylistic eclecticism). It pleads for the urgency of art in a prosaic age especially by invoking Shakespeare as a crown witness, indisputably no "dumb little cutie."

Yet Shakespeare is present only as a fading past. The aesthetic priority he represents is slipping away inexorably, and *Der Park* notably refuses to adopt a cultural conservative posture of preserving the traditional text as a marmorated object of veneration. Instead it maintains the tension between the represented figures blind to the consequences of the erosion of culture and its own metacritique of the disappearance of the traditional horizon. The experience of modernity always derived from the distance to a traditional order of the past, a distance that was interpreted negatively as a loss of orientation or applauded for its emancipatory potential. In either case, the traditionalist reference provided posttraditionalist modernity with its substantial values. *Der Park* describes the postmodern as the stage of modernity in which that possibility of temporal referentiality dwindles to nil. Both inherited conservatism and the orthodoxy of emancipatory narratives lose their grounding, since neither the sovereignty of the political state nor the sovereignty of the autonomous personality can convincingly cite a relevant historical model. It is as if the crisis were not solved—on the contrary, it certainly continues—but its character of crisis, a situation of disorder inviting closure, were forgotten.

Der Park begins with the failure of art. Dressed in the tricot of a circus acrobat, Helen sits outside the opening of a tent and shivers in the cold. Georg's question makes the thematic matter clear: "*Was macht die Kunst?*" Helen's reply glosses the contemporary aesthetic situation; she has fallen from the trapeze and refused to climb back up. An altercation has ensued, and she irately denounces the whole enterprise: "This shitty little amateur circus. . . . A sheer waste of time. They're just a bunch of would-bes. Dilettantes! Big talk, no action" (11). The tirade is not only an attack on the established institution of art, the *Kunstbetrieb,* that motivated the reference to *Gross und Klein* to which I pointed a moment ago. It is more emphatic, an announcement of the end of art, a radical leave-taking: the show won't go on. Thus the contemporary drama commences with the knowledge of its own impossibility, and it sets that paradox as the object of its investigation. *A Midsummer Night's Dream* begins with a promise that it can keep only with duplicity. *Der Park* starts by underscoring the duplicity of any performance and then proceeds, without legitimacy, to pose questions: what has displaced art and where has art fled?

The question is posed insistently by a visual absence: an empty trapeze swings above the opening scene. In the final scene, it swings above the empty anniversary celebration, bearing no one at all, certainly no artist. Yet one time it is occupied by the "man in black," Wedekind's *vermummter Herr,* whom Strauss transforms explicitly into an allegory of death. The figure is dialectical. Marked by death, this sterile society, devoid of lust, will tolerate no aesthetic pleasure; thanatos has vanquished eros who has fled the field. Without death, however, the locus of art, the abandoned trapeze, would remain perpetually empty, for the Enlightenment denial of mortality and nature rendered art impossible in a society of "*Bewusstsein und Geschäfte*" (16).

The dual signification of death ensconced in the aesthetic trapeze relies on a complex chain of intertextuality. In a work constructed so thoroughly as a perpetual commentary on the Shakespearean text, the new title can be adequately understood only with reference to the immanent set of substantive issues: death, the end of art, and the refusal of cultural conservatism. The title is an invitation; Helma's plea to Wolf is addressed to the audience: "We simply can't treat the park as something that doesn't concern us! We have to go in it!" (43). The exhortation makes the subtext evident, another invitation, Stefan George's "*Komm in den totgesagten park und schau.*"[5] The symbolist poem insists on the unimpaired vitality of an aesthetic realm; it defends literature against the allegation of death—"*totgesagt*"—by demonstrating the untenability of the accusation. Asserting an irreducible permanence of the aesthetic object, it implicitly announces the immortality of art, always impervious to death: as if art were only neoclassical beauty, as if death were not already gnawing away at the foundation of modern art. Strauss invokes George in his title in order to reject this unshakable aestheticist faith: *Der Park* suggests that death and a knowledge of mortality are essential elements of art. Yet the death that flies through the air has little to do with the historical decadence of the early twentieth century, to which George himself was close. This death guarantees art and denies it simultaneously, like Paul Celan's "*Meister aus Deutschland*," playing the violin in a fugue for the corpses who populate Strauss's stage.[6] The only poetry possible after Auschwitz—I take this to be the sense of Adorno's dictum—is one that explores its own impossibility, its own lack of identity in terms of the classical subject-object unity. The black man of death swings across the stage like an eraser, obliterating the same aesthetic text he needs to stage his performance.[7]

The immanent and objective incoherence of art in *Der Park*, which is presented initially as Helen's subjective failure, seems to stand in contrast to the successful aesthetic projects of *A Midsummer Night's Dream*, i.e., Shakespeare provides a standard with which cultural criticism claims to measure the inadequacies of contemporary modernity. In that distant past, Puck's wizardry could resolve the amorous meanderings of the Athenians, Oberon's deception could still master Titania's intransigence, and the epithalamium could provide a compelling closure to the multifold conflicts of the drama. Yet Strauss invokes Shakespeare, as I have already put it, not only as standard but as culprit as well: the vagaries of aesthetic representation are in fact already apparent in *A Midsummer Night's Dream*, subverting the ostensible teleology of action. Aesthetic confusion is present, in a humorous vein, in the efforts of the artisans to perform the tragedy of Pyramus and Thisbe, and, more seriously, in the vicissitudes of Puck's interventions. For charged with the task of reconciling the two pairs of lovers, Puck blunders and makes matters worse, as Oberon complains:

> What hast thou done? Thou hast mistaken quite
> And laid the love-juice on some true-love's sight.
> Of thy misprision must perforce ensue
> Some true-love turned, and not a false turned true.
>
> (3.2.88–89)

Art that inhibits eros must already maintain a secret tie to death, and conversely, the society in which love fails will discover a parallel failure in art: the critical moment, the turning point of Shakespeare's play, already encompasses the judgment passed on modernity by *Der Park*. In addition, however, the very possibility of Puck's deviating from Oberon's command is crucial, no matter how the servant eventually scurries to put things right by following his master's second set of orders. Just as Hermia announces the rebellion of the modern individual, insisting on the freedom of her soul against inherited authority, Puck's mishap points to the impending emancipation of art from the institution of patronage. Prefiguring the modern artist, Puck discovers the possibility of disobedience and the pursuit of autonomous aesthetic projects, no longer encumbered by the exigencies of political representation. Simultaneously, however, he discovers the complexities that preclude an immediate translation of artistic will into an aesthetic work. Emerging from premodern structures of dependence, the modern artist discovers subjectivity and autonomy and, at the same time, loses them to the opacity of language and the limits of subjective intentions.

Against the background of *A Midsummer Night's Dream*, *Der Park* addresses the crisis of art as a problem of modernity that began to appear in the Elizabethan text. There however it could still be resolved by the relatively unimpaired vitality of the mechanisms of absolutist authority. In contrast, modern art cannot fall back on the power of a Theseus to solve its legitimacy crisis. Strauss traces three competing possibilities of modern art and explores their fates in contemporary culture. Unlike his Shakespearean predecessor who was only peripherally concerned with affairs of mortals while he carried on his bouts with Titania, the new Oberon is primarily committed to an Enlightenment project of aesthetic education. Exposure to the sight of beauty will permit an insipid humanity to overcome the emptiness of its existence, from which all meaning has fled, and recover the fullness of a utopian pleasure: "We want to be the first to wake the deeply buried wishes and melt the frozen sobriety" (16). His strategy, as already indicated, is the "*Augenblick,*" the moment of aesthetic vision, which however is only vision, i.e., the visual representation of beauty that refuses to engage directly in the material transformation of life practices. Thus, when he catches Titania taking the project of erotic resuscitation too literally by making love to the black boy, he warns her with a classically Kantian admonition: "If you destroy the picture, you'll destroy its glow" (19). For to be autonomous art must remain without interest or tangible pleasure.

This steamy escapade of Titania was no accident. Her critique of contemporary social relations is always more heated than Oberon's philosophical discourse: "Is this lust?" she cries; "Do they have any sexuality?" (15). Such passion leads her to denounce the ineffectuality of Oberon's insistence on aesthetic autonomy: "What do you want to do? Here below you can't do anything but show yourself off in the form of a sudden fullness. Your powers are restricted" (15). Her alternative suggestion entails a direct participation in erotic encounters. She pursues men, searching for an ultimate consummation; the aesthetic project turns out to have a reciprocal character, for not only will Oberon and Titania attempt, by different means, to carry love into the world; their own survival depends on the reflection of an aesthetic glow from mortals. Oberon tries to prevent her repeatedly, insisting that the immediacy of aesthetic representation imagined by Titania can only desiccate her utopian potential: "You should be able to appear without getting involved. You stop being Titania of the moon, you lose your nocturnal power when you get accustomed to such incomplete love!" (20). The conflict between the two corresponds to that between the autonomous and avant-garde models of the work of art, the former insisting on the separation of the work from material practice, the latter, motivated by an unremitting passion for transformation, taking part in the quotidian activities of human experience. For the avant-gardist Titania, Oberon seems effete; for Oberon, the advocate of aesthetic autonomy, Titania's activities are well-meaning but pointless and, in any case, beyond the pale of art. Both critiques turn out to be valid. By the conclusion of the play, Oberon has failed to initiate cultural progress through the "*Augen-*

blick," and can no longer recite the Shakespearean lines he could render so well at the beginning: "I know a bank where the wild thyme blows, / where oxlips and the nodding violet grows . . ." (14, 119). Driven by desire, Titania appealed to the artist Cyprian to build her a construction with which she could seduce a bull as a lover; the result is violence and suffering, as Oberon puts it: "Titania turned into a bloody myth!" (82). Her effort to surpass aesthetic autonomy results in a regression to barbaric myth. It is her half-animal son who carries on a monologue in the final scene, the failed celebration of her marriage, the failure of her erotic avant-gardism.

Cyprian marks the third alternative. He is the genuine heir to Puck, the artist servant of Oberon who finally capitalizes on the artistic independence that began to emerge in Shakespeare. The artist is no longer exclusively subservient to the aristocratic patron and can make use of his talents for his own purposes. That of course is the logic underlying the classical-romantic aesthetics of autonomy. It is also the logic of the marketplace. Without the guarantee of patronal support, the artist presents his work to the market and quickly commodifies the creative process. Cyprian is the artist of the culture industry. He appropriates the transcendental knowledge received from Oberon and mass markets figurines with an apotropaic power; in the play they function as aphrodisiacs. Similarly he is willing to serve Titania, from whom he receives the black boy in exchange; the exchange mechanism again is the organizing principle of his aesthetic activity. Thus his declaration of independence from his erstwhile lord who has been displaced by the democracy of money: "I'll serve you gladly, sir, but not only you. Now I serve the masses as well. I found a new lord there, whom I must accommodate" (83). The aristocratic Oberon can only despise Cyprian's capitalist equality as "*greed for mere success*" (83). The culture industry surrenders the immanent values of the aesthetic work, and especially the utopian project with which both Oberon and Titania set out. Consequently Oberon reclaims the powers he had invested in Cyprian, whose objects d'art lose their magical force. Simultaneously he abandons his privileged position and his aesthetic essence and enters the world of the mortals as an equal.

The aesthetics of classical autonomy are demonstrably ineffectual, the interventionism of the avant-garde has failed, and the mass marketing of the culture industry succeeds only in trivializing aesthetic substance. *Der Park* provides no answer, but there is faint suggestion of a final option. The drama opened with Helen, the failed artist sitting outside the circus tent. In the penultimate scene, the same tent is in the background with an illuminated opening. At the conclusion, Titania and Oberon, who has taken on the life of an ordinary human without supernatural powers, walk toward it, turning their backs on the petty squabbles that have dominated the discussions, and Oberon's last word is a defiant "*Ja.*" The affirmation expresses a final allegiance to a utopian project whose home is in the circus. Oberon has been unable to realize the transcendental project in the alienated culture of modern society, but it remains a desideratum, if only as a never fully articulated normative goal that radiates throughout the world from behind. The text of the play has repeated the same logic: it incorporates elements of traditional high culture (especially the Shakespearean material), the avant-garde (theater of cruelty), and commercial theater (a language borrowed from the boulevard entertainment), and it subjects them all to a radical critique. This is a work concerned with the inadequacies of its own constituent moments. Describing the failure of the three aesthetic options of modernity, it relegates them to a past, and this historicizing gesture locates the text itself in a postmodern position, i.e., after modernity which it looks back on with an anatomical, not a nostalgic, eye. However, maintaining the utopian substance of the aesthetic project, no matter how problematic its realization may turn out to be, the play inscribes itself as part of that same modernity and locates the postmodern within it.

The condemnation of Cyprian points to the valuelessness of a consistent commercialization of art. In contrast, the alternative versions of utopianism advocated initially by Oberon and Titania are linked to explicitly political strategies: progressive reform and radical action. Each corresponds to a possibility during the historical decade in the wake of which the cultural structures investigated in *Der Park* were constituted: classical social democracy and student-movement activism. "Postmodernism," if the term has relevance in the Federal Republic, refers to a retrospective vision of the sixties, and, more broadly, to a loss of faith in the projects of radical social transformation conceived by activist intellectuals.

Nevertheless, *Der Park* carries out an emphatically political exploration, although it eschews the explicit tendentiousness that often characterizes West German drama. Measuring it against *A Midsummer Night's Dream,* one cannot fail to recognize how thoroughly it insists on one traditional understanding of emancipation: the aristocratic ruling class of Athens has been abolished, and the drama presents a formally leveled society. Yet the eradication of heteronomous rule has not ushered in the realm of freedom. The ancient sovereigns have been banished, but the modern individuals are hardly in control of their lives, are perhaps even less in control than the youth of Athens. Like their forebears in the Greek forest, they are trapped in a terrifying isolation. Yet while Shakespeare's figures still participated in a linguistic community of comprehension and exchange, Strauss's are caught in perpetual misunderstandings and banalities. Their personality structures reproduce the authoritarianism that formerly adhered to the political state, but because no sovereign center, no Duke of Athens, provides a focus for political controversy, the crisis is infinitely shattered. The political drama therefore refuses to proclaim the urgency of a single overriding political issue—no such stance is any longer legitimate. Instead it investigates the microstructures of oppression.

The society in which formal political identity and traditional patriarchy have been eroded by enlightenment produces fragmented actors in search of an irrational retotalization, to be provided by some recycled mythology or by one or the other of the compulsive neuroses of contemporary capitalism. Helma is the perfect consumer, buying into Cyprian's marketing strategies with hebephrenic delight. While Helen nurtures a vicious racism, Wolf indulges in a morbid patriotism that renders him nearly catatonic, and Titania's reluctant suitors, unwilling to love, all don uniforms of the *Bundeswehr,* rather than the more traditional ass head that Puck formerly provided. The point is not that *Der Park* emphatically criticizes these gestures from some political Archimedean point; they are cited rather as symptomatic of the fruitless efforts to achieve identity in a culture which frustrates the constitution of a genuine one.

Oberon understands the threat of this irrationalist potential. His project of aesthetic education was intended at least to postpone it: "In the end we will be honored and receive greater rewards than those who will certainly follow" (16). The same fear of these strange gods, a mythic violence in competition with the beneficent Oberon and Titania, recurs later when he berates Cyprian for abusing the magic gifts: "Ignite no soul before you know that, in place of love, not another, darker kindling will ignite" (82). Cautious Oberon understands that history provides no universal guarantees. Fragmented society might be rescued by the splendor of the aesthetic "*Augenblick,*" but it might also fall victim to some unknown beast, slouching toward

catastrophe. Utopia or barbarism: the former is intimated by the return to the circus tent, the latter is expressed most strongly in Helen's
outburst at the height of the lovers' disagreements:

> Men? You call for men? Ha! Men must first wage wars to learn
> again how to love women! . . . Does no one still want to con-
> quer another? . . . Oh no, you simply can't, you can't! You talk
> it over and decide to agree. These days you make agreements
> and prefer to rot through and through, in your bones and mar-
> row and manhood, in this lax and lazy age of peace. Lazy, lazy,
> lazy! (79)

The lines could not help but provoke current political sentiment in
1983 at the height of the West German missiles debate. Yet the text is
not tendentious; its point is that modern society denies the individual
autonomy and vitality, making reactions such as Helen's nostalgia for
belligerence likely.

That interpretive ploy, a standard move vis-à-vis a dramatic text,
attributes the articulated position (the critique of peace) to the dramatic figure and not to the author. Yet there is more at work in the
passage, which stands in close relation to the Shakespearean model.
A Midsummer Night's Dream commences with the obliteration of the
memory of a violent past; Theseus has won Hippolyta by force but
hopes henceforth to live in marital comity. The state maintains a monopoly on violence, but it presents itself as the agency of peace. Hel-
en's speech points out the mendacity of this claim and modern political representation in general. Politics have indeed ceased to be the
center of individual consciousness; hence the absence of Theseus and
Hippolyta in Der Park. The state is no longer visible, and the premodern excesses of absolutism have been blunted. But the state has certainly not withered away. Its citizenry are still its subjugated subjects,
helpless as ever and weak, prevented even from calling the omnipotent
state into question because of its protean ubiquity. Wolf's forgetting
the French Revolution is one case of the false consciousness that becomes socially necessary once the state becomes inaccessible to effective criticism. This false consciousness corresponds to the dialectic of
neoconservatism that strengthens the state apparatus by diminishing
its visibility.

Helen's provocation is not essentially a matter of right-wing fanat-
icism, as it is misunderstood by Georg. On the contrary, calling for
violence, she calls into question the monopoly on violence claimed by

the state since Shakespeare's Theseus. Her cry therefore amounts to an anarchist manifesto which, coupled with the program of aesthetic utopianism, constitutes the objective content of the play. The speech denounces the mistreatment of Hippolyta and the legacy of unquestioned power, be it in the form of Elizabethan absolutism or the modern welfare state. For the state has monopolized power in order to maintain oppression and persecute that soul that "consents not to give sovereignty." Helen's anger gives expression to the rational moment latent in the manifest irrationalism which Oberon rightly fears. It is the rationality of a constantly frustrated love that rejects the complacency of a culture without passion or desire, affects which have been undermined by the process of civilizational rationalization. Strauss refers to "an industrious society, nearly as far from holy things as from the timeless poem (and a little tired out)" (n.p. [7]). It is Weber's capitalist modernity, economically affluent, culturally impoverished, and always on the verge of a mysterious irrationalism and new prophets.

The crises of art and politics in *Der Park* point to a general crisis of representation. The utopian substance of the aesthetic project has not been translated adequately into a textual body and retreats into the paradisiac enclave of the circus at the rear of the stage from which the audience, positioned outside of Eden, is spatially banished. The democratic substance of the Enlightenment project has similarly found no appropriate body politic; the absolutist ruler has disappeared, but only because subjugation has been universalized. This shared problematic, the inability to achieve viable modes of aesthetic or political signification, is rooted in the lability of representation already inherent in *A Midsummer Night's Dream;* references to that material in *Der Park* bring it to the fore in the original, pursue its logic, and constitute the genuine intimacy of the two texts.

The Elizabethan crisis of order follows from the introduction of difference—the changeling, the control of whom is the basis of the dispute between Oberon and Titania. The clean slate of power is destablized by the presence of the Indian boy as a mark transformed into a token of exchange. For it is the exchange of the mark, who is never present on stage, that permits the provisional restoration of order at the conclusion of the drama. I say "provisional," since Oberon's blessing, cited earlier, makes clear a continued effort to defer the signs of writing: "And the blots of Nature's hand / Shall not in their issue stand." The activity of the drama depends on the introduction of India ink, the diacritical figure, into the literary text, but the labor of the text entails asserting its erasure and exclusion. The text begins as writing but tries to deny this origin, as if it were really a spirit of a different sort.

A Midsummer Night's Dream therefore describes modernity mobilizing writing as a device that initiates social action, but the same modernity insists on the denial of the materiality of its writing. It is a linguistic community that calls itself into question by refusing the specificity of its own language, to which it falsely imputes a universalist transparency. This contradictory structure of representation has a corollary in the economic realm. The successful pursuit of individual happiness, the emancipation of the amorous soul from patriarchal authority, turns out to presume the control of the body of the other. The body of the changeling is sacrificed to Oberon in order for Hermia to control her own body and sleep with Lysander. Beneath the bourgeois freedom of the modern citizenry, the material domination of an underclass, which is already located in the Elizabethan text in an oriental realm of imperialist expansion, is carried out, although always denied in the representational practices of the hegemonic order. Hence the imperative of denigrating the alternative representational strategy, the dramaturgic assumptions of the artisans, who are mocked because of their naively realist refusal to engage in the standard fictional codes of substitution and exchange.

Modern society, which replaces traditional authority with the anonymous authority of the market, relies on the ideological representation of value while denying the agency of its production—the absent figure of difference, the writer and the laborer. Der Park draws attention to this problematic in A Midsummer Night's Dream by bringing the changeling onto the stage as "der schwarze Junge," a silent employee of the recreation department, the third-world worker in the metropolis, condemned to cleaning up the litter in the park. Ignored by all the Europeans, the yuppies and the punks, he is the figure of negation, and his genealogy is perfectly clear. Like his Shakespearean ancestor, he belongs initially to Titania and is the object of desire no longer of Oberon himself but of Oberon's recalcitrant servant, Cyprian. Again an exchange takes place, but it leads to no resolution: the black boy, refused by all, refuses Cyprian's seduction and kills the artist. His genuine identity becomes clear immediately after the murder when, in the next scene, the man in black, the allegorical figure of death, makes his first appearance and predominates during much of the rest of the drama.

I want to suggest that in its treatment of the changeling *Der Park* provides the crucial gloss on *A Midsummer Night's Dream*, effecting, in a strikingly literal sense, a mortification of the original work and bringing its truth content to the fore. Ostensibly a peripheral ornament in the Shakespearean version of the fable, the changeling is recognized as death and turns out to be the organizing principle of enlightened modernity and of its strategy of representation. The absolutist ruler has been deposed but only to be displaced by Hegel's "absolute lord," death, who is the agency of absence: the absence of the writer and the absence of the laborer.[8] Condorcet looked forward to the victory of enlightenment over death; *Der Park* demonstrates a mythic cult of death as the motor of enlightenment that always denies the earthly happiness that it claims to provide. It has relied on the sacrifice of the differential victim of violence and has thereby only reproduced the myth of violence it hoped to escape. Thus the crisis of modernity is misunderstood if it is posed in terms of myth and enlightenment as mutually exclusive alternatives. That opposition uncritically accepts the naive Enlightenment's self-understanding as the opposite of myth and its equally self-serving and specious distinctions between magic and science, religion and philosophy, etc. A genuinely critical project would begin by recognizing the mythic structure of enlightenment itself in order to consider whether enlightenment might escape its own enthrallment with myth.

As a culture of writing advocated by literary intellectuals, modernity is nevertheless implicated in a desire to escape language—as shown by Oberon's fear of diacritical marks—and it produces a deathlike silence. As capitalist exchange, modernity depends on difference but asserts a formal equality indebted to the sameness of death. *Der Park* locates this self-subversion of the Enlightenment, the structure of representation that promises universal individuality while simultaneously pulling the ground out from under each particular individual in order to open up a grave. Modernity modernizes the mythic imperative of human sacrifice, which is to say, it continues the practice in a sublimated form, and it therefore prevents itself from achieving the community of free individuals it was proud to promise.

Der Park also provides a critique of modernity by invoking a normative ideal of society as a genuinely free association. Thus the final, disturbing line: "Have you understood me, or are you only listening in? [*Haben Sie mich verstanden oder lauschen Sie nur?*]" (127). The text accuses modernity of failing to complete its own legitimate project, an intersubjectivity of rational comprehension that could replace

the traditionalist order of the past. *A Midsummer Night's Dream* concludes with a labile celebration of marriage and social cohesion based
on a forced reconciliation, on the violent irrationality of absolutist
power. *Der Park* concludes with a failed celebration in the modern
world of rationality as sublimated violence. Against the background
of the Shakespearean text, it rearticulates the challenge of reconciling
enlightenment and pleasure, reason and love. It is Bottom, whose
name locates the origin of democratic projects, who understands best
what is at stake: "And yet, to say the truth, reason and love keep little
company together nowadays. The more the pity that some honest
neighbors will not make them friends" (3.1.130–33).

CHAPTER NINE

Imperial Encounters:
The Instrumentalization of Culture
and Transnational Practice

RECENT work in the sociology of literature has shifted critical attention away from traditional concerns of literary scholarship such as the authoritative meaning of particular texts or the biographical parameters of their genesis. Instead the notion of literature as an institution points toward other areas of research as the setting for a materialist history of culture: writers' organizations, the book trade, censorship, literacy, salons, etc. Yet in addition to this extendable list of discrete forms and activities, the term "institution" also suggests the norms which define a hegemonic model of literature within a given cultural setting, i.e., a model that is by definition never identical with real practices but which constantly describes the borders of normalcy, thereby allowing for the possibilities of acceptance and transgression.[1]

It would not be difficult to construct a similar institutional account of philosophy that would include both the set of actual places and deeds—university institutes, intellectual circles, lecture series, private gatherings, and public conferences—and the normative status attributed to the discipline. Yet in the classical bourgeois culture of Austria during the second half of the nineteenth century and the first few decades of the twentieth, these two normative ideals, the literary and philosophical institutionalizations, were linked and often indistinguishable from one another within a wider set of idealized values labeled "culture" or *Bildung*.

An institutional approach to cultural material will necessarily tend to disprivilege a traditionalist discussion of the particular meaning of a work of art or the intentional substance of a philosophical inquiry. It will instead attempt to describe the normative status ascribed to cultural activity in order to demonstrate the resonance between the particular work and its institutional context; for the critical significance of a work is likely to depend on the degree to which it can call the conventionality of its setting into question. Two sorts of questions consequently arise: (1) the Brechtian question Cui bono, or How does

155

the specific institutionalization of culture function within simultaneous social practices? and (2) the Adornian scrutiny of Stendhal's *promesse de bonheur,* the utopian potential of cultural works, or How can particular instances of institutionalized cultural practice (works of art, philosophical writing) subversively call into question their own institutional preconditions and thereby the heteronomy of "precondition" altogether?

For Weber the emergence of a set of cultural values designated as "eternal" and carried by an elite defined by its proximity to culture, a *Geistesaristokratie,* was a consequence of the bifurcation of class society and therefore dependant on the presence of the state as the sole legitimate agent of violence, i.e., high culture means state power. This state power is exerted both domestically and internationally; in the *Zwischenbetrachtung* to the essays on the sociology of religion written in 1916, the defense of cultural values clearly requires a strong state which participates in the "world dominion of unbrotherliness" (*"die Weltherrschaft der Unbrüderlichkeit"*), that is, the carnage of the war.

The complicity of values designated as eternal in the production of a cultural elite robs those values of the substance which Weber would deem appropriate: an ethic of solidarity. Given his particular account of modernization as the separation of value spheres and an irreversible process of rationalization, he can envision a critique of this institutionalized culture developing only exogenously in a Nietzschean revaluation of values that might be carried out by "new prophets." Yet in fact the critique of institutionalized culture had long become thematic within institutionalized literature itself. In *Young Törless* (1906), Musil describes his hero's experience of the hegemonic form of culture in the following manner:

> Now, in Törless's hearing the name Kant had never been uttered except in passing and then in the tone in which one refers to some awe-inspiring holy man. And Törless could not think anything but that with Kant the problems of philosophy had been finally solved, so that since then it had become futile for anyone to concern himself with the subject, just as he also believed there was no longer any point in writing poetry since Schiller and Goethe.[2]

Culture, transformed into authority, discourages further cultural activity, aesthetic or philosophical, and leads apparently to a self-dismantling of cultural production or even to the auto-da-fé that Canetti would describe in a novel three decades later. In fact, Canetti's *Die Blendung* (*Auto-da-Fé*) is the final text I will examine here; Stifter's *Nachsommer* (*Indian Summer*) is the first, and in between I will turn to several pieces of literary and nonliterary writing with a dual intention: to describe the transformation of "culture" as it is institutionalized and instrumentalized within particular social projects and to suggest that this instrumentalization has to do with a particular transnational practice that Hugo von Hofmannsthal labeled, without any critical undertone, "cultural imperialism" (*geistiger Imperialismus*).[3] How does the appropriation of cultural material in a project of intercultural domination transform culture, and what sort of critical response is possible from instrumentalized culture itself?

Considerable evidence suggests that in *Nachsommer* (1857) Stifter intended less an idealization of a halcyon prerevolutionary Austria than a sort of literary critique of political economy; extrapolating from the success of a bourgeois revolution, which he would have greeted, Stifter asks what sorts of cultural contradictions an unfolding of capitalism might engender and what regulative mechanisms might be instituted in order to preserve social order. The universalization of bourgeois class relations is evident in the class membership of all the central figures, but more important is the articulated project of a globalization of bourgeois economic relations on the basis of scientific progress, unencumbered informational exchange, and a perpetual commerce with commodities:

> "What will it be like when we can send messages across the whole earth with the speed of lightning, when we ourselves will be able to reach the most diverse places on earth with alacrity in the shortest of times, and when, with the same speed, we will be able to transport great shipments? Will not the goods of the earth then become common property through the possibility of easy exchange, so that all will be available to all?"[4]

In Stifter's utopia, communism and consumerism become indistinguishable.[5] Commodities are universally available—or they will become so, as soon as the transparency of the market is imposed on all opaque points of resistance: "Today a small country city and its hinterland can close itself off with what it has, and what it is and what it knows: soon it will no longer be so, it will be torn into the universal intercourse."[6] Universal intercourse (*allgemeiner Verkehr*) is Stifter's capitalist cosmopolitanism. Its establishment will not be easy; small cities or even countries might resist the expansion of the metropolitan market system, and the various centers will likely enter into competition with each other. To meet this challenge, Stifter goes on to explain how only a cultural rearmament, an educational *Nachrüstung*, will be able to guarantee victory in the impending struggles: "Owing to the demands of universal contact, it will then be necessary for even the least member of society to know more and to have greater abilities than today. Those states which through the development of reason and culture first acquire this knowledge will be foremost in wealth, power, and splendor and will even place the existence of the other states in question."[7]

A more explicit account of the exigency to reinstitutionalize culture is hardly imaginable. Cultural activity is no longer simply a matter of a personal culture, the old bourgeois cultivation of a private interiority, but rather a moment in a transnational expansion of economic activity that may encounter resistance and is therefore prepared to mobilize "culture" as a mechanism with which to pursue its project.

This account of the status ascribed to culture in *Nachsommer* may well be incompatible with the more individualistic descriptions evident elsewhere in this *Bildungsroman*, the presence of which it would be foolish to deny. There is of course no reason to assume that a single model of cultural institutionalization has to prevail throughout the text. On the contrary, it appears that a privatistic culture coexists within the novel with a postindividual culture appropriated for a transnational project. Do the specific forms of privacy and individuality in *Nachsommer* already imply the imperialist expansion? Does the structure of educational culture in the course of Heinrich's discourse with Risach already betray its pending instrumentalization and refashioning for the extension of the market? Without attempting anything like an exhaustive reading of the novel, I want to point out four crucial features of institutionalized culture in *Nachsommer* that bear on its integration into the globalization of commercial relations.

First of all, it is impossible to overlook a process of formalization of cultural material that robs it of any particular substance. This becomes especially evident if one compares Stifter's work with the paradigm of the genre; in *Wilhelm Meister* the encounter with *Hamlet* constitutes a crucial experience contributing to bourgeois personality development, while for Stifter, Heinrich's attendance at a performance of *King Lear* has no further consequences for the production of subjectivity. The other literary works mentioned in the text, most notably the *Nibelungenlied* and the *Odysee,* make similarly perfunctory appearances, as if Stifter merely intended a semiotic display of cultural possessions unencumbered by any concomitant interpretations. The potentially diminished status of culture caused by this formalization is compensated for by a second feature, a reauraticization of cultural material. Works of art are endowed with a sacred glow, suggesting a nearly apotropaic functionality, i.e., the corollary to the Enlightenment disenchantment of nature is the assertion of the magic substance of art. This holds especially for the classical statue in the Rosenhof as well as for the libraries in which books are enshrined like holy relics, for adulation, not for reading. This increased power of art allows it, third, to become the mechanism with which an abstract order can be imposed on a potentially disorderly world: the reader watches Heinrich project the image of Nausica onto Natalie. Culture, which will be mobilized to colonize distant lands, begins by colonizing the life world nearby and repressing its identity, just as the formalization process already described can be understood as the self-colonization of culture. Finally, it is crucial to underscore how Stifter's appropriation of culture for an imperialist project is not yet explicitly tied to any national identity. His goal remains the expansion of a (truncated) Enlightenment rationality and not the aggrandizement of anything like Austrian state power, national spheres of influence, or racial *Lebensraum*—all features which emerge at later stages of the imperialist project.

In another context, it would be possible to trace the effects of the instrumentalization of culture in the reified character of the interlocution between Risach and Drendorf that constitutes the bulk of the novel. However, now I want to turn to a second voice, twenty years after the publication of *Nachsommer,* which is emphatically more liberal but in which the complicity of national culture and colonial practice is also considerably clearer. Karl Emil Franzos attended school in Czernowitz, studied in Graz, and eventually settled in Berlin, but most of his writing is concerned with the social and cultural problematics of the eastern sections of the Austro-Hungarian Empire, a terrain he designated as "*Halb-Asien.*" That term, which provides the title for a collection of his ethnographic essays from the mid-seventies, is itself implicated in an orientalist project with political import. For just as Freud would endeavor to displace the id with the ego, Franzos advocates the replacement of Asian irrationality with European—which is to say German—identity: "In the political and social conditions of these regions, one finds a peculiar confrontation of European culture and Asian barbarism, European progress and Asian indolence, European humanism and a so primitive and cruel discord among nations and religions that must appear to the Westerner to be not only foreign but implausible or even incredible."⁸ This syncretic character of the underdeveloped East represents a challenge to all that is good in the occidental tradition—liberalism, progress, humanity—and Franzos poses as the journalistic anthropologist who will report on both the hideous backwardness of the savage world and the inevitable progress of the civilizing beneficence of culture:

> I have tried to accompany the spirit of culture and progress [*Bildung und Fortschritt*] on its crusade in the East as a devoted but honest reporter, who is objective enough not to treat a successful skirmish as a victorious battle, who will openly concede every defeat, no matter how painful, and who will not depict the opponent as blacker [*schwärzer*] than he is. An objective representation of contemporary cultural relations in the East—this is, as I have said, my primary goal. However, I am not satisfied with a mere documentation of the victories and defeats of those enlightened powers. Rather I permit myself to offer them my modest strategic suggestions, on the basis of my close knowledge of the terrain. I indicate the positions which must be taken, if the current pseudoauthority [*Scheinherrschaft*] of that beneficent power in the East is indeed to be transformed into an authentic rule. I am pleased with what has already been won and report on it gladly; however, I consider it more useful to dwell extensively on that which must still be conquered [*was erst erkämpft werden muss*]. Consequently I place in the foreground of my depictions all that which is still Asiatic in the East.⁹

Militant liberalism or liberal imperialism? Franzos allies himself explicitly with the project of cultural modernization, the military character of which he makes adequately clear with his own choice of metaphors. He complains that the Austrian government has been remarkably unsuccessful in civilizing its backward hinterland, and twelve years later, in the 1888 introduction to a new edition of the volume, he will wax even more bitter over the failures of Viennese politics. The "*Culturtragen nach Osten*" has made no significant progress since the reign of Joseph II, and *Halb-Asien* is still characterized by poverty, illiteracy, superstition, and all the other symptoms of the nonmodern syndrome. For Franzos, there is only one solution, and that is a massive transfusion of culture, and the only culture that can succeed is German culture. Although he repeatedly insists that he does not advocate a German political annexation of the East, he argues passionately that only German culture can adequately restructure the demi-oriental *"Culturverhältnisse,"* and establish the hegemony of a Western social system within a process of developmental modernization.

What are the consequences for culture? What happens to cultural material once it is appropriated for a project of modernization linked to the expansion into a foreign terrain? As much as Franzos may deny any German chauvinism on his part, culture takes on a decidedly national identity, and his canon is considerably more parochial than Stifter's. Franzos is certainly still committed to the value of *Humanität*, but for Stifter humanism implied a universal education, while for Franzos German particularity becomes the medium for human universality. Furthermore, this emphatically national culture will be transplanted outside its initial national realm and, curiously enough, not lose any of its relevance, i.e., the substance of culture—so goes the suggestion—is blind to the particular geographical context. Culture can cross borders with ease—or is the practice of border crossing itself the crucible of this "culture?"

The imperialist project of transnational power relies on the imagery of a universal culture that provides an alibi for expansionism. Objects of culture consequently assume an antinomic identity structure; they are increasingly signs of national cultural identity, i.e., signposts of a particular imperialism, which however, claiming universal significance, become the vehicle for transnational imperial encounters. The imperialist functionalization of culture means that it is reconstructed in a manner to allow it to claim priority in other national territories. Universalized "culture" can harbor ideals that seem to be guaranteed precisely by this sort of decontextualization. The utopia in (German) works of art thrives on the distance from the realities of (Eastern European) misery. Culture functions as a vessel of hope, a collection of timeless values that retain their viability, no matter how counterfactual their claims.

In a feuilleton first published in 1875, Franzos describes the five volumes of Schiller in the small eastern village of *"Barnow bei Tarnopol in Oesterreichisch-Podolien."* None, Franzos claims, is found in the only local library, belonging to a Polish Catholic monastery, the collection of which is parochial and dogmatic. Four belong to various social types, whose relationship to Schiller the enlightened liberal describes in order to characterize cultural and social conditions: the Polish aristocrat bought the full Cotta edition for reasons of social prestige but does not open it; the local doctor acquired some Schiller for his wife but discovers in them his own lost dreams; the wife of the local judge lives out her passionate nature vicariously in Schillerian fantasies; and a Jewish moneylender uses Schiller to hold onto the last vestiges of a secular education that he had commenced but was compelled to terminate. Culture apparently allows at best for a sentimentalist escape from the constraints of the "half Asian" surroundings. It is, however, the fifth volume of Schiller, a collection of his poems, that demonstrates how even in Barnow, *deutsches Wesen* can initiate a cultural *Genesen,* for gathered around it are a Polish Catholic monk, a Ruthenian Greek Orthodox peasant, and an Orthodox Jew: "*Then they read the 'Ode to Joy' and then they shook each other's hands, and their eyes filled with tears.*"[10] Christians and Jews from the Maas to the Memel come together under the sheltering wing of culture in a universal brotherhood, or, in other words, culture as the guarantor of universalism becomes politically empowered as the plausible alibi for boundless expansion: earthly borders dwindle into insignificance when viewed from the heights of eternal ideals.

This fictional celebration of Schiller, tolerance, and culture took place, as Franzos would have it, on November 10, Schiller's birthday. He comments:

> Only his birthday is celebrated, and that's just fine, for what do we care about Schiller's death? For us, he was only born—he never died and never will die, as long as men yearn and thirst. Perhaps a horribly satisfied day will come, when Schiller will have died; some signs point in this direction, others do not—in any case, that day is far away. Today he still lives for millions and is reborn every year for thousands and thousands of hearts and is for them a true savior and redeemer [*ein rechter Heiland und Erlöser*], who raises them up out of the depths of prejudice and sullen deprivation to the heights of free humanity.[11]

It is incorrect to disregard a statement like this by attributing it simply to an epigonic taste or midcentury conventions, no matter how hopelessly *dix-neuvième*. For a vital legerdemain of power is at stake. Cultural material—"Schiller"—is being transformed before our very eyes into a cipher with which "*Millionen*" are integrated into a cultural hegemony. The agents of institutionalized culture (here, Franzos) carry out a cultural metamorphosis that concludes with an annexationist project. Within Germany and Austria as well as in areas of other ethnic populations, projects of political integration are henceforth waged through cultural constructions. This transformation leaves its marks on culture: it is definitively national, "made in Germany," but it has universal relevance—Schiller never dies. The substance of culture is preserved as eternal values that cannot be called into question by any particular social immediacy. Once culture becomes that irresistible, then one might as well go to war for it: to battle for cultural modernization in the East in the 1870s or for culture against civilization in 1914.

My point is not that all works of art, literature, and philosophy, that is to say "culture," are fully complicitous with imperialism but that the study of culture may be missing the point by restricting itself solely to interpretive investigations of discrete objects. For these objects are always produced and received within an established institutional setting, and this hegemonic designation in turn is linked to the production of national identity. National identity, furthermore, cannot be adequately understood if it is reduced to some natural, geographic context; it is a moment in a political imagination that is capable of appropriating cultural objects (even against their intent) and integrating them into a transnational practice. Thus even for liberals like Franzos, the invocation of Schiller boils down to a European counterpart to the white man's burden or North American manifest destiny. And this dynamic can be demonstrated with particular clarity in Austro-Hungary, owing to the urgency of the problem of multinationalism.

During the 1890s, the multivolume work *Die oesterreichisch-ungarische Monarchie in Wort und Bild,* initiated by Crown Prince Rudolf, appeared. It is a representative statement on the multiplicity of national cultures within the empire, with one or more volumes devoted to each of the many geographical terrains: the Tyrol, Hungary, Galicia, Istria, Vienna, Trieste, etc. I can hardly even suggest what a political decoding of its massive material would entail, as worthwhile as such a project might be for the cultural history of the fin-de-siècle. However, its specific mode of institutionalizing culture is indicative of the historical moment: the various ethnic groups are viewed as autonomous carriers of culture, although the unity of the Hapsburg realm is maintained. References to the dynasty are generally positive—one reads, for example, of *"the glorious reign of Maria Theresia,"* although a certain degree of liberal criticism is evident (symptomatic of the political tendency associated with Rudolf).[12] Nevertheless, even the recognition of a plurality of cultural traditions is itself part of a political mobilization: the early appearance of Rumanian manuscripts in the Bukovina, for example, is emphasized, apparently in order to counter pan-Slavic claims, i.e., Hapsburg political power is prepared to countenance the claims of non-German culture, as long as it can be instrumentalized in its own multinational project against the czarist expansionism that was anathema for Central European liberals. Consequently the Rumanian material is designated as cultural and proto-national, while the Old Church Slavonic, displaced by Rumanian, is suggestively represented as precultural and primitive.[13]

A more explicit example of the appropriation of cultural material for the transnational practice of Hapsburg power is evident in the section on Bohemia, where the discussion of German literature begins with the following account: "Cosmas, the venerable historian of Bohemia, reports that at the arrival of Dietmar, the first bishop of Prague, the clerics began to chant the Te Deum, but the duke and the nobles began the song: *Christ uns genade,* kyrie eleison, *und die Heiligen alle helfen uns,* kyrie eleison,—while the commoners and uneducated folk chanted only kyrie eleison. That was in the year 973: the oldest evidence of German song in Bohemia."[14] The point is to use *"deutscher Gesang"* in order to establish a German ethnic claim on Prague (and my point is not to comment on the substance of that claim but to indicate the role ascribed to cultural material in the assertion). Culture becomes the tool with which power announces itself, and—as in the Bukovina—is a matter exclusively of high culture. There is apparently no need to establish the presence of a popular German presence; the assumption is that it is the force of high culture that guarantees political legitimacy, since the identification of high culture and culture *tout court* has not become problematic. After the war, the collapse of the imperial state, and the establishment of formally democratic regimes, culture would be redefined as popular culture, ethnic customs, folk costumes, and the like; in the 1890s, however, culture can still fulfill its political function best when it is highest and, significantly, when its territorial location can be underscored. Therefore it becomes crucial to emphasize the specific birthplaces of authors or to mention literary works that thematize particular landscapes: culture as Baedeker.

The dialectic of imperialism and culture can account for the transformation of Stifter's abstractly universal humanism into the antinomic construction of an introverted cultural nationalism and an extroverted cultural imperialism by the early twentieth century. The appropriation of culture for territorial projects of political power induces changes in the organization of culture, by which is meant, however, solely high culture: the great works of the elite as the locus of authentic values. It is not until the mass mobilization of the First World War that an explicit reformulation of culture is undertaken that qualitatively revises this hierarchical structuring. In order to generate ideological paradigms sufficient to explain the demands for military sacrifice, intellectuals rearticulate the cultural project: the battle for culture becomes the battle for the people's culture which in turn endows participation in the war effort with a democratic appearance. The de facto defense of the empire and imperialism is inverted, by the magic of culture, into the defense of the people. Whether the "people" loses in 1918 is a matter of debate; the fate of the empire is a matter of record; in any case the prewar notion of culture as high culture has been irreparably damaged and replaced by vague notions of mass participation, "a matter for the people," as Kafka put it in a diary entry of December 25, 1911, "*eine Angelegenheit des Volkes.*"

This metamorphosis is nowhere clearer than in Hofmannsthal's oeuvre. His work unfolds as a movement from aestheticist symbolism to explicitly social concerns, what he calls "*das erreichte Soziale.*" This corresponds in general to a generic shift in his literary activity from hermetic poetry to various dramatic forms, intended to have a broader popular appeal (opera, the Salzburg Festival, the later morality and political plays): culture for the happy few gives way to a populist model of a mass audience.

Without attempting to investigate further the vagaries of Hofmannsthal's cultural-political practices, I want to underscore the critical importance of the moment of the war. For it is in the war that the propagandist Hofmannsthal arrives at explicit formulations of the relationship between culture and imperialism and between culture and "*das Volk.*" In place of earlier bourgeois notions of individual development and the cultivation of private interiority, one finds, not surprisingly, that culture becomes a particular mode of collective expression, national identity, and that national identity, in turn, instrumentalizes culture in order to assert its own international priority: "Austria first became spirit in its music, and in this form it has conquered the world." [15] *Geist* or culture is the objectification of the nation, not of the individuals Mozart, Beethoven, or Schubert, and the nature of culture, its universal impulse, insists Hofmannsthal in 1916, leads it to global supremacy. Certainly this cultural expansionism goes hand in hand with a more mundane economic and military policy, "our expansionism, which can certainly be called colonialism, even though it is intra-European." [16] The ideological defense of the Central Powers as the party of culture against Western civilization and czarist barbarism is modified by Hofmannsthal so that within the cultural camp a division of labor is established between the technical rationality of Germany and the aesthetic-cultural priority of Austria, where the imperialist project is most consistent and therefore most cultural: "Austria is the special duty of the German spirit within Europe. She is the field, appointed by history, of a purely cultural imperialism. . . . Austria must be recognized again and again as the *German duty in Europe.*" [17] Austria represents the priority of a German element over the plurality of other national identities on the continent as well as being the model for maintaining this privilege through cultural imperialism—rather than through brute force alone. Clearly Hofmannsthal is mobilizing culture in a two-front war: as part of the explicit war effort against the declared enemies outside the German alliance and, implicitly, within the alliance, as a mechanism to assert Austrian particularity against imperial Germany.

Hofmannsthal produces Austrian particularity by insisting on the regionalistic identity of literature which always emerges from a geographical landscape, a claim that would soon be institutionalized in Vienna by the Germanist Josef Nadler in his territorial account of literary history. The provincialization of literature leads in turn to a pseudodemocratic privileging of the provincial population, the peasantry, as the carrier of authentic culture. This argument allows Hofmannsthal to mobilize the peasantry in the cultural war effort, while still insisting on the difference between Austria and allied Germany, a double functionalization of culture: "[Austrian literature] grows . . . as a populist construct [*ein volkstümliches Gebilde*] in its greatest representatives: the art poet Grillparzer, and so much more folklike [*volkshaft*] in the actor Raimund, the actor Nestroy, the peasant son Anzengruber, the backwoods boy Rosegger, and Stifter, the son of the Bohemian forest. When one considers the strongest representatives of our literature, one can speak of a poetry of peasants [*Poesie der Bauernsöhne*], which can be counterposed to the filiation of pastors' sons that gave to the German people so much of its cultural property."[18] The conservative character of Hofmannsthal's project is evident in the fact that he ultimately describes culture as the collection of aesthetic texts by major writers, and the list of writers he particularly reveres constitutes the standard lineage of Austrian literary history. This does not differ significantly from the prewar understanding of culture, except perhaps that the insistence on national identity has grown considerably more shrill. The material of culture, the kinds of objects included in the hegemonic canon, remains the same. Nevertheless Hofmannsthal does initiate a revolution in the representation of culture, i.e., in its normative institutionalization, insofar as he insists on the character of culture as *volkshaft* and derives the cultural achievement of particular figures from the rural origin of the *Bauernbuben* and *Waldsöhne*.

The valorization of cultural objects understood to represent a populist national identity amounts to a pseudodemocratization of culture as part of its mobilization in the war effort. While the literary texts (redefined as *volkshaft*) that collectively add up to "culture" are the same familiar canon of the elite, "culture" has changed in a real way insofar as Hofmannsthal uses the populist redesignation as a mechanism with which to articulate an anti-intellectual irrationalism. Populist culture is, for Hofmannsthal, clearly antithetical to intellectual labor, which is dryly cerebral and therefore ultimately inauthentic. For Stifter and Franzos, literary culture was, in different ways, contiguous with a broader ratiocinative project of learning and enlightenment; in contrast, for Hofmannsthal, genuine literature, the expression of the folk, is qualitatively different from any conceptual cognition: "The spirituality of the educated class [*die Geistigkeit der Gebildeten*] can be compared to a tablet on which terribly much has been scribbled and written over and erased and written over again. The spirituality of the folk is a wonderfully pure tablet, on which a few precepts have been recorded with pure markings that last for centuries."[19] Despite this apparent gesture of democratization that privileges the knowledge of the people over elite culture, Hofmannsthal goes on to claim that popular knowledge has to be interpreted by the intellectually mature [*geistig Mündigen*] who have "the duty to interpret these signs for the people," i.e., the people alone, trapped by the imposed irrationalism of Hofmannsthal's definition, appears consequently incapable of understanding itself and requires the leadership of another elite group, allegedly different from the old *"Gebildeten"* and designated now as the *"geistig Mündigen."* The ostentatiously anti-elitist exorcism of the old mandarins flips over into a self-serving defense of a new leadership that Hofmannsthal deems necessary. For the *Volk*, despite the centrality attributed to it in cultural production, is condemned to silence because of its ontological naïveté; hence my designation of Hofmannsthal's cultural practice as pseudodemocratization: "In the natural depths, in which the people finds its being [*in den Naturtiefen, in denen das Volk west*], just as in those dark depths of the individual, where the border between the mental and the somatic grows hazy, reflection and knowledge are out of place and only desire and faith are at home." [20]

Integrating the masses into culture results in a concept of culture devoid of any rational component and in an image of a *demos* whose unchanging essence may be the ground on which culture grows but which is otherwise prohibited from any verbal participation in the body politic. This exclusionary structure results from the simultaneous effort to wage a modern mass war while retaining traditional social stratification. Culture becomes the mechanism with which an illusion of participation is generated precisely in order to deny participation in political power. Hofmannsthal's manipulation of the concept of "culture" therefore yields important insight into the genesis of the culture industry. Culture is appropriated for political purposes— generating mass loyalty to the empire—rather than becoming the field on which the desire for emancipatory political transformation might be articulated. The "aestheticization of politics" which ensues reduces the people to the silent spectators of the theatricality of the state. [21] The more the folk is declared to be the source of culture, the more is its autonomy denied and its access to power refuted. The converse is crucial as well: the more plausible the establishment of a democratic society (and that would certainly include a redefinition of national identity in a manner that would preclude transnational aggression), the more frequently does one encounter a conservative insistence on culture as a fundamental ontology (*"wo das Volk west"*) or as an immutably synchronic structure or as the adequate expression of the naturally subrational plebes.

In the prewar period, cultural representations were functions of the exigencies of the multinational empire: the demonstrations of a Rumanian national tradition or a German presence in Bohemia. During the war, culture became a mechanism to legitimize the mass mobilization. Afterward, during the twenties, culture is again refunctionalized according to the needs of a new transnational practice, i.e., Austrian identity is reformulated, and Austrian culture is concomitantly redefined. Hofmannsthal's erstwhile populist direction undergoes a sudden radicalization; for where Hofmannsthal had maintained the objects of high culture and simply declared them *volkshaft,* the official postwar representation of culture foregrounds genuine popular material, i.e., folk culture, peasant costumes, rural architecture, local customs, and the like. Is this a consequence of a democratic impulse in the first republic? An alternative interpretation is suggested by at least one key text, *Österreich: Sein Land und Volk und seine Kultur,* edited by Michael Haberlandt and introduced with a "Preface by the Federal President" Michael Hainisch, giving the 1927 book a semi-official status.

Hainisch in fact admits that he has nothing to say about Austrian culture, but he makes an ulterior motive perfectly clear: "Therefore I will say nothing about Austria, but only wish this book success in convincing foreigners to visit our country."[22] Austrian culture—or the new representations of Austrian culture—has the ultimate goal of increasing the tourist industry. After 1918 the imperial multinational concerns lose their relevance and the reduced Austrian state is forced to turn itself into an object of international vacationing—a new transnational practice. Hence the emphasis in the volume on the sorts of things that intrigue vacationers: the natural environment, the weather, and, especially, the newly discovered picturesque character of peasant culture, which was by no means foregrounded in the volumes on the Hapsburg Empire. It seems as if this peasant culture is not at all authentically traditional but a twentieth-century production of a calculated marketing mechanism. The consequence of this transformation of culture is that in these five hundred pages on Austria's culture, traditional high culture is treated in about fifty, with most emphasis on architecture and music (typical tourist material); Austrian philosophy is discussed in one short paragraph.

Yet tourism is not the only transnational parameter that determines the institutionalization of Austrian cultural identity here. A perhaps even more important issue is the insistence on particularly close ties to Germany. The editor begins his foreword by proudly presenting his work to "the educated Austrian population and the fraternal German people." The same alliance of Austrian *Bildungsbürgertum* and Germany is reenvisioned, with more rhetorical flourish, at the end: "May this work . . . awaken the Austrian population to a renewed love and comprehensive appreciation of its fatherland and may it become a household volume for families in our regions and especially in educated Viennese circles. We earnestly hope that it will contribute to a just and sympathetic understanding in Germany [*in reichsdeutschen Landen*] of the German-Austrian brother country and its sorely tested folk [*seines schwergeprüften Volkes*]."[23] Clearly cultural identity is being constructed to ally the domestic needs of a conservative bourgeoisie, which likely perceives itself as besieged by the Viennese Austro-Marxists, with an international project of integrating Austrian particularity into the German *Reich*. Thus Eduard Castle concludes his chapter in the volume, a relatively untendentious survey of Austrian literary history, with a programmatic definition of national identity:

> The Alpine regions, forced by the unfortunate peace treaty [*das unglückliche Friedensdiktat*] to go it alone—something they had never been politically or economically or culturally—are struggling to survive. To all the well-intentioned voices who constantly tell us "Be Austrian!" we can only reply: "We can be nothing more than what we have always been: the German outpost in the southeast."[24]

Culture has become the culture of the folk and the landscape, both of which are intimately tied to the greater identity of Germany. Austrian culture—the year is 1927, eleven years before the annexation by Nazi Germany—is apparently just one fractional aspect of the German cultural world, reduced to a national-physical presence. It is hardly surprising that this cultural self-representation ends up including a crucial chapter on biological anthropology, replete with photographs of typical peasant crania, measurements of body size, and descriptions of physical types. A good deal of effort is devoted to demonstrating the racial continuity of the Austrians with the Germans; their consanguinity is only relativized, insofar as the Austrians are designated as a mixture of what is described as Nordic and Dinaric races, which the author assures us is *"eine sehr günstige Rassenmischung,"* i.e., "a very favorable racial mixture." It turns out, in fact, that the stereotypical distinctions between Austrians and Germans, which today still form part of popular prejudice, are rooted in their allegedly peculiar racial nuances:

> Even if the Dinarian is livelier, warmer, and less withdrawn than the [Germanic], he nevertheless has a sense of order, displays a masculinely forceful manner, and is capable of enthusiastic demonstrations of heroic deeds. . . . There can be no doubt that the Austrian population, if consciously trained to cultivate its positive attributes, will hardly lag behind a purely Nordic group: in the reunification, to which the friends of an *Anschluss* look forward in both countries, the Austrians will certainly be a very valuable part of the whole people [*ein sehr wertvoller Bestandteil des Volksganzen*]. Even now, its artistic traits are highly valued in the *"Reich"* and undoubtedly represent a cultural enrichment for that extraordinarily gifted people already living within the current borders of the empire.[25]

In order to legitimate a politics of *Anschluss*, culture is transformed into racial identity, and Austrian particularity is explained as a minor variation on the Germanic character: even though the Austrians are a tad more sensuous and aesthetic—clearly an echo of Hofmannsthal's ascribing to Austria a cultural priority over the technical rationality of Germany—they too can be orderly, heroic, and masculine. After all, it is all the same gene pool: "Only because of the common blood is it possible that all those who, in these confusing times which have been, in part, purposefully imposed on us, have lost their leadership [*steuerlos geworden*] still cherish the same ideals." [26] Cultural identity takes shape as the expression of hegemonic political interests. First it is emphatically addressed to the *"Gebildeten"* threatened by the perceived disorder of the postimperial society that has become *"steuerlos."* Culture is a discourse that allows for the conservative self-representation of the *Bildungsbürgertum* within the class conflicts of the late twenties in Austria. This conservatism is tied, second, to nationalism and anti-Versailles ressentiment, combined with an orientation toward *Anschluss* that relies on a racial reduction of culture. Finally the exigencies of tourism force an emphasis on local color and peasant culture that resonates successfully with both the domestic conservatism and the proto-*völkisch* Germanophilic racialism. Seventy years earlier Stifter had imagined that imperialist expansion and competition on an international market would lead to a heightening of high-cultural productivity. By 1927, however, a higher stage of that imperialism effects a self-demontage of culture, which barely survives as tourism and hematology, and an eagerness to jettison any specific Austrian identity.

My term "transnational practice" has provided a locution for the various reformulations of national identity made necessary by political-economic vicissitudes. Let me recall the trajectory which has been sketched out: from Stifter's abstract anticipation of a world market in 1857, through the liberal colonialism of Franzos in the seventies and the imperialist nationalisms of the Hapsburg volumes in the nineties, to Hofmannsthal's mass mobilization in the First World War and the postwar conservative anticipation of an annexation that eventually took place in 1938. The corollary to these transnational practices is the perpetually revised institutionalization of culture: from Stifter's universal *Bildung* to an idealist German culture in Franzos, to the national literatures of the multinational empire, to Hofmannsthal's *volkshaft* culture, and, finally, to ethnic regionalism in the twenties—from Homer to *Heimat,* from *King Lear* to *Lederhosen.* The autonomy of culture disappears in what critical theory refers to as a *falsche Aufhebung,* a false sublation; writing in 1929 from the standpoint of traditional culture, Freud alludes to this tendency as *Kulturfeindlich-keit,* a "hostility to culture." The suspicion with which he regards the optimistic claims of socialist reformism in *Civilization and Its Discontents* is overshadowed by his concern that a right-wing instrumentalization of culture could unleash an aggressive potential in human society leading to war and destruction. He concludes with an admonition that has lost none of its relevance today: "The fateful question for the human species seems to me to be whether and to what extent their cultural development will succeed in mastering the disturbance of their communal life by the human instinct of aggression and self-destruction."[27] His account is comprehensible only against the background of institutionalized culture taking on increasingly aggressive features within the matrix of imperial encounters whose violent character is apparent long before the official outbreaks of wars. Instead of carrying out the civilizational project of eros by guaranteeing social cohesion through aim-inhibited libido, culture—which ought to overcome aggression—redirects aggression toward the ego. On the phylogenetic level, this means that culture becomes the mechanism with which human aggression is aimed at humanity.

The transformed institutionalization of culture is however not simply external to individual literary texts, the collection of which we continue to designate as "culture." I began with a reference to Musil's account of reified culture in *Young Törless;* now that we know that the particular form of cultural appropriation has to do with national identity and imperialism, the critical problem of the novel becomes the investigation of the relationship between the sadistic persecution of Basini and Beineberg's Nietzschean fascination with Indian religion. Or more largely: between the authoritarianism of the boarding school and its location in a colonized, vaguely Slavic world at a "small station on the long railroad to Russia." [28] The instrumentalization of culture and transnational practice—Musil's novel apparently calls into question the hegemonic understanding of culture and pursues its critique by foregrounding its setting within a web of geopolitical stratagems.

I will not pursue that reading of *Törless* any further but will conclude now with an even more cursory reference to Canetti's *Auto-da-Fé*. Reified culture appears there as Peter Kien's compulsive self-encapsulation in the iron cage of bibliophilic scholarship. The text suggests various alternatives: openness, intersubjectivity, collectivity, the leitmotif of a celestial blue, the mass. For my purposes it suffices to indicate that Kien's insistence on order, closure, and isolation is intimately tied to his mandarin fascination with classical Chinese material. A cipher for academic learning and education in general, sinology is the medium in which imperialist violence returns to the metropolitan capital, transformed into the barrier which precludes human solidarity: "Of that far deeper and most special motive force of history, the desire of men to rise into a higher type of animal, into the mass, and to lose themselves in it so completely as to forget that *one* man ever existed, they had no idea. For they were educated men, and education is in itself a *cordon sanitaire* for the individual against the mass in his own soul." [29]

This is one of the points at which Canetti's impassioned diagnosis of Austrian thought and Western culture announces itself with admirable clarity: institutionalized culture as a blockade, an embargo, against a collective human potential. Canetti's own term reveals the intersection of cultural and political dynamics, for the term *"cordon sanitaire"* signified, in a then-common parlance, the postwar construction of the East European nation-states—including the Republic of Austria—as buffers against Bolshevik Russia in order to halt the spread of what the West regarded as an infectious ideology. [30] The construction of nation-states, motivated by international conflicts, also means the construction of national identities, which is to say national cultures. A study of an aspect of a national culture therefore short-circuits its own claims if it takes the contextual setting as a sort of natural given, for just as culture is lodged in a specific institutionalization, national identity too is a historical product of conflicting practices.

CHAPTER TEN

The Peace Movement and the Avant-garde

WHILE preparing this chapter, I received in the mail a copy of a newsletter entitled *Peace Education at Stanford*. I take it as an expression of at least one tendency within contemporary antimilitarist activism (I think there are others as well) and wonder if it can offer any insights into the relationship between the peace movement and aesthetic culture, especially the legacy of the avant-garde. Below the masthead, the following program appears:

> PEACE EDUCATION AT STANFORD (PEAS), a group of students and other community members, maintains an open forum on peace issues. We are devoted to seeking viable, non-violent methods of conflict resolution. This search requires greater communication, tolerance and understanding between people at both the interpersonal and international levels. We are working to address these needs through our participation in Peace Studies at Stanford, our quarterly newsletter, and our weekly discussions. Most importantly, our group is creating a supportive community from which we draw friendship and strength in our efforts to promote Peace Education.[1]

The brief text may seem innocuous to a degree that borders on the irrelevant—is there anything here with which anyone could take issue?—but it in fact displays certain key commitments that prove crucial for a broader consideration of the relationship between the peace movement and avant-gardism. One is struck first of all by the apparently absolute priority of peace: the group's self-definition mentions no other concerns. No attention is directed toward social issues or questions of culture. Not that every activist group need concern itself with every social problem—or art: that would be a rather silly demand. The point is that within the peace movement and within this text, a sense of the profound urgency of disarmament in the face of the nuclear threat tends to overshadow other material, especially those themes that have traditionally occupied the protest subculture.

This exclusion of simultaneous dimensions of social existence, which might disturb the unity of the peace "community," corresponds to a second feature indicated by the text: the insistence on harmony as the internal and external organizational principle of the group. It is composed of "community members" who approach each other with "greater communication, tolerance and understanding." The activities are educational and always verbal: a newsletter and discussions. "Most importantly" the group is described as a "supportive community," which is a source of "friendship and strength." Half ideal speech situation, half congregation, it is the locus of a discourse on peace and approaches its environment in a nonthreatening manner. Its goal is "to address . . . needs," i.e., not to raise demands, and this address is largely internally directed, i.e., nearby opponents or competing institutions are not attacked. Not concrete results, only "methods" are sought, and these still-to-be-determined methods are designated in advance as "non-violent." One wonders why the author seems to be bending over backward to provide the assurance of the group's own nonthreatening character. Why is the hypothetical possibility that violence might be an appropriate method to achieve peace disqualified from the start, despite the desire to "[maintain] an open forum"? The rhetoric suggests that the group is operating on the basis of an implicit (and perhaps one-sided) nonaggression pact with its institutional surroundings.

This hypostatization of nonviolence is indicative of a further feature of the text and of important tendencies within the peace movement. The inquiry into war and peace in international affairs is conflated without mediation with the practice of "peace" on the local level. Likely differences between international and interpersonal relations disappear in an abstract methodology of "conflict resolution." Political issues will tend to lose their political character, as they are transformed into matters of individual social morality. This one-dimensional conflation of two different materials is reminiscent of both the insistence on the principle of harmony and the disappearance of all differences in the shadow of the priority of peace. This conflation is indicated allegorically in the masthead itself: at the left one sees an open pod out of which peas (PEAS) are floating to the right, drawn as increasingly large circles, the last of which turns into the globe—"Think globally, act locally," the familiar ecological slogan.

The passage does not address the problem of aesthetics directly, but it may indicate a basically negative relationship between the peace movement and the cultural avant-garde on two counts: (1) as already mentioned, the absence of any interest in (modern) art or aesthetic culture in general, and (2) the insistence on "discussions" and an "open forum" as an implicit counterprogram to avant-gardist claims to leadership. On the basis of the text, a stronger argument could be mounted for the second point than for the first, but in both cases, the evidence is inconclusive. I will return to them—the aesthetic avant-garde and avant-gardist leadership—in a systematic manner below. Now, however, it will be useful to take a look at a brief article printed in the newsletter which testifies to the experience of at least one peace activist in regard to culture and politics and their interrelationship. Entitled "Thoughts on Action," it begins with a report of the response evoked by a speech of Helen Caldicott: "I was angry. I was afraid. I would disappear with the earth and everything that I love and care about would never be here again." This sense of crisis provokes a review of the experience of culture as a rigid separation of aesthetics and ethics: "Art meant for me beauty in itself. Politics meant action. Active art was such a difficult endeavour." Difficult, perhaps, but now unavoidable, as the author comes to the realization that a program of engagement is the only possible response to the severity of the nuclear threat: "A life of contemplation can only lead me towards stagnation. A life of action will make me believe that there is a purpose in life, in beauty, in art."[2]

As a symptomatic example of peace movement prose, the text can stand on its own, especially because of its confessional character as an aphoristic interior autobiography. Its religious character is obvious. Hearing the evangelist's prophecy of doom, the author undergoes a conversion process, moving from a past state of "constant struggle," doubt, and worry to a missionary zeal and a set of self-assured convictions. One again finds the absolute priority of peace, now in the form of the threat of absolute destruction articulated in the privileged speech of the natural scientist. As in classical conversion texts, it is the vision of death and damnation, apocalypse and final judgment, that initiates the motion of the soul. I do not want to deny the objective reality of the possibility of nuclear destruction. The point is instead that tendencies within the peace movement experience this reality within a religious framework and therefore may draw religious or moralistic rather than political consequences.

The force of the conversion furthermore engenders an anger that is transformed into a commitment to activity that becomes the ultimate source of meaning. The author can "believe that there is a purpose in life, in beauty, in art." These three categories, which in hindsight now appear to have been previously devoid of meaning (a distortion of personal history?), take on significance solely as functions of peace activism. The logical consequence is that life, beauty, and art must be forced to sacrifice their particular substance and become mere vehicles for a religious/moral project. This leads to a final consideration, the specific character of aesthetics in the text. Even in this postconversion account, art in the past is seen as having maintained a relative independence from other areas of interest. Yet the antagonism between aesthetic and political interests now appears as an intolerable contradiction that is finally overcome once both art and politics are *aufgehoben* within Caldicott's message. Art, which was once "beauty in itself," and politics, which was once both "peace and justice"—i.e., not only peace—become indistinguishable within a "life of action." The ease with which the author concludes with a list of "life, beauty, art" suggests that their specific characters are repressed. All that is different becomes the same, like the conflation of interpersonal and international relations in the programmatic paragraph: a romantic repression that ignores the differences between peas and the globe.

Violence and the Aesthetic Avant-garde

If these passages suggest some possible hostility on the part of the peace movement to the avant-garde, it is important to examine the relationship in a more systematic manner. I want however now to reverse the examination: instead of continuing with an examination of the peace movement, I will ask whether the historical avant-garde has had some natural affinity or hostility to the peace movement, pacifism, or antiwar movements. This is of course only a superficial reversal, for if it turns out that the avant-garde has been no reliable friend of peace, then the peace movement had no particular reason to appeal to the avant-garde because their goals were ultimately irreconcilable. I will examine the status of peace within the two decisive forms of the avant-garde in the twentieth century already described above: the avant-garde of aesthetic innovation and the political avant-garde of intellectual leadership, especially Leninism.

It is hardly surprising that the political substance of avant-garde aesthetics constitutes a particularly crucial concern for Marxist and neo-Marxist critics. It comes as more of a surprise however that several of these neo-Marxist accounts, which otherwise advocate extraordinarily different and even mutually exclusive positions, share a common evaluation of the avant-garde, which is described not as a carrier of peace but as the locus of belligerency and violence. In the late 1920s, Georg Lukács returned to literary criticism after nearly one and a half decades of exclusive devotion to philosophical and political matters, during which he had moved from the neo-Hegelianism of *The Theory of the Novel* through the subjectivist communism of *History and Class Consciousness* to a modified Leninism. He entered the debates in the German Bund proletarisch-revolutionärer Schriftsteller as the defender of a program that would soon be institutionalized as "socialist realism." In his critiques of Willi Bredel and, especially, Ernst Ottwalt, he presents the nineteenth-century bourgeois aesthetics of Balzac and Tolstoy as a norm, indicating a fundamental hostility to the avant-garde and modernism, i.e., the full range of aesthetic innovation that appears on the European scene some time around the turn of the century. In addition, Lukács's criticism evaluates aesthetic content in terms of his own political commitments. Consequently one finds him condemning innovative literary currents, at least in part, through an analysis of their purported political message.

The classical locus of this critical practice is the German expressionist debate. It is of no concern here whether German expressionism was objectively part of the historical avant-garde or, alternatively, the swan song of nineteenth-century aesthetic culture. For the participants in the aesthetic-political debates of the 1930s and for Lukács in particular, expressionism functioned as the cipher for all the new artistic movements, and its relationship to contemporary political conflicts became a burning issue, especially after the establishment of the Nazi dictatorship. Given this context and Lukács's own critical model, it follows that Lukács quickly focuses on the political programs and statements of the expressionists (rather than on the specific aesthetic character or "form" of their works). Interestingly, he does not take the easier road of underscoring the widespread enthusiasm for the outbreak of the First World War among expressionist writers in order to argue for a basic affinity between the avant-garde and militarism. Instead he addresses the pacifism of the expressionists after 1916 and especially around 1918; Lukács's rhetorical strategy is to invert the empirical affinity between expressionism and pacifism into a political danger:

> The passionate struggle of the expressionists against the war was objectively only a mock battle, even when their literary

works suffered prosecution in wartime Germany. It was a
struggle against war in general, and not against the imperialist
· war, just as the expressionists struggled against "middle-
classness" in general, and not against the imperialist bourgeoisie, and as in the further course of development of war and revolution they directed themselves against "violence" in general
and not against the concrete counter-revolutionary violence of
the bourgeoisie.[3]

Clearly, the literary-critical analysis of expressionism is relying here
on a political assumption regarding the inadequacy of pacifism:
expressionist pacifism becomes a universal hostility to violence which
leads the expressionists to oppose violent, revolutionary politics, an
opposition which in turn transforms them into "objective" allies of
the counterrevolutionary bourgeoisie. Expressionist pacifists, like the
Independent Social Democratic Party (USPD), refuse to engage in a
genuinely revolutionary politics and therefore become pillars of the
counterrevolutionary order: "The objective affinity of method, which
at some points amounted to actual identity, was due to the fact that
both tendencies, USPD and expressionism, while remaining on the
class foundation of the bourgeoisie, sought to avoid a confrontation
with the underlying causes by their attacks on the symptoms."[4] For
Lukács the fact that expressionism (again, the cipher for the whole
aesthetic avant-garde) remains "on the class foundation of the bourgeoisie" is not just shrugged off as naïveté, quietism, or apathy. The
allegedly superficial pacifism plays a role in the restoration of the capitalist order by preventing successful opposition to counterrevolutionary terror. The argument assumes an inescapable choice between
revolution, which requires force, and a counterrevolution which
maintains itself by violence.

It is important to give attention to the historical context of Lukács's
essay, "Expressionism: Its Significance and Decline." When it was
written in 1934, Hitler had been in power for a year, the concentration camps were already functioning, and the opponents of the new
regime were being slaughtered. The claim that an absolute rejection of violence serves to stabilize an exponentially violent order certainly could seem plausible, and Lukács pushes the argument to its
extreme:

As a literary form of developed imperialism, expressionism
stands on an irrational and mythological foundation; its crea-

tive method leads in the direction of the emotive yet empty de-
clamatory manifesto, the proclamation of a sham activism. . . .
Expressionism forms a legitimate part of the general "November legacy" of national socialism. For despite its rhetorical gestures, it was unable to rise above the horizon of the 1918 Weimar republic. Just as fascism is the necessary result of the
November betrayal of the German working class and the revolution by the SPD and the USPD, it can also take up this November legacy in the literary field.[5]

For Lukács, the political substance of expressionism is indicated less
by its ostentatious pacifism than by an immanent affinity with fascism:
the avant-garde as the carrier of reactionary violence. Again it is important to distinguish between two strands which Lukács intertwines:
the political critique of pacifism and the aesthetic-political evaluation
of the avant-garde. He proceeds first from certain assumptions about
the political function of pacifism in the German revolution and in the
face of militant fascism. Is it fair to question the value of pacifism—
say, in France during the 1930s—or to cite the political trajectory of
the author of the impassioned antiwar novel *Voyage au bout de la
nuit?* If Lukács is understood as claiming that pacifism amounts to
appeasement and therefore collaborates with aggression, he turns out
to be the predecessor of today's defenders of a strong military defense.
Behind this historical irony lies a good deal of the history of the cold
war. In this discussion, it is however the second strand that is of interest, the contention that expressionism, modernism, or the avant-garde
has (for whatever complex political reasons) a fundamentally violent
identity, even when it claims to reject violence. This is a crucial claim,
and it is noteworthy for the same connection is made by Adorno,
Lukács's arch-opponent in the neo-Marxist discourse, despite the profound differences in their critical models and their historico-political
commitment.

While Lukács has gone down in intellectual history as the Marxist
defender of the bourgeois tradition of the eighteenth and nineteenth
centuries and especially realism, Adorno is regarded as the Marxist
protagonist of Modernism and the avant-garde. Instead of the former's canon of Goethe, Balzac, and Tolstoy, the latter presents a modernist constellation of figures such as Kafka, Valéry, and Beckett. Yet
significantly Adorno does not insist on a fundamental antagonism between pre-avant-garde aesthetics and contemporary art. On the con-

trary, he is able to integrate, for example, both Goethe and Balzac into an aesthetic model constructed in terms of modernist principles:[6] antirepresentational self-referentiality, formal rationalization, and the immanently contradictory construction of the work. In the place of Lukács's concentration on the mimetic totality of the work's content, Adorno suggests that abstraction has historically been the medium for an aesthetic critique of material conditions, for a determinate negation of society: the work of art as the "sundial of history."[7]

Adorno's history of abstraction amounts to the projection of modernist aesthetics backward onto early works which are consequently read as precursors of cubism or twelve-tone music. Adorno is not always consistent on the scope of this projection. In the *Dialectic of Enlightenment* he constructs an anthropology of aesthetic activity which grounds nonreferentiality in the prehistory of civilization and the differentiation of a primitive identity of science, religion, and art. Some twenty years later, his *Aesthetic Theory* points to the collapse of the universal system of belief in the Renaissance and the Reformation and the gradual separation of art from courtly and religious tutelage. In both accounts, however, the central issue is the emergence of the principle of aesthetic autonomy within a process of secularization, and it is this autonomy which still designates the essential features of modern art. This is not to imply that all autonomous art is the same; there is a history of aesthetic material in Adorno's account, as there is a history of the social context, which is always present in negative form in the autonomous work. The point of this brief excursion into Adorno's aesthetic theory is to prepare the ground for a further pursuit of the question of the avant-garde and violence. For unlike Lukács, Adorno accords no importance to the explicit political allegiances of artists. The social import of art lies instead in its aesthetic substance, i.e., its principled distance from society, its autonomy. Do historically advanced works with their claims to radical autonomy decode as pacifism, or do they—as with Lukács but for different reasons—come out fighting?

Maybe both, but it's not quite that easy. In Adorno's account the imperative of autonomy means the distance which the auratic work of art maintains from the immediacy of everyday life. This distance is initially not escapism but a gesture of protest against a society of domination, and this critical stance simultaneously contributes to the immanent character of the work. Autonomous art is therefore simultaneously a rejection of real suffering and a utopian inscription of an alternative social order in which autonomy might be realized. Adorno arrives at this approach both through his reception of German idealist aesthetics refracted in neo-Hegelianism (here a crucial point of intersection with Lukács) and his response to the crisis of Marxism after the First World War: the expected revolution which does not happen in the West and goes awry in the East disallows an unbroken faith in the emancipatory potential of the working-class movement whose utopian ideals—a free society, freed from the principle of ownership[8]—are transferred to the work of art where they are preserved in hibernation. As much as Adorno resists positive descriptions of a future society, it may be possible to push him on his utopian claims. His vague designations include autonomy, freedom, and an end to suffering; it is probably not farfetched to assume that these values also imply nonviolence and an end to war, i.e., the claim is plausible that the *promesse de bonheur* allegedly carried by the work of art (which is always an avant-garde work) also means peace, although this goes beyond the letter of Adorno's text. It also runs the risk of imputing a positive content to the aesthetic utopia that is defined precisely by its nonreferential character: Adorno's avant-garde has nothing to do with a tendentious pacifism (just as he is a vocal critic of tendentious socialist art). Nor does it have anything to do with a pacifist cult of immediate harmony, since the work of art remains authentic only by preserving contradictions and registering suffering within its own formal principle, as Adorno makes adequately clear in his polemics against classicism.

So far the discussion of Adorno has come up with some rather ambivalent results. Adorno's aesthetic utopia may imply peace but not a tendentious pacifism. To the extent that pacifism focuses on only one dimension of human suffering, it succumbs to a culture of reification that ignores the social totality at the center of which the Marxist Adorno places the question of ownership. If the hypothesis of a positive relationship between the (avant-garde) work of art and peace is therefore at best tenuous, what about a relationship between art and violence? Certainly, the work remains a depiction of a utopia which cannot be imagined as beset by war. Yet Adorno's own account of autonomy is itself dialectical. Initially, autonomous art is a critique of oppressive material conditions, but within bourgeois society this art undergoes an alienation that robs it of its critical character and transforms it into a separate realm of Culture with a capital C. Its function is inverted, as it becomes an ornament to institutionalized suffering: autonomy as the lie with which heteronomy defends its crimes.

Autonomous art, in its reified state, becomes complicitous with violence. It becomes ideology once it is appropriated as an affirmative vessel of eternal values, rather than as a utopian anticipation of qualitatively new social relationships. For Adorno, it does not however have only this external relationship, an alibi function, to violence. The very notion of autonomy is itself the potential source of the worst violence. In his essay "On the Question: What Is German?" (an implicit commentary on Wagner's essay "What Is German?"), Adorno addresses the allegedly German and definitely Wagnerian cult of autonomy, i.e., doing something "for its own sake." Wagner attributes this value to the national character; Adorno regards it as an expression of the underdevelopment of capitalist market relations in nineteenth-century Germany. The relative independence of cultural activity from commercial concerns permitted an unadulterated devotion to the internal consistency of philosophical and aesthetic works. Yet this autonomy, according to Adorno, culminates not only in Hegel and Beethoven: "The great German conceptions in which autonomy, the pure For-its-own-Sake, is so extravagantly glorified were all available, too, for the deification of the State. . . . The urge for boundless domination accompanied the boundlessness of the idea, the one was never without the other." [9] The point is not that some historical accident explains how the language of the *Phenomenology of the Spirit* slips into a defense of the Prussian state. Adorno is undertaking a fundamental critique of the historical potentials of the principle of autonomy which is at the root of the model of the self-referential work. Autonomy, it turns out, is not just critique or utopia. It becomes a program for destruction, as soon as absolute independence turns into a universal misanthropy and an imperialist intolerance for otherness: "Even inhumanity is not alien to the For-its-own-Sake, in its implacably uncompromising lack of concern for others. It manifests itself in a certain overbearing, all-embracing violence, even in the greatest spiritual structures, or especially those, in a will to dominate. . . . The Absolute turned into absolute horror." [10]

At stake is the contention that autonomy always bears an aggressive potential which threatens to turn into violence. For autonomy—the auratic character of authentic art—is for Adorno the sine qua non of art in general and of the avant-garde of the twentieth century in particular. No matter how utopian, no matter how peaceful the hope may be which is inscribed in the formal integrity of the work, its radical immanence, which guarantees this utopia, can generate dystopic destruction. The real scandal in Adorno's aesthetic thought is not the often quoted and often misunderstood dictum that "writing poetry after Auschwitz is barbaric" but the suggestion here that poetry before Auschwitz was barbaric as well, that it led to Auschwitz because its claim to autonomous sovereignty was always less than a step away from a claim to command. As much as Adorno values autonomous art and participated in a mandarin reverence for high culture, there is an unmistakable iconoclastic streak in his thought, clearly influenced by Benjamin, which leads to a profound distrust of art, treated as a constant ally of an unredeemed world of suffering.

The argumentative strategies of Lukács and Adorno could not be more dissimilar, their political and aesthetic goals more irreconcilable. Yet treated in terms of an inquiry into the relationship between the avant-garde and peace, they come up with surprisingly and disturbingly similar allegations. Expressionism becomes fascism, autonomy becomes the Holocaust: in both cases the respective cipher for the avant-garde ends up as the carrier of extreme violence. One might be tempted to make short shrift of this result by way of an intellectual-historical relativization: two highly cultured Marxist intellectuals witness the rise of fascism and genocide, and it is only comprehensible that their thought takes a pessimistic turn. Yet this response, no matter how legitimate, evades the real challenge to question whether the avant-garde may not in fact truly have some necessary link to violence. This line of thought is confirmed, perhaps unintentionally, by the later neo-Marxist position of Peter Bürger in his *Theory of the Avant-garde*. A demonstration of a connection between the avant-garde and violence within Bürger's model would be particularly interesting, for unlike Lukács in the expressionism essay and much more than Adorno, Bürger excludes any explicit thematization of the political intentions or functions of art. For Adorno, autonomy is a characteristic of each work of art, considered in its singularity; for Bürger, the problem is the relative autonomy of the subsystem of art within bourgeois society, and he proceeds to sketch a history of that subsystem in terms of the production, reception, and function of art—but not its politics. A bourgeois institution of art arises in the late eighteenth and early nineteenth century; art is no longer a function of ecclesiastical or courtly representation, but an expression of bourgeois self-consciousness, produced by individual artists for individual reception. In its theoretical articulations in German idealism, the work is separated from everyday life practice and becomes "purposeless," i.e., autonomous.

A history of increasing autonomization stretches from Weimar classicism to late-nineteenth-century symbolism and aestheticism, characterized by complete separation and self-referentiality. While Adorno
would suggest a continuation of this trajectory, Bürger describes a
break when, once the model of bourgeois autonomy is completely
filled out, it becomes susceptible to attacks by the historical avant-
garde (dadaism, cubism, surrealism) which attempts to overcome aestheticist isolation through a radical reconciliation of art and life. Duchamp's urinal or the cubists' collages integrate material from everyday life directly into works of art in order to challenge the autonomy
of art, and this "attack on the status of art" is the dialectical corollary
to the program to transform life in terms of the values previously sequestered in art: beauty, sensuality, and freedom.[11]

Unlike Lukács, Bürger does not examine the explicit or implicit
political allegiances of the avant-gardists. Unlike Adorno, he does not
investigate the political/historical ramifications of an aesthetic category (autonomy). Instead he provides a description of a rupture in the
social subsystem "art," and this exclusion of explicitly political material contributes no doubt to the importance of the study for current
work on the sociology of literature and art. It is however remarkable
that, despite this exclusion of politics, a terminology creeps into Bürger's account that points to a linkage between the avant-garde and
violence similar to that found in the other critics. For Bürger consistently describes the avant-gardists as carrying out an "attack" on the
bourgeois institution of art, a term of violence which is perhaps
echoed in the suggestion that avant-gardist practice must entail "raising demands." Similarly the specific characterizations of avant-gardist
aesthetic activity share this tone: provocation and shock. The relationship both to the established institution and to the contemporary
public is in no way peaceful; Bürger's model is the confrontation between artists and public in the dadaist events. Provocational artists,
destroying traditional aesthetic values, antagonize a threatened public
which responds with violence.

Three critics with three different approaches and very different
understandings of the avant-garde all register its affinity to violence.
This of course does not mean that the avant-garde is somehow en-
amored with war (although there would be cases that demonstrate
such a connection). It does mean however that peace or pacifism or
the peace movement may not be a useful category with which to
understand the aesthetic avant-garde. Is the hypothetical affinity of the

avant-garde to violence restricted to the aesthetic avant-garde? "Avant-garde" has another connotation as well, i.e., political leadership. Is it peaceful?

The Vanguard Party

Bürger ascribes to the avant-garde the project of revolutionizing society through an attack on the institution of art and the corollary separation of art and life. Leaving aside the specifics of this program, it is undeniable that many strands in the aesthetic explosion of modernism (understood in the broadest sense) shared the common hope that aesthetic innovation would generate social change. The new society therefore appeared as a product of the carriers of aesthetic change, i.e., the intellectuals especially writers and artists. This claim to intellectual leadership was nourished by the historical situation at the end of the First World War, when political revolutions and aesthetic innovation seemed to coincide. This explains the foregrounding of political allegiances in a wide range of avant-gardist movements: futurism and fascism, surrealism and communism.

A few examples from German literary history can illustrate this claim to intellectual leadership. The politicization of literature, a central feature of Weimar culture, did not mean just that authors began to participate in politics; they may have always done that in more or less private manners. The point is that suddenly writers began to claim for themselves a privileged voice in the public sphere. This is particularly clear in the so-called activism of Kurt Hiller. In a volume published in 1920 entitled *Geist werde Herr,* i.e., let the spirit (that is, literature) become master (that is, political ruler), he exhorts the intellectuals to abandon their traditional antipolitical isolationism and engage themselves directly in matters of public concern:

> You are not superfluous, and least of all in this age of a
> triumph of bodies. Germany, our beloved homeland, is calling
> you; as does humanity, our even greater beloved. Is not the
> world roaring for collapse and new constructions? Building the
> future—whose job is that if not yours? You are the spirit, you
> are the leaders, you are the power.[12]

Hiller eventually formulates this privileging of the intellectuals as a program labeled "logocracy," the rule of the word or the spirit, in the passage quoted counterposed to the triumph of the body. In the context of political upheavals, a new social order must be constructed, and writers are nominated the natural leaders in this transformation. Heinrich Mann's pamphlet of 1923, characteristically entitled *Dictatorship of Reason,* makes a similar claim:

> Politics is a matter of the spirit. The mature treat it as an ethical obligation. Economy is mechanical and remains so. Whoever accords primacy to economy can hope for no innovation, certainly none that is humane and hardly even any for the economy. Progress is possible. Its slogan is: Politics first![13]

Again politics is treated as a domain that belongs to the spirit, which is to say the writers. Furthermore, the realm of spiritual politics is characterized as superior to mundane material concerns, such as economy, which is denigrated as merely "mechanical." Authentic change can emerge not from an economic logic of development but solely through political intervention, to be carried of course by writers as political leaders. This dichotomy of politics and economy, typical for the period, echoes the Leninist treatment, which will be discussed below: the political leadership, which Mann associates with the spirit and Lenin with theory, is the source of authentic change, while economic tendencies remain trapped within the limitations of the material body (Hiller) or mechanical repetition (Mann). Lenin's attack on "economism" is indebted to the same evaluation.

Thomas Mann provides a different account. One can hardly expect the writer who consistently analyzed the proximity of disease and creativity to denigrate the aesthetic substance of the body. Yet he does repeat the invocation of the author as a privileged speaker in the body politic. In his 1926 "Speech on the Founding of the Section for Poetry in the Prussian Academy of the Arts," he contrasts the ease with which French authors always addressed social concerns with the reluctance of traditional German authors to participate in politics. Since the collapse of the monarchy, however, a politicization has set in, due not merely to external events but to an unraveling of the inherited antipolitical stance:

> [The German author soon discovers] that his loneliness and isolation were an *illusion,* a *romantic* illusion. . . . He discovers that he has been an expression, a mouthpiece; that he spoke for many, when he believed he spoke only about himself and for

himself. He discovers . . . that not only are works of art and the spirit socially received, but they are already *initiated* and *conceived* socially. . . . The German poet discovers his sociality.[14]

Mann welcomes this entry of the writers into politics, which had always been a hidden potential in the cult of autonomy. Again, however, it is not merely an entry into politics but a claim to a privileged status, for the writer purportedly does not merely pursue particularist interests, i.e., "speak for himself." He is rather the oracle of the universal interest of the nation and can therefore claim to be above partisan strife. As a seismographic indicator of the general will, the writer stands on a par with parliament and can compete with it on the basis of his own representational claim. Like Hiller and his own brother Heinrich, Thomas Mann locates the writer in the realm of political debate and simultaneously accords to him the status of leader.

These leadership claims for writers are a particular example of a broader early-twentieth-century variation on the avant-garde phenomenon: the intellectuals as political vanguard. Its purest manifestation is found in the Leninist program for the revolutionary party. At the turn of the century the Russian left was marked by a division between a growing working-class radicalism pushing for reforms and supported by older activists and, on the other hand, an intelligentsia increasingly familiar with the international Marxist discussion. In fact the former group as well was familiar with Marxism, especially revisionist currents in German social democracy and their emphasis on "economist" reforms coupled with an antitheoretical stance. Against this program centered on the immediate material conditions of the working class, Lenin argues in *What Is to Be Done?* for a party that would subsume the economic question under larger political concerns and therefore address issues not directly linked to the point of production (e.g., censorship, the draft) with the long-term goal of overthrowing the czarist autocracy. Such a political project, he argues, demands precisely the advanced theoretical consciousness that the reformist economists would be eager to jettison:

> The national tasks of Russian Social-Democracy are such as
> have never confronted any other socialist party in the world.
> We shall have occasion further on to deal with the political and
> organizational duties which the task of emancipating the whole
> people from the yoke of autocracy imposes upon us. At this
> point, we wish to state only that the *role of vanguard fighter*

can be fulfilled only by a party that is guided by the most advanced theory. To have a concrete understanding of what this means, let the reader recall such predecessors of Russian Social-Democracy as Herzen, Belinsky, Chernyshevsky, and the brilliant gallery of revolutionaries of the seventies; let him ponder over the world significance which Russian literature is now acquiring; let him . . . but be that enough![15]

The opening line of the passage serves not only to underscore the legitimate distinction between social democracy in the relatively liberal West and in the czarist police state. It also heroizes the Russian situation and justifies the subsequent call for a heroic discipline: the Russian party must act as a vanguard, not a mass organization. The ideological corollary to this institutional structure is the primacy of theory which Lenin presents as a privileging of literature. He mobilizes support for his proposal by invoking a panoply of forbears who are all writers, i.e., writers, as carriers of theory (for the Germans: the "spirit"), prefigure the vanguard party of the revolution.

Because of this purported necessity for a theoretical vanguard, Lenin must posit a specific relationship between the party of the working-class revolution and the working class itself. Just as Hiller accords priority to the spirit over the body, and Heinrich Mann denigrates the mechanical character of economy, Lenin treats the intellectual leadership as the authentic source of revolutionary consciousness which could never develop in the merely economistic struggles of the working class reformers: "We have said that *there could not have been* Social-Democratic consciousness among the workers. It would have to be brought to them from without. . . . The theory of socialism, however, grew out of the philosophic, historical, and economic theories elaborated by educated representatives of the propertied classes, by intellectuals." [16] Because of its theoretical function, the party is distinct from the class with its reformist instincts, and because, as Lenin admits, the Leninist program for a revolutionary avant-garde is a product of bourgeois intellectual life, it apparently reproduces the heteronomy of bourgeois class relations within the socialist movement. The principle of the avant-garde turns out to be not that new after all but only continues a traditional division between a small elite and a disenfranchised mass. This critique may hold at least for the Leninist version of the avant-garde, as Pavel Axelrod noted critically as early as 1907: "The mass of the proletarian members of the party exists as a sort of plebeian estate, while the intelligentsia play the role of an aristocracy or patricians by controlling all the internal and external affairs of our party-state and by protecting the plebeian strata from all corrupting influences from without." [17] Luxemburg attacked Lenin along similar lines for his "ultracentralism," and Plekhanov accused him of confusing "the dictatorship of the proletariat with a dictatorship over the proletariat." [18]

The etymology of *avant-garde* begins with a military usage, and I have examined the implicit linkage between an "avant-garde" and violence in several critical writers. The same reverberation recurs in *What Is to Be Done?* Lenin argues that social democrats, with their political (not just economic) goals throughout society, must not concentrate solely on the workers but penetrate all social groups; his military phrasing is the call to "dispatch units of their army *in all directions*." [19] Later he states explicitly that "the thing we need is a military organisation of agents." [20]

It is possible to account for this military organization of the revolutionary avant-garde as a response to the police-state conditions in czarist Russia. Similarly it is possible (although not convincing) to explain the so-called militarization of the economy in 1918–20 against the background of the civil war and the foreign invasion. Yet there may be more to the relationship between the Leninist vanguard theory and the militarization of the revolution that led to what Cornelius Castoriadis has referred to as the "stratocracy," i.e., the priority of the military in the Leninist state. [21] Such a thesis would severely undermine the plausibility of the various claims that Soviet militarism is a response to the Soviet perception of "encirclement."

Lenin's own "Military Programme of the Proletarian Revolution," written in September 1916, may indicate the likelihood of such a connection. Faced with the carnage of the First World War, antiwar socialists in Holland, Scandinavia, and Switzerland began to call for disarmament, implying a break with the traditional program of the nineteenth-century left for an arming of the people in a popular militia. Lenin argues against disarmament and pacifism, insisting that "socialists cannot, without ceasing to be socialists, be opposed to all war." [22] He proceeds to list three types of war which, because of their revolutionary character, deserve the support of socialists: anticolonial wars of national liberation, revolutionary civil wars, and—after a successful revolution—wars in defense of a revolutionary socialist state. A principled rejection of all wars can only mean a renunciation of all revolutionary hopes: "The 'social' parsons and opportunists are always ready to build dreams of future peaceful socialism. But the very thing that distinguishes them from revolutionary Social-Democrats is that they refuse to think about and reflect on the fierce class struggle and class *wars* needed to achieve that beautiful future."[23]

The argument obviously anticipates Lukács's critique of expressionist pacifism and the antiwar position of the USPD. Absolute pacifism implies a refusal to employ violence to carry out a struggle against a violent opponent, the armed, antirevolutionary bourgeoisie. It is an "opportunism" because it exploits a natural hostility to war in order to renounce the class struggle and the long-term revolutionary goals. It is ultimately a sort of escapism that abandons the project of radical social change. Lenin hammers away at this point: "The main defect of the disarmament demand is its evasion of all the concrete questions of revolution. Or do the advocates of disarmament stand for an altogether new kind of revolution, unarmed revolution? . . . 'Disarmament' means simply running away from unpleasant reality, not fighting it."[24] Obviously the military terminology in *What Is to Be Done?* is not peripheral to the politics. The military seems to have a special status within the avant-garde project of Leninism. Similarly "The Military Programme of the Proletarian Revolution" suggests that the Leninist conceptualization of the proletarian revolution is necessarily military. It still remains to be seen, however, how the precise connection is constituted.

A clue may be found in the critiques of Leninism within the socialist movement. Axelrod's comment, cited above, points to the perpetuation of bourgeois class structure within the Leninist party. The same complaint is elaborated in A. Kollontai's pamphlet on "the workers' opposition." Written in 1921 for the tenth party congress, it points to the development of a bureaucracy and a class of Taylorist experts who are quickly taking control away from the authentically working-class institutions. This development is presented as a retreat from the alleged unity of party and class in the first months of the revolution:

> During the first period of the revolution, who would have spoken of the "leaders" and the "lower levels?" The masses, that is, the working masses, and the leadership centers of the party made up a single whole. The needs that emerged from life and struggle at the lower levels were given precise articulation and a

clear and scientifically grounded formulation in the leadership centers of the party. A confrontation of leadership centers and lower levels did not occur and could not occur. Today this confrontation exists, and neither agitation nor any "intimidation" measures will be able to banish the emergence of a typical new "social stratum" of soviet and party leaders from the consciousness of the broad masses.[25]

Kollontai contrasts the current contradiction between leaders and masses with an alleged unity during the initial phase of the revolution. She does not explicitly suggest that this dichotomy might follow from the principles presented in *What Is to Be Done?* Whether this reluctance has to do with a personal or political affinity to Lenin, the influence of the relatively "anarchistic" April Theses and *State and Revolution,* or an authentic experience of the mass uprising in 1917 cannot be of concern here. The point is that she describes the emergence of a split between the representatives of the vanguard party and the working class, a split that is a key element in the Leninist design of the vanguard party. It is a split, furthermore, that transforms the party leaders into bureaucrats and the workers into passive followers, which Kollontai associates with a specific political potential:

> When the masses grow distant from the "leaders," when a distance, an abyss, appears between the leadership centers and the masses, then this means that all is not well in the leadership, especially when the masses are not silent but step forward, defend themselves and their "slogans." The leadership centers can distract the masses from the straight path of history, which leads to communism, only when the masses are silent and submissive and follow their leaders in passive trust. That was the case in 1914 at the start of the world war, when the workers believed their leaders and decided: "They know the path of history better than we do. Our instinctive feeling to protest the war deceives us. We must be silent, repress this feeling and follow those above us."[26]

For Kollontai, the problem is not the presence of a leadership party in general (as it was for anarchists and syndicalists) but rather an ossification of the relationship between party and class. The party loses contact with the masses, while the masses fall into a depoliticized passivity and consequently follow the party directives without reflecting on them. This bifurcation, accelerated by the spread of bureaucracy and the growing influence of technical specialists, runs counter to an authentic communism, which would rely primarily on the creative force of the class and its own initiatives. Similar critiques of the continuity of bourgeois authority patterns within Bolshevism were current in Western European "left communism," especially in the writings of Anton Pannekoek, Herman Gorter, and Otto Rühle. Kollontai suggests however in this passage that an excessive subordination of the masses to the party, which was a major result of the "militarization of the economy," generates a potential for war which the workers would otherwise naturally resist. Her organizational goal seems to be a reversal of the Leninist privileging of the theoretical vanguard; in her account, the workers, left to their own, come rather close to correct political judgments and are thwarted only by the party leadership. Consequently her remark on war apparently confirms the suspicion that the project of the vanguard party has something to do with militarization: Lenin's "military organization of agents" agitates against pacifism, while Kollontai's class without leaders "spontaneously" opposes war.

Some interesting tentative results: the aesthetic avant-garde appears to be the carrier of a violent potential, and vanguard politics points to a potential militarization. The common denominator may be the heteronomous social context. For Adorno denounces the alibi function of the aesthetic category of autonomy, purportedly emancipatory but in fact ideological, in terms that are structurally homologous to the left-communist denunciation of Leninist leadership claims. Both the aesthetic and the political vanguards attempt to appropriate a power that is potentially directed against the rest of society which is then written into a subordinate position. This leads to a second parallel. Each avant-garde, which presents itself as the authentic historical subject, adopts a program to transform the social object in its own image: the aestheticization of life or the militarization of the economy. Finally each avant-garde, trapped in a perpetual assertion of its own privilege, is forced to modify its emancipatory pretenses and enters a process of ossification. The artistic avant-garde, which intended to revolutionize the bourgeois institution of art, has become the aesthetic meat and potatoes of established taste, and the revolutionary party transformed itself with equal rapidity into a new autocracy. I label this last similarity the "reification of the avant-garde," another version of a recuperated modernism.

The Reification of Peace: Anti-Aestheticism and Antipolitics

Neither in the dadaist provocations nor in the Bolshevik party does the project of the early twentieth-century avant-garde seem to have a specific relationship to a substantive notion of peace, let alone the pacifist movement. If then, as suggested at the outset of this chapter, the peace movement has no particular interest in either aesthetic innovation or radical social change, one could simply conclude that the lack of interest is mutual. At best it is a case of apples and oranges with no shared program; at worst, sheep and goats, moving into opposite camps—because the potential for violence in any avant-garde must necessarily repel the peace activists.

However, it may be worth exploring another line of analysis. After scrutinizing the absence of a definite affinity to peace in the avant-garde (the violence of aesthetic innovation, the militarization of the party), one might ask whether the peace movement displays any signs of avant-gardism and how it addresses the classical projects of the historical avant-gardes, i.e., critique of traditional art and revolutionary social change. There seems to be at first a very easy case to be made for the anti-avant-garde character of the peace movement. Given its assumption that humanity and civilization are threatened with total destruction, the peace movement does not find it necessary to identify with any particular cultural program. Its goals include the preservation of all civilization, and it by no means distinguishes between pre-avant-garde and avant-garde culture. Such a distinction would certainly seem trivial in the shadow of the imminent danger. Consequently the text "Thoughts on Action" speaks only of "beauty" and "art," and it lists "French, German and Cuban authors" in an abstract series with no additional characterizations; it is concerned with the protection of culture in general and does not differentiate between good and bad, high and low, old and new art.

The peace movement's disregard for the specificity of the aesthetic avant-garde is mirrored in its distance to the claims of the political avant-garde. The same dynamic operates again: with nuclear war looming on the horizon, other social issues tend to lose their erstwhile urgency, and the distinctions among competing political groups pale. Left-wing sectarianism of the early seventies is replaced by a sort of popular-front pacifism, carried neither by the "working class" nor by a "vanguard party" nor by "marginal groups" but by "humanity" in general in defense of its general interest. This statement is not meant as a commentary on the objective sociological composition of the peace movement which is probably not at all a representative cross section of humanity; the point is rather that the ideological self-representation of the peace movement is marked by a tendency to suppress alternative social or political goals in order to pursue the common goal of preserving humanity from a nuclear end.

In addition to this exclusion of political material not directly related to peace, the peace movement's rejection of traditional political avant-gardism is evident in its organizational self-understanding. Vanguard politics means the Leninist party with its "ultracentralism" (Luxemburg) and the hierarchical division of labor between "the leadership centers" and "the lower levels" (Kollontai). In contrast, the peace movement describes itself as egalitarian: in the PEAS program one reads of an "open forum" and "community," and the placard outside of the Greenham Women's Peace Camp insists that they have "No Commanders."[27] Similarly, the West German Green party repeatedly underscores its commitment to grass-roots democracy or "*Basisdemokratie*" and attempts to prevent the development of a leadership cadre through the application of a rotation principle to its parliamentary representatives. All these examples are of course a far cry from Lenin's call for a "military organisation of agents."

After the tentative description of the incompatability of the avant-garde and the peace movement, a query into common features seems risky, but some questions remain. Do they share a starting point that lies somewhere before the extreme differentiations outlined so far? Are their rhetorical origins, the gestures with which the mobilizations of their respective constituencies commence, similarly structured? In fact, they all begin with similar invocations of a crisis, the significance of which is always heightened through the allegation of causal connection to war. The historical aesthetic avant-garde thematized the cultural crisis of nineteenth-century Europe and linked the bad taste of bourgeois philistinism in the arts to the burgeoning militarism that exploded in the First World War, as if a preference for epigonic painting necessarily implied a predilection for trench warfare and mustard gas. The political vanguard addressed a political-economic crisis of capitalism that purportedly led through its highest stage, imperialism, to the highest stage of imperialism, war: from free-trade zones to free-fire zones. The peace movement too describes a crisis, an apparent immobility in the international arms control negotiations and the contradictions in military strategy, and it insists that this crisis of deterrence can quickly slide through a new cold war into a colder nuclear winter.

I have set these three argumentative lines in parallel without intending any judgment on the plausibility of their claims. The point is rather that the claims are made within a shared rhetorical structure—the invocation of a crisis that has the potential of leading to an ultimate end—and this common practice may explain why, despite its anti-avant-gardist pretenses, the peace movement acts very much like the historical avant-gardes. The historical practice of the avant-garde movements must be distinguished from their programmatic intentions to revolutionize their institutional objects, i.e., established art and the state. Through the rhetorical invocation of an ultimate catastrophe, the avant-gardists relegate all other material to a secondary status and devote themselves solely to the privileged project: the attack on the work of art or the seizure of state power. The repressed material may disappear from consciousness but not from history, and if it returns, as repressed and therefore not revolutionized, it can impede the intended transformational process and lead to a merely "modernized" status quo ante. The attack on the traditional work of art leaves the art market (and the market economy) untouched, which quickly recuperates the avant-garde as an improved commodity. The Leninist seizure of state power occludes the hierarchical class character of society which subsequently distorts the revolution and generates an updated repetition of the autocratic state. In both cases, the invocation of an existential threat, which denies all nuances and violently demands full subordination, undercuts the successful completion of the foregrounded tasks. It is as if the ruse of reason intervened by way of artificial negativity and cast the dadaists as agents of the Museum of Modern Art and the Bolsheviks as Taylorist experts hired to streamline the czarist police. Is the peace movement trapped in the same eternal return?

No one can miss the rhetoric of absolute crisis in the advocacy of the peace movement. It is the starting point of "Thoughts on Action" and other current accounts of disarmament, which is presented not as an abstract desideratum but as a fundamental prerequisite of any continued survival. This maximalist imagery quickly turns however into a minimalist program for the reduction and abolition of weaponry rather than into a critique of the causes of militarism. There are of course many former leftists engaged in the peace movement, and they often carry with them vestiges of their social analyses, but the hegemonic position within the various national movements has been an abstract opposition to the presence of nuclear arms. Yet if one assumes that weaponry is not an accident but a result of social forces, then a removal of missiles from Central Europe (the demand of the German peace movement) or a freeze on the production of nuclear weapons (the demand of the American movement) without an attack on the causes of armament would only clear the ground for a renewed and "modernized" operation of those forces. The causes of armament are not thematized because of the urgency of disarmament in the face of the nuclear threat, i.e., the vision of the absolute crisis blocks an analysis of its origins.

If, hypothetically, the argument were to be made that capitalism is the cause of militarism, then the peace movement would be pushed to the left and lose its mass base and popular-front character. If, alternatively, one suggested that bureaucratic socialism leads to a stratocracy, then one runs the risk of appearing to agree with Reagan and Thatcher. If, finally, the arms buildup were related to geopolitical rivalry, one would be trapped in the complicated debates on Poland, Afghanistan, Lebanon, and Central America that might distract from the overriding threat. The peace movement's insistence on the unquestionable priority of its single goal—clearly a modified claim to vanguard leadership—blinds it to the complicated sociopolitical context in which it operates and consequently impoverishes its own political analysis. The only explanation of the arms problem that is widely shared in the peace movement, E. P. Thompson's exterminism thesis, is, characteristically enough, a tautology, i.e., weaponry escalates because of the history of weaponry; it is necessarily a tautology because the primacy of peace eclipses all other material.

The reification of peace as the sole good and the subsequent truncation of the peace movement's analytic capacities maneuver the movement into a political helplessness. A case in point is the response of the West German peace movement to the declaration of martial law in Poland.[28] The rhetoric of the peace movement depends largely on what I have elsewhere described as a "discourse of authenticity" that posits an abstract self confronted by a threatening other and which consequently treats the arms problem as the imposition of foreign, i.e., American, missiles on German national "soil."[29] In its implicitly nationalist phrasing of the foreign policy issue, the German movement contrasts, for example, with the American peace movement in which a natural scientific discourse about the effects of radiation, extent of destruction, ecological consequences, etc., predominates. Given the West German perception of the issue in terms of national or European selves challenged by superpower "others," the events in Poland and the banning of Solidarity would seem to have been a likely moment to mobilize demonstrations of protest; in fact, the Polish events might have been grasped as a welcome opportunity to prove the evenhandedness of a movement that is always attacked from the right as Soviet-inspired. Yet the response by the peace movement to Poland was extraordinarily weak, and not because Poland was perceived as somehow unrelated to the priority of peace. On the contrary, the potential of a relatively autonomous Poland was understood as intimately tied to the question of peace in Europe—but in a negative manner, i.e., because a radical Solidarity and Polish nationalism challenged Russian hegemony, and because the Soviet Union will not tolerate the dissolution of its sphere of influence and will eventually invade, the declaration of martial law was implicitly and, often enough, explicitly treated as a step toward the stabilization of peace. The West German author Peter Schneider comments:

> Peace is reduced to the avoidance of atomic war. Peaceful life becomes the hostage of the fear of massive death. Gradually any situation short of atomic war becomes acceptable. Nothing makes this process clearer than the reaction of the German public to the military putsch in Poland. In short, public opinion in West Germany accepted, if not condoned, martial law in Poland in order to preserve world peace. I address this accusation particularly to that part of the public which, thanks to its critique of the military dictatorships in the West—Chile, El Salvador, Turkey—would have had the moral legitimacy to protest against the coup in Poland. Instead, liberal commentators—not to be confused with opponents of *détente* like Strauss and Reagan—used all their energy to warn against "provocative phrases" and "verbal radicalism." This project was so exhausting that they barely had the strength left to designate or even recognize the events in Poland.[30]

The vanguardism of the peace movement leads then first of all to a political tunnel vision. The reification of peace as an absolute and isolated goal renders all other goods secondary, including freedom and justice. The West German peace movement can understand the exigencies of Solidarity as little as North American pacifists can presumably

provide an adequate analysis of a practical response to the violence of
the Nicaraguan Contras. The vanguardist privileging of a single goal
means the prohibition of any others. The same apocalyptic rhetoric
generates a further vanguardist feature, the absolute priority of engagement for the individual activist. For Lenin, the revolutionary
"agents" were professional revolutionaries, fully devoted to the party.
For the dadaists, aesthetic revolution was an all-encompassing life
practice. For the peace movement, all dimensions of everyday life are
determined by the urgency of the situation. The author of "Thoughts
on Action" describes how she once participated in politics and art as
two separate, though certainly not unrelated, activities; after hearing
Caldicott, she subordinates art to politics and reduces politics to peace
activism. This is not just a single exception. Consider how the following account of the Greenham protest places the commitment to peace
at the center of the identity of the activist, rendering all other personal
traits peripheral:

> The peace camp's more than just a brave gesture of defiance.
> It's an experiment in nonviolent resistance, the taking of re-
> sponsibility by ordinary people, not just for what's being done
> in our name, but for how we behave to each other. It was cer-
> tainly my instincts that brought me here—a deeply based con-
> viction that nothing in the world is more important than peace
> and that what's going on over there, behind those gates, is evil
> and only adds to peril.[31]

The Leninist would hardly speak of "instincts," although the dadaist
might, but they would both agree with the peace activist that "nothing
in the world is more important than" the respective goal of each. Each
moreover would share the Manichaean division of the world into
bravely defiant heroes or, in this case, heroines and an evil lurking
behind the gates, a division which serves to heighten the urgency of
personal commitment.

The avant-gardist always lives the politics pursued. Just as the ul-
tra-centralism of the Leninist party becomes the shape of the revolutionary state, the goal of international disarmament is mirrored in the
ostentatious insistence on the nonviolent character of the peace activists themselves. An analytic recognition of the difference between the
two levels disappears, as the spirit of Greenham indicates: "Nonviolence is not just the absence of violence or simply a tactic, but a total
approach to living, both an ideal to aim for and a strategy for

change. . . . Means and ends merge into one another and cannot be separated, so that anything won by violence has the seeds of the violence contained within it."[32] The congruence of means and ends suggests that the distance between the individual activist (carrying out "means") and the principles of the movement (the envisioned "ends") also disappears. The abolition of weapons in the international realm is consequently indistinguishable from a nonviolent "conflict resolution" on the personal level. However, the institution of the principle that the only good peace activist is a pacifist must require a considerable quantity of repression: by excluding nonpacifists from the movement and by compelling each participant to stifle any natural violent rage. Furthermore whenever a violent outbreak does occur, be it physical, verbal, or emotional violence, the peace activist who subscribes to the pacifist credo and the equation of personal and international violence must be overwhelmed by a wave of guilt and social ostracism, as if she had just pushed the nuclear button. Because of the vanguardist logic, the Leninist who by breaking party discipline betrays the revolution, and the pacifist whose personal violence is tantamount to a megaton explosion, face massive psychological recriminations.

This psychological pressure translates as a burden of guilt, a theme that runs through much peace movement literature and often gives it a religious, confessional touch. Once ends and means converge and the individual is fully responsible for peace, then a process of self-accusation sets in, for each individual continues to pursue a life that cannot at every moment be fully determined by the political goal:

> It is hard to accept that *each individual* is to blame for nuclear weapons—ourselves, our families, our friends. Thousands of people do not want them and genuinely feel the present situation is not of their making. This year the government will spend 16,000,000,000 pounds or so on "defence." This works out at about 18 pounds a week for every family. The army, navy, airforce, weapons manufacture and research are all paid for with our money, from income tax, VAT, tax on cigarettes and drink. Of course, not everyone has equal power to effect a change—most of us do not have the same power as a cabinet minister, for example—but we all have the power of refusal in our own lives. If the government makes decisions we do not like we can go along with them—however reluctantly—or we can stand out against them and make our opposition clear. If

we do not stand out against nuclear weapons, then we are—
however reluctantly—supporting them.[33]

The absolute priority of the goal and the absolute submission of the
activist to the cause—two features of vanguard politics—are transformed here into a variation on the Weberian notion of "inner-worldly
asceticism," with a vaguely Puritan undertone. Participation in the
sensuous pleasures of the world—wealth, tobacco, and alcohol—
leads quickly to a complicity in "evil." This original sin applies to all,
regardless of social station, but one can hope to escape this nexus, at
the center of which is the government, through a constant testimony
to a dissident faith: the Calvinist elect as the paradigm of the modern
avant-garde?

Besides the reification of peace as the single goal and the reification
of the activist, fully subsumed in the movement, the peace movement
displays a third feature of vanguardism, the privileging of a leadership
group. This seems to run counter to the pronouncements of the peace
movement where there are allegedly "no leaders" and the "community" is an "open forum." However, again a distinction must be made
between the ideological self-representation and the historical action of
the political movement. In fact the claim to universal representation—
the peace movement as the expression of humanity in general—draws
on classical bourgeois ideology, which masks particular class interests
with the fiction of equal access and linguistic transparency. The ideal
speech situation posited by the PEAS program is open to all who are
prepared to participate in the university-based discourse. Greenham
was open to all women who had the resources to leave their occupations and devote themselves to the protest. Of course all activism
makes personal demands on the participants and is therefore selective;
the problem arises when this process of selection is masked and the
activists begin to deny the specificity of their own social status. Once
a select group of "agents" presents itself as humanity, the Leninist
dynamic has set in: the party replaces the class, the central committee
replaces the party.

The emergence of a leadership stratum, despite claims to the contrary, is evident elsewhere as well. In West Germany, the rotation principle is constantly challenged, as a cadre group of political experts
gradually develops. Meanwhile, in the United States and England, the
leadership function of natural scientists is unmistakable: in the "open
forum" of discussion, natural scientists have a privileged access to the

language and relevant information and consequently occupy a position of authority. In all cases, the intelligentsia rises to the top and employs a rhetoric of catastrophe in order to mobilize a mass following which, stunned by the visions of horror, is condemned to a subordinate passivity. Because of the primacy of peace, the masses at the base are prohibited from raising additional, social issues. Because of the demands of personal commitment, each individual is ensnared in a psychology of guilt. The ideology of egalitarian transparency turns out to be the medium of heteronomy, which is the paradigmatic structure of every avant-garde.

Trapped in its own rhetoric of catastrophe, the vanguardist peace movement is immobilized, particularly after the failure to block the stationing of the cruise and Pershing missiles in Western Europe and the hopelessness of the freeze initiative in the United States. Its internal contradictions may have already rendered it a mere footnote to the history of the early eighties, and it could disappear the moment the superpowers agree to a new arms treaty; its future after the agreements of Reagan and Gorbachev is shaky indeed. The leaders of the peace movement may end up, as leaders do always, as managers in a scientific/arms control bureaucracy. The end of the peace movement, the end of this avant-garde? But there is another radical antiwar potential, speechless because lacking the liberal linguistic competency of the intelligentsia, beyond the pale of a moralizing pacifism. It is found where, as Kollontai insisted, a natural aversion to war is linked to a distrust of any leadership, especially one that represses the social question and transforms criminal policies into a debilitating ethic of collective guilt. The failure of the peace movement—the failure of another avant-garde—leads to more interesting questions: how to move beyond the antinomies of the avant-garde, the "leadership centers" and the "lower levels," to a point where the division of labor between leaders and followers no longer determines the structure of society.

CHAPTER ELEVEN

The Vienna Fascination

The Discovery of Central Europe

ANOTHER specter is haunting Europe and has even made it to Manhattan. Seventy years after his assassination on a sultry afternoon in Sarajevo, His Excellency the Archduke Franz Ferdinand has returned and has brought with him a danse macabre, a multinational celebration of a long-gone multinational empire. First sighted in Venice in the Palazzo Grassi in the summer of 1984, he reappeared quickly in an old haunt, the Künstlerhaus in Vienna, and then moved on to conquer the world: the Centre Pompidou in Paris and the Museum of Modern Art in New York.

As the end of the century approaches, the fin-de-siècle is rediscovered. How can one explain this Vienna fascination? Let me leave aside the baroque confabulations and the metaphysical meditations on the imminent collapse of another empire and offer instead a more sober suggestion. After Alexander and King Tut, China, the Vatican, and the Impressionists, Vienna was another blockbuster show, one more once-in-a-lifetime chance, a strenuous effort to bedazzle a jaded public which otherwise has neither patience nor interest for the impressive but nonsensational permanent collections of the major museums. The mega-exhibit is a tourist attraction, and the expansive galleries, which, under normal circumstances, are as empty as a church on Monday morning, are abracadabra filled with the hustle and bustle of the curious, the cursory, and the culture-vulture crowds. These are hard times for high culture—beam me up Scotty, there's no art down here—so the museum administrations wax ecstatic when the attendance statistics speed off into hyperspace, justifying the hypertrophic subventions: a venal calculation no one should underestimate in a cruel age of budget cutting.

Was Vienna really only just another opportunity for the culture bureaucrats to get a quick fix? This account sounds close to a vulgar Marxism, boorishly reducing cultural complexities to penny-ante parsimony. Vulgar or not, it is indeed an economistic explanation that remains abstract, helplessly blinded in the darkness of a night where all the cats are Klimt. Despite the shared constraints of contemporary museum politics, each museum handled the material differently. In Italy, Austria, France, and the United States, imperial Vienna never wore the same dress twice. Its appearance was as protean as the devil in *Doctor Faustus*, marked each time by the unique concerns of the respective beholder. The Venetians limited their retrospective to the two decades before 1918, as the subtitle of the exhibit put it: from the Secession to the fall of the Hapsburg Empire. A barely hidden irredentist nostalgia recalled a former political geography that included the north Italian provinces in a central European confederation (a similar archeology of the Dual Monarchy is evident, for different reasons of course, in the Hungarian vision of the director Istvan Szabo, whose film *Captain Redl* even includes a homage to Emperor Franz Joseph I). In contrast, the new Viennese representation of old Vienna cast a wider net, the period 1870 to 1930, both artificial dates, obvious stand-ins for the hidden political markings: the *Ausgleich* with Hungary in 1867 and the civil war of 1934. While the official periodization disguised the political agenda, it simultaneously described a historical range that allowed for equal time for competing political groups, so characteristic of the Austrian social partnership: the conservatives could indulge in the imperial aura of the good old days before 1918, while the socialists basked in the memories of the First Republic and the welfare-statist municipal policies of Red Vienna. But both groups could join hands at the patriotic center of the exhibit, where, in front of a bust of the Empress Elisabeth, the blood-stained uniform of the archduke from that sultry day in Sarajevo was stretched out in full glory. Was this art?

Outside of the successor states of Austro-Hungary, the Viennese material underwent further metamorphoses. In one of the final fortresses of autonomy aesthetics, the Museum of Modern Art, emphasis was placed on artistic innovation, the legacy of the major painters, Klimt, Schiele, and Kokoschka, and Vienna appeared as one of the crucibles of aesthetic modernism. Yet the Parisian exhibit fore-grounded Viennese irrationalism, hieratic ornament, mythic excess, and the allegories of psychoanalysis: Vienna as the birthplace of post-modernism, evidently the diametrical opposite of the New York version.[1]

These four permutations of Vienna are indicative of particular local concerns which lead to extraordinarily divergent appropriations of the cultural-historical material, as if fin-de-siècle Vienna were objectively nothing at all, or only an empty screen onto which the various groups of empowered cultural administrators could project their own specific interests. One might even label this solution itself a Viennese account, recalling Mach, Wittgenstein, and perhaps even Freud, insofar as the perceptions of the material are reduced to just so many subjective impressions and discrete illusions, with no fundamental grounding. The variations on the Vienna of the past would then turn out to be an open catalogue of varied local cultural concerns of the present.

This pluralist model of interpretation has much to recommend it, especially its diagnostic value in the examination of the specificity of really-existing cultural groups, but it may not be the whole story. Does it not miss the Vienna forest for the trees? By shattering the material into four separate perceptions, it ignores the fact that in all four cases it was the same object, no matter how unique each disguise, that attracted the attention of the viewer. In Venice, Vienna, Paris, and New York, there was a shared concern with the legacy of turn-of-the-century Austria, and it may be worth our while to consider whether one can uncover an agenda that is as common as it is hidden.

Let me proceed with this admittedly tenuous inquiry through a mixture of negation and free association. If not Vienna, then what? International interest in the culture and history of German-speaking Europe centered, for many decades, on monumental political questions: the causes of the First World War and, later, the rise and fall of the Third Reich, and the latter topic returned in hundreds of films and popular novels. It was Hitler and by no means the Archduke Franz Ferdinand who fascinated a collective imagination, which in turn never perceived Hitler as in any significant way Austrian. This interest, the specific phantasmagoria of the cold war, underwent a modification when the generation of the sixties discovered an elective affinity with the cultural revolution of the twenties, the Weimar Republic, the theater of Brecht, expressionism, the radical avant-garde, and, in more popular packaging, the cachet of the cabaret.[2] The reason for this shift in interest is rather obvious and need not be belabored: the common denominator is a confluence of cultural experimentation and a political radicalism.

As early as March of 1968, Peter Handke pointed to things to come in an article provocatively entitled "Horváth Is Better Than Brecht," a phrase that challenges one to discern a political impetus beneath the

Vienna fascination that displaced the Weimar Republic of the student movement.[3] Yet the four exhibits appeared to eschew any obvious political grandstanding, either excluding political material altogether or including only brief, contextualizing remarks regarding local political movements. The exhibit in Vienna mentioned Karl Lueger and Viktor Adler, but the Austro-Hungarian politicians of international stature like Ferdinand Beust or Gyula Andrassy were nowhere to be found. Vienna may have been the home of aesthetic innovation and/or social modernization, but in its various representations, it remained a polis without politics, outside of international relations, cut off from global entanglements. One cannot envision early-nineteenth-century Vienna, Metternich's Vienna, without considering the international diplomacy of European politics; in the images of late-nineteenth-century Vienna, it was almost as if modern art and social movements had displaced international political concerns. This tendency was amplified by the reduction of Austro-Hungarian culture to a single municipality, the capital city, as if nothing had taken place elsewhere in the monarchy or the rest of the world. And it is precisely this foregrounded separation of the insular metropolis from the rest of the world which can help explain the Vienna fascination and the gothic return of Franz Ferdinand.

The denial of politics, which nearly engendered an unintended provincialization of the represented metropolis, Vienna, was embedded in two related descriptions. The first, deriving from the political culture of the empire, locates Austria at the crossroads of the European north and south, east and west, where Germans, Slavs, and Latins meet; it is mediator, the middle power, the neutral terrain between the surrounding cultural-political zones: it is Central Europe, ideally separate from the great powers that surround it. This tradition was then revived after 1945 and, especially in the context of the state treaty of 1955, in a second version. To use the phrase of the Austrian president, the "Austrian example" entails neutrality, a Central European buffer zone pledged to retain its political autonomy from the superpower blocks in the East and the West.[4]

The Vienna fascination was the cultural corollary to the "Austrian example." It corresponded to a reconsideration of the possibility of a specifically European or, more properly, Central European political and cultural identity, defined outside of and against the spheres of influence of NATO and the Warsaw Pact. A glance at recent political discussions confirms this suggestion. Interviewed in the West German

tageszeitung after the American bombing of Libya, the British journalist Fred Halliday called for a dissolution of NATO and, nearly
echoing the Austrian president, invoked the model of an "Austrian
solution" for Western Europe. At the same time, a conference was
being held in Vienna to clarify the contemporary relevance of the concept "*Mitteleuropa*." Finally, to choose one text of the West German
peace movement that can stand for many, the volume *Neutralität für
Mitteleuropa: Das Ende der Blöcke* by Jochen Löser and Ulrike Schilling (1984) proposes the term "Australism" as an alternative to the
pejorative labels "neutralism" or "Finlandization." The authors insist
programmatically that "despite existing ideological and political differences, all Central Europeans living between France and the Soviet
Union have developed stronger common interests that enable them to
shape their coexistence autonomously in a confederated Mitteleuropa
as a neutral community of sovereign states." They look forward to
declaring Vienna the center of what they call a "peace zone Mitteleuropa," and they conclude by calling on the Soviet Union to seize the
initiative, as it allegedly did during the negotiations of Austrian neutrality in 1955, and take diplomatic steps "to open up an Austrian
perspective for all Central Europeans."[5]

The Vienna exhibits and the Austrian example: the place may be
the same, but the geographical congruence may not be enough to
make a compelling argument. What after all does Egon Schiele have
to do with the discussion of Central European neutrality, except for
the apparent accident of location? The political hypothesis just outlined seems to suffer from nearly the same reductionism pointed out
in the earlier discussion of museum budgets. Yet this political connection is crucial, although it becomes convincing only in tandem with a
second, cultural hypothesis. Fin-de-siècle Vienna is fascinating because the cultural-historical material it includes provides a rich field
for exploring the anomie and labile identity formation in twentieth-
century modernity. It frames the tension between scientific rationality
and aesthetic utopianism, and it records the disorientation of civic
consciousness, the transformation of the bourgeois citizen into the
modern consumer. The political move—pointing to the Austrian example in order to make the case for Central European neutrality—
may entail a response to that cultural confusion, an effort to find a
collective identity, or, alternatively, it may exacerbate that confusion,
to the extent that neutrality may imply a denial of genuine political
challenges and conflicts.

In his introduction to the Vienna catalogue, Carl Schorske summarizes his seminal account of fin-de-siècle culture. Two separate Austrian legacies, the rationalism of the Josephine Enlightenment and the aesthetic irrationality of the baroque Counter-Reformation, combined briefly in the "cultural synthesis" of the middle of the nineteenth century, carried by the liberal bourgeoisie which nurtured a traditionally aristocratic aesthetic culture while pursuing its own project of capitalist modernization.[6] For Schorske, this synthesis collapsed owing to the subjective aftershocks of the crash of 1873 and the rise of antiliberal social movements on the right and the left. Viennese modernism itself turns out to be inherently antiliberal, the revolt of a younger generation against the culture of the "founders" of the 1860s. Reason and art, Josephinism and the baroque, which had once appeared to be compatible, again polarized. Hence the antinomy of an archrationalist modernism in the works of Alfred Loos and Karl Kraus and, on the other hand, the subjective irrationality of the secessionist painters and the writers of Young Vienna.

Schorske's description is rich and valuable, but its most important consequences become clear only if it is thought through in terms of broader social and cultural processes. The two separate traditions he identifies, rational and aesthetic culture, certainly have specific manifestations within Austrian history, but the dichotomy is characteristic of European modernization in general and the separation of particular value spheres, i.e., the autonomization of art and science. Furthermore the crisis of midcentury liberal culture—including the stock market crash and the rise of the social movements—cannot be convincingly regarded as a deus ex machina, an inexplicable accident that befell the Austrian bourgeoisie. On the contrary, it was a consequence of the truncation of the project of modernization, the reduction of Enlightenment rationality to instrumental reason and the logic of the market, the transformation of political liberalism into the economic liberalism of laissez-faire doctrine.

While scientific reason and autonomous art remain normatively incompatible, all the Vienna exhibits demonstrated how the modernization of late-nineteenth-century capitalism demanded an ever-increasing aesthetic stylization of everyday life: from the World's Fair in 1873 through the Makart parade of 1879 to the birth of the culture industry in the Viennese operettas and the industrial aestheticization of practical objects in the Wiener Werkstätte. While the genres and forms of the objects of institutionalized art—the domain of high culture—were undergoing the radical transformations associated with classical modernism, artistic considerations spread into other spheres of social activity, populating the world with consumer objects and replacing traditional patterns of identity formation, including political consciousness. The result included social movements like Christian Socialism and Austro-Marxism, organized to administer the new expanses of an aestheticized social sphere.

To the extent that turn-of-the-century Vienna includes aesthetic innovation (Klimt, Kokoschka) as well as ubiquitous aestheticization (Makart, interior design), it anticipates both the modernist and the postmodernist positions in the contemporary critical discussion. Hence part of its cultural fascination today. To the extent however that Vienna points to the collapse of a liberal rationality and political identity, it dovetails with the political hypothesis already described. For the various political proposals for Central Europe as an alternative to East or West or whatever suggest, especially in the twentieth-century, that Central Europe is the carrier of a special cultural mission, contrasted with, for example, an empty rationalism or an atomistic individualism or an anticultural barbarism ascribed to other political units. One might even say that the very notion of culture as a discrete, venerated, and somehow redemptive domain of human activity is a specifically Central European product, a product of various Central European aspirations. It is this cultural substance, legitimating the mission of a political Central Europe, that might have been under scrutiny in the exhibits of fascinating Vienna.

The Politics of Neutrality

The political attention currently being paid to the notion of Central European autonomy is largely a result of the West German peace movement and the debates over the stationing of the cruise and Pershing missiles. Because these matters have received considerable public attention in recent years, a short version will suffice. In a speech in London in 1977, West German Chancellor Helmut Schmidt pointed out a growing strategic imbalance in Europe. Given the numerical superiority of the Warsaw Pact conventional forces as well as the presence of the Soviet medium-range nuclear missiles (SS-20s), the United States would be able to resist a hypothetical Soviet invasion of Western Europe only by relying on its intercontinental nuclear potential.

In other words, the military balance would force the United States to escalate a local European conflict into a global nuclear war. Yet strong political pressures would make any American president reluctant to risk a Soviet retaliatory attack on American cities simply in order to defend the allies in Western Europe. Therefore the American claim to defend Western Europe would lose its credibility unless an alternative, a model of flexible response, were instituted in the form of middle-range nuclear missiles for NATO. Such missiles would, so the argument went, allow for a defense of Western Europe without attacking the territory of the Soviet Union from North American launching sites.

In 1979, NATO adopted the so-called double decision, the program of deploying these middle-range missiles starting in 1983 unless the other track of the double decision, the pursuit of negotiations in Geneva, turned out to be successful. From the start, the double decision was extraordinarily controversial, especially in West Germany, where the left could argue that the new missiles implied the possibility of a nuclear conflict that would be played out solely on German territory. Flexible response appeared to be less a defense against a Soviet invasion than a temptation for American strategists to launch a first-strike attack, since, in the eyes of the West German left, the major threat to peace was not Moscow but Washington. This perception was of course heightened after the presidential election of 1980 and the commencement of the Reagan administration with its thinking-out-loud about winning a nuclear war, and the debate was embittered by a sense of persecution: according to some West German commentators, one or the other or both superpowers looked forward to a limited war precisely because it could be waged in Germany. The critique of the missiles therefore slid easily into a vision of encirclement, which in turn generated calls for a German national or Central European resistance to the threat from abroad, especially from the United States.

Despite the burgeoning of the largest mass protest movement in postwar German history, the missiles were continued to be stationed since the end of 1983. This development has to be seen in the light of two larger factors: the decline in the doctrine of nuclear deterrence, with its critics on the left and on the right, and the thorough collapse of détente between the superpowers during most of the Reagan era. As long as a peaceful coexistence seemed possible, the division of Europe inherited from the Yalta Conference had at least the virtue of keeping the European peace. Yet as real belligerence and verbal sparring increasingly marred international relations in the early eighties, the massive stationing of American and Russian troops in Central Europe came to look more and more like a tinderbox waiting to explode. This perception was strengthened by every characteristic foreign policy move of the Reagan administration: support for the Nicaraguan Contras, the invasion of Grenada, the insistence on SDI, the bombing of Libya, and the renunciation of SALT-II. The result was that in West Germany (and in Great Britain) the Reagan administration successfully produced political opposition movements eager to dissolve NATO and explore various models of European neutrality.

The rejection of American foreign policy and NATO was incorporated into the platform of the Green party and strongly colored the new program of the Social Democrats. Even conservative politicians began to complain about the imbalance in the Atlantic alliance.[7] Yet more important than these specific examples was the reopening of a fundamental foreign policy debate in the Federal Republic, a reexamination of the Western orientation, the German national question, and the status of Germany in Europe.

Figures as diverse as the editor of *Der Spiegel,* Rudolf Augstein, the filmmaker Werner Herzog, and the neutralists Löser and Schilling called for a new German patriotism.[8] To some extent this was of course another case of West Germany imitating contemporary American developments, even though it was a patriotism directed primarily against American foreign policy. It was however not directed against the neighboring European states. On the contrary, the resurgence of the German national question was generally linked to models for a neutral sphere in Central Europe. Among the competing—and often overlapping—proposals, one can differentiate (1) an ecological-fundamentalist opposition to all state structures, a position that is susceptible to cooptation by the right-wing populism of the so-called national revolutionaries, and (2) the relatively realpolitical efforts by the parliamentary fraction of the Greens to promote détente and thereby indirectly to contribute to a diminishment of European tensions. It is however a third position which is most interesting in this context: drawing on the rediscovery of the German national question by the New Left, proposals emerged advocating a nonaligned, neutral, and demilitarized zone in Central Europe to be achieved by a process including a peace treaty between the allies of the Second World War and Germany; this already implies the next step, the constitution of a German government, usually envisioned as a confederation of the two

German states; and finally a confederation of Central European states. Thus in 1984, Otto Schily proposed a Central European Peace Union to include the two Germanys, Austria, Czechoslovakia, Hungary, Poland, the Netherlands, Belgium, and Denmark. Löser and Schilling added Rumania, Yugoslavia, and Luxemburg. Their long-term goal is an autonomous "Europe of states between the Urals and the Atlantic," recalling the peace movement's slogan of a nuclear-free zone "between Poland and Portugal."[9]

The arguments for Central European neutrality have to do with the avoidance of a superpower confrontation and the self-determination of the European peoples. The arguments against neutrality point to the long-term strategic consequence—the diminished American presence, the strengthening of the Soviet military position, and a possible "Finlandization" of Central and Western Europe. The advocates of neutrality in turn reject this term as a cold war myth. Their proposed revisions of the geopolitical status of Europe include bitter attacks on what is called "Social Democratic status quo politics," the alleged colonization of the Federal Republic by the United States, and Adenauer's historical tilt to the West in the postwar period. Löser and Schilling look even further back, calling for a combination of Bismarck's accommodation with Russia and Stresemann's European perspective of Locarno. Elsewhere a rapprochement with the East has been discussed in terms of a "new Rapallo." These competing references indicate both the fluidity of the contemporary discussion of German national identity and, perhaps more important, the embeddedness of this contemporary discussion in an extensive history of considerations of German territorial organization in relation to Central European politics. The point is not that the advocates of neutrality or a German confederation are simply repeating positions familiar at least since the establishment of a unified German nation-state, but that their proposals derive from a long-standing tradition and similar strategic considerations. It is therefore useful to recall some of their precursors.

Denouncing Adenauer's opting for a "small" West Germany rather than a neutral and reunified state and, at the same time, calling for some sort of Central European confederation between East and West, the contemporary proponents of neutrality echo similar critics of the Bismarckian small-German solution that produced the modern German nation-state by excluding the erstwhile other German country, nineteenth-century Austria. Some of the arguments of one of the leading *grossdeutsche* publicists of the 1870s, Constantin Frantz, sound remarkably familiar. Consider first the geopolitical claim: Bismarck's small Germany—today one would say "divided Germany"—played into the hands of a great power, czarist Russia, whose expansionist drive could have been blocked only by a confederation of Germany and Austro-Hungary.[10] This argument is probably specious and historically untenable; it is cited only as an anticipation of contemporary claims that a German confederation could diminish superpower influence in Central Europe.

Second, in terms of domestic politics, Frantz asserted that the small-German solution in the form of a Prussianized Germany necessarily led to a centralized and militaristic state. His confederate alternative implied a decentralized military, since each of the German principalities would have retained its own army. While the result might be a technically less effective defense system, a general demilitarization and a decline in international tensions would likely follow.[11] Again, a certain affinity to the contemporary neutrality discussion is unmistakable: European peace through Central European confederation.

Frantz lodged his vision in the standard antiliberalism of the 1870s (the same antiliberalism which, according to Schorske, propelled Viennese modernism). This antiliberalism included a hostility to Enlightenment individuality and civil libertarian legislation (today's "human rights"); a rejection of laissez-faire capitalism in the name of corporativist economic structures; and, related by image and innuendo to the two other aspects, a conservative anti-Semitism. Instead of Bismarck's centralized small Germany, Frantz advocated a genuine *Reich,* a term he used to indicate both an internal particularist differentiation and a potentially expansionist dissolution of external borders. While other nations, indebted to Roman law, might culminate in statist organizations, the properly German political form included both regional autonomy and universalist claims. Such a *Reich* finally has a special historical role, as Frantz puts it: "Germany shall become the real foundation for the whole European peace system and for the gradual establishment of a European confederation, which will find its model in the German confederation. Not for nothing does Germany lie in the middle of Europe; and it is therefore predestined to become the general mediator."[12]

Frantz clearly walks a thin line between a neutral internationalism and a chauvinist expansionism; here the former is probably an alibi for the latter. The constellation of antiliberalism and political confederalism reappeared decades later in a somewhat different form, when

Bismarck's German *Nationalpolitik* had been transformed into an imperialist Wilhelmine *Weltpolitik*. As early as the 1890s, one finds the social reformer Friedrich Naumann, for example, reproducing the same ambivalence noted in Frantz's European speculations. In the "National Social Catechism" of 1896, Naumann defines his concept of "the national" as "the drive of the German people to spread its influence across the globe," but he soon links this sort of expansionism to a defensive strategy of "gathering the middle powers so that the world powers do not strangle everything." [13] The world powers were of course England and Russia.

While Frantz described his model of regional decentralization with reference to the medieval *Reich*, Naumann urges his *reichsdeutsche* compatriots to learn from the federalism of the Austrian model. The program of an alliance of "middle powers" comes to mean a political organization of the nationalities of Central Europe, an extrapolation of the Austro-Hungarian arrangement. It must be loose enough to respect local autonomy but cohesive enough to resist the pressure of the hostile encirclement of 1914. In Naumann's words:

> This is *Weltpolitik:* participation in the emergent international system. The German people does not want to be pushed aside in this process. It does not want to leave the regulation of human organization on land and sea to the syndicate of the old colonizers; it does not want to be isolated and crushed between Romans and Slavs; it therefore must defend itself and therefore sends its sons into battle, fearing nothing, sacrificing all. [14]

A fairly typical and not especially egregious example of the enthusiasm at the outbreak of the First World War, the passage emphasizes the image of Germany "between Romans and Slavs," between West and East. The image will remain crucial for the reconstitutions of German national identity and for the geopolitical discussion of Germany's role in Central Europe as the defender of local particularity against superpower empires. For it is Naumann himself, in his book *Mitteleuropa* (1915), who introduces the term Central Europe as a political rather than merely geographical concept, the confederation of Central European states against the alien threat on both fronts: "After this war we will be able to move mountains. Now or never will we establish a unity of East and West, Mitteleuropa, between Russia and the Western powers." [15]

Naumann's geopolitical project was intimately tied to a specific

economic program, the moderate anticapitalism of the Christian Social movement, and his model of a Central European confederation
tended necessarily to include certain distinctive domestic features. In
order to facilitate a multinational political organization, Naumann
recognized the importance of conceding a good deal of local autonomy, especially in matters of culture, such as education and religion.
A European mosaic of regional nationalities however implied a premodern resistance to secularization and cultural differentiation within
any given local community. Thus Naumann specifically rejects the notion of an international culture of modernity, the abstract "railway
man." [16] Confederation apparently amounts to a collection of conservative and parochial groupings, marked by the same hostility to liberal
individualism that Frantz had expressed.

This cultural conservative antiliberalism becomes particularly
problematic in the case of the Jewish population. Because they were
by and large still untouched by Zionism, the Jews were the only European ethnic group (with the exception of the Gypsies) who lacked a
specific territorial orientation. Thus they were the likely carriers of a
genuine Central European mentality, just as in Austro-Hungary they
tended to be particularly attracted to the multinational concept rather
than to local nationalisms. Yet precisely because Naumann envisions
a *Mitteleuropa* organized around local cultural autonomy, he cannot
recognize the Jews as a genuine cultural community, urging them instead to choose a host culture into which they could assimilate. He
defines the Jewish question as a social rather than a national question,
a position which is especially problematic, since his political program
foresees an empowerment of nationalities rather than social groups,
let alone individuals. [17]

The antiliberalism and anti-Semitism inherent in Naumann's Central European confederation are compounded by an antidemocratic
structural feature. Given the wide range of political cultures in the
Central European area, stretching from liberal aspirations in the West
to nearly feudal conditions in the East, Naumann is reluctant to establish a central parliamentary organ. For that would imply a shift toward electoral democracy bound to frighten off the conservative participants. Therefore Naumann proposed a confederation that would
manage its shared economic and foreign policy concerns through non-
elected commissions that would not even be responsible to an elected
legislature. Although he takes pains to apologize to the liberal-
democratic constituencies, it is evident that his version of *Mittel-*

europa necessitates a reduction of political culture to the least common denominator.[18] In practice, this would have meant a step back even from the minimal parliamentarianism of the German Empire, although it would have been compatible with Naumann's own economic corporativism. Frantz, by the way, made a similar move, when he complained that Bismarckian centralism transplanted Western political forms and imposed them onto the specificity of German conditions.[19] Underlying the argument is an indeed specifically German ideology that democratic institutions are characteristic expressions of a West European (Roman in other versions) culture that have no universal validity and, in particular, no organic resonance within the German context. Variants of this claim resurfaced after the First World War in conservative attacks on the Weimar Republic, allegedly foisted onto the Germans by the victors at Versailles; in left-wing arguments that the Federal Republic is a creature of Western machinations; and in the relativist neutrality of the former secretary-general of the United Nations, the proponent of the "Austrian Example," eager to point out that democracy is not a universal goal and that Western critiques of third-world dictatorships are therefore beside the point.[20]

Some of Naumann's ideas recur in the political thinking of Max Weber during the First World War, recently published in the new collected works. Especially in the crucial speech "Germany among the European World Powers," delivered in Munich on October 28, 1916, the features of a traditional discussion of German national identity and international relations become admirably clear. Like Naumann, Weber presents the German war effort as a matter of self-defense, thereby rejecting the attacks from the allied camp as well as from the emergent domestic antiwar movement. Yet, and again like Naumann, Weber devotes considerable energy to a denunciation of the expansionist fantasies of the Pan-German League, whose emotional politics, Weber fears, could ultimately harm the German national interest.

For Weber, that real national interest is, as for Frantz and Naumann, a consequence of Germany's geographical location in the center of the continent. Flanked by major powers in the East and the West, it will always have to pursue alliance policies in both directions, which will require a maximum of flexibility. If however Germany were to alienate one major power thoroughly, for example England through an annexation of Belgium, it would become thoroughly dependent on the other power, Russia, which is to say, fully subordinate. German national interest therefore implies preserving an autonomy from East and West, in order to maintain a perpetual competition between the rival powers.

In addition to this vision of Germany, in alliance with Austro-Hungary, as a neutral or third power between East and West, Weber insists on Germany's role as the defender of small nations against the hegemonic claims of a pan-Slavic Russia and the colonialist empires of France and England. Only Germany, as the largest of the Central European nations, will be able to provide "a counterbalance to the superpowers" and prevent a division of the entire world between the East and the West. Otherwise he predicts a sorry fate for humanity, destined to fall into the clutches of either "the boredom of Anglo-Saxon conventionality or the desolation of Russian bureaucracy."[21] While Frantz packaged his account in the antiliberalism of the 1870s and Naumann relied on the corporativism of Christian Socialism, Weber characteristically insisted on a political heroism. In his eyes, fate and geography had charged Germany with the duty of defending freedom, and Germany could not escape the challenge. If Germany refused its geopolitical role or if Germany had refused even to become a world power by resisting the unification of 1871, the Germans would still be trapped in the global conflict: "The states of the Rhine Confederation would be fighting for French interests, the others would have become a Russian satrapy or, as in the past, they would have provided the theater of war."[22] Thus unless Germany could assert its autonomy in between East and West, it would become the victim of both East and West. This argument, which Weber made seventy years ago, is proof enough that the contemporary discussion in the wake of the peace movement regarding NATO and neutrality represents a continuation of a traditional German foreign policy calculation and debate regarding the status of Germany in Europe.

In this account, East and West are treated as symmetrical evils, mirror-image superpowers threatening imperial domination. Weber of course understands that their political cultures are different, but the difference is ultimately irrelevant, since he conceptualizes German foreign policy—indeed the politics of any nation—as the pursuit of a central and undifferentiated national interest. Such a bilateral foreign policy, which would address the needs of Germans of the right and the left as members of the same nation, ought not to be contaminated by heterogeneous concerns, more appropriately handled in other contexts. Hence his insistence on an international perspective that is blind to any considerations of secondary values:

There have been times when some have been sympathetic to co-operation with England *because* they were liberal. Now that is over, once and for all. Similarly there have been parties which shamelessly flattered Russia *because* they were conservative.
. . . Men who mix their domestic antipathies into our policy in war and peace *are for me not national politicians,* and a genuine coalition with them is impossible. Our specific international position and our foreign interests alone should determine our foreign policy.[23]

As he does in discussions of cultural modernization, Weber here too insists on the separation of value spheres: the serious pursuit of foreign policy entails an exclusion of all other interests and concerns. Between East and West, Germany ought to consider only its international advantage and bracket any reflection on political values. The admonition presumes that an autonomous Germany could engage in shifting alliances with the flanking superpowers without gradually succumbing to either sphere of influence and without any consequences for its own domestic constitution. This assumption was probably already fallacious in 1916, and it has become more so in the intervening period.[24] The time is not at all over "once and for all" when German politicians linked foreign policy to domestic considerations, and this in turn is the link between Weber's reflections and the contemporary debate on neutrality. It remains to be seen however to what extent subsequent proponents of neutrality between East and West repeat Weber's decoupling of foreign policy from the alternative models of political culture.

As different as the accounts of Frantz, Naumann, and Weber may be, a set of characteristics emerges that seems to relate to their models of a neutral Central European political identity. The confederation notion appears at times to have an emancipatory character, to the extent that it promises to defend local particularity and the autonomy of weaker national communities. However, this emancipatory gesture is combined with authoritarian structures, the retreat from liberal and democratic principles tentatively established during the nineteenth century. The status of ethnic minorities remains ambiguous at best, and the very discourse of a place between East and West seems to be marked by a sense of persecution that it is apt to invert into an imperialist expansionism of its own.

Some of these negative features resurfaced after the First World War in the efforts of the Pan-Europa movement to revise the Treaty of Versailles on politically conservative terms.[25] To what extent do they reappear in the current neutrality discussion as well, given its efforts to revise the results of the Yalta Conference? The point is not to suggest that the contemporary positions are identical with those of Frantz, Naumann, and Weber, which are themselves very different from each other. Yet given a similar understanding of the East-West conflict, a similar invocation of the Austrian model, and a similar call for a Central European confederation centered in Germany, the possibility of a substantive continuity cannot be rejected out of hand.

The proponents of Central European neutrality claim to be eager to escape the reciprocal recriminations of cold war rhetoric. Yet one cannot help but find a curious asymmetry here, a reluctance to criticize the countries of the Warsaw Pact. For, as with Naumann, an advocate of confederation will tend to refuse to measure a local political culture by external standards. The pursuit of confederation necessitates a cultural relativism that resists judging political conditions in terms of universal norms. This agnosticism turns out to be compatible with the Weberian separation of geopolitical interests from alternative value spheres: European policy becomes ideally sequestered from an internal scrutiny of the individual European states. Consequently nondemocratic states cannot be criticized for a lack of democratic rights. In the contemporary literature on neutrality, one therefore finds trivializations of Western attacks on Soviet human rights violations, a position extraordinarily close to Frantz's antiliberalism. The human rights campaigns are treated as just so much propaganda, not worth pursuing since they only add to international tensions.[26]

This proclivity to self-censorship, which may already represent a sort of Finlandization of a neutral West Germany, was evident in the response to the declaration of martial law in Poland discussed in the previous chapter: because it was assumed that the Soviet Union could not longer afford to allow Solidarity to grow, Jaruzelski's coup was greeted as a guarantor of the European peace to the extent that it forestalled a Russian invasion. A neutral peace, it seems, would tend to include a high degree of tolerance for the repression of local oppositions.[27]

A similar reluctance to criticize the Soviet Union has generated heated debates in the West German writers' union.[28] It is worth noting that this extraordinary moderation of public criticism may not be only a result of an implicitly pro-Soviet sympathy or an inverted anti-

Americanism but a consequence of the neutrality model altogether. What does it mean to ask if parts of the West German left press are already acting as if they were in a neutral state? Would a declaration of neutrality, recognized in terms of established international law, have consequences for the freedom of the press and formally guaranteed civil rights?

It turns out that precisely this question has been raised in the literature on the Austrian example, which, as has already been pointed out, is frequently cited as a model for a future neutral Central European confederation. A standard interpretation, *The Permanent Neutrality of the Republic of Austria* by Alfred Verdross, insists that the legal neutrality of a state does not necessarily mean the neutrality of the press. Nor does it necessarily restrict the freedom of opinions of the citizenry. This principle was underscored in a declaration of the Austrian government of October 26, 1955. Yet while the law of neutrality does not directly impinge on the press, it does oblige the government to protect the general policy of neutrality by taking domestic measures to ensure that the state will not be dragged into foreign conflicts. This could therefore imply a regulation of public debate, so as to prevent any possibility of the erosion of impartiality in the case of international disputes. Thus Verdross: "As a matter of principle, a permanently neutral state itself has to decide what measures are to be taken in order to lend credibility to its neutrality and to protect it against internal and external dangers. During the Second World War, Switzerland, for instance, imposed certain restrictions on the press in order not to be dragged into the war through a one-sided attitude on the part of the press." [29] One presumes therefore that a neutral Germany, modeled after Austria (which was explicitly modeled after Switzerland), would be eager to prevent its press from adopting a one-sided attitude on, for example, the question of human rights in Eastern Europe. The bitter critique of the Western press expressed by the Austrian president, a strong advocate of neutrality, confirms this conjecture. [30] It is as if some Central Europeans would be prepared to adopt the quip by Bismarck which Weber quotes in the speech discussed above: "Eventually every land is after all responsible for the windows broken by its press." [31]

It appears then that the contemporary advocates of neutrality for Germany and/or Central Europe do in fact inherit a good deal of the legacy of the Central European discourse of the past: a vacillation on liberal civil rights, a resounding silence on the question of Soviet Jews (an issue of such central importance to the French left), extremely limited support for the democratic movement in Poland, and a pro-phylactic self-censorship in public debate. It is as if the culture of neu-trality already anticipated the likely consequences of an American re-treat and the extension of Soviet hegemony into a nonaligned Central Europe. For the neutrality of Central Europe could be effective only if it were armed to the teeth—Germany is not comparable to neutral Switzerland with its natural topographical defense—something none of the advocates of confederation propose. Can a hypothetical Central Europe substitute for its absent military prowess a sort of cultural legitimacy that would guarantee the loyalty of its citizens? For Weber precisely such a cultural identity motivated the sacrificial devotion of the German soldiers to the imperial state in the First World War.[32] Historically, Central Europe has often claimed to be a privileged vessel of culture, and turn-of-the-century Vienna was perhaps its center. Is there a viable culture of neutrality today—or is the discourse of neu-trality itself a symptom of a cultural crisis?

Central Europe and Culture

In the introduction to the Vienna catalogue, Schorske provides a vivid example of the tensions in late nineteenth-century Austria by exam-ining the transformation of the representation of culture in some of Klimt's most famous paintings.[33] The depiction of the interior of the Burgtheater of 1888/89 is executed with a moderate historical realism, proof of the early Klimt's surprising proximity to the work of Makart. One looks into the public along a slightly diagonal line from the stage to the back of the hall. The construction of the tiers of balconies, shrinking toward the background, emphasizes the depth perspective, and the ornamental decoration of the ceiling is clearly detailed. The audience is gathering for a performance, and the formal attire as well as the stern demeanors hardly conveys any particularly electric excite-ment. It is indisputably a rather stiff crowd, the representative public of the liberal "founding years" growing old, with none of the Diony-sian enthusiasm which would soon characterize the young modernists, including Klimt himself.

However, the ultimate architectural monument of liberal nine-teenth-century culture lay elsewhere, in the new university building on the Ringstrasse, the splendid home for Enlightenment rationality, scientific exactitude, and an unbroken faith in human progress. Although opened in 1883, its most highly symbolic feature, the representation of the disciplines on the ceiling of the auditorium, was not completed until the new century had begun.

Schorske provides a detailed account of the controversy that followed the unveiling of Klimt's painting of "Philosophy" in 1900. It outraged the liberal public and the rationalists on the university faculty, for it audaciously gave expression to a new culture of aesthetic irrationalism that seemed to contradict the taste and all the cultural values of the middle-class establishment. The clarity of Renaissance perspective has been abandoned, ambiguous shapes float mysteriously in and out of a glowing darkness, and mythic figures loom out of a starry sky. Here is Schorske's description:

> Everything earthly has disappeared, dissolved into a dark and infinite cosmos, which seems to melt together the immeasurable expanse of the heavens and the cloudy obscurity of hell. A confusion of bodies of suffering humanity slowly passes by, aimlessly spread throughout the viscous emptiness. Out of this cosmic twilight arises an indifferent Sphinx, itself a concentration of atomized space. Only at the very bottom of the picture is there a suggestion of a thinking spirit—Klimt called it "Knowledge." [34]

The distance between the two paintings, *The Burgtheater* of 1888 and *Philosophy* of 1900, epitomizes the transformation of Austrian culture in the period and indicates the primary connotation of the label "fin-de-siècle Vienna." The nineteenth-century tradition deriving from the Enlightenment seems to come to an end, displaced by modernist inquiries into ambiguity, psychological interiority, and the irrationality of myth. Whether this rupture was indeed the end of the Enlightenment *tout court* or, alternatively, a consequence of the Enlightenment or even a radical reformulation and extension of the Enlightenment—and arguments can be made for all of these positions—is for the moment less important than the fact that this rupture was lived as a radical break, a generational conflict in which the modernist progeny turned their backs on a rationalist legacy, denounced, emphatically enough, as the culture of the fathers.

While the secessionist painters and the writers of Young Vienna treated the culture of the turn of the century as a temporal novum— i.e., the transition from a nineteenth century of reason to a subjectivist modernity—elsewhere the same antinomy was spread across an ahistorical terrain. Vienna, or more generally, Austria, became identified as the authentic locus of aesthetic culture, a southern utopia contrasted with the dry rationality of a Prussian north. For example, Naumann eagerly invoked this topos in his argument for a *Mitteleuropa* organized around a confederation of Germany and Austro-Hungary. While Berlin can provide technical know-how and a disciplined work ethic, it must turn to Vienna for taste and aesthetic refinement. Only such a Central European combination of talents would encompass a complete culture able to produce what the practical Naumann has on his mind: attractively designed industrial goods able to compete successfully on the international market. *Mitteleuropa* will not be able to survive economically unless it incorporates Austrian art:

> We [Germans] have more horse-power and you [the Austrians] have more melody. We think more in quantities, the best of you in qualities. Let us join together both of our abilities, so that the real neo-German culture will, thanks to your help, take on the touch of gracefulness that will make it palatable abroad.[35]

An interesting variation on Naumann's wartime plea to combine German technology and Austrian art is present in the essays of his contemporary Hugo von Hofmannsthal, writing as a propagandist of the Imperial War Ministry in Vienna. Like Naumann, Hofmannsthal insists on the north-south differential and the aesthetic privilege of Austria. Yet while Naumann's goal is to use cultural arguments to bolster his program for a Central European alliance, Hofmannsthal is eager to insist on the specificity of the Austrian contribution to the combined war effort. Germany will not be able to establish a stable political regime unless its military predominance on the continent is coupled with a cultural component. Thus Hofmannsthal: "Austria is the special duty of the German spirit within Europe. She is the field, appointed by history, of a purely cultural imperialism. . . . Austria must be recognized again and again as the *German duty in Europe*."[36]

Both Naumann and Hofmannsthal identify Austria as the specific carrier of Central European culture, but for the latter "culture" is much more than the cultivation of industrial design. It is rather the domain of the "spirit," the insistence on the priority of intellectual, aesthetic, and religious values, without which any political community will remain fundamentally labile. Hofmannsthal's "cultural imperialism" is therefore the medium with which the Austrian Empire has been able to stabilize (or so Hofmannsthal thinks) a multinational confederation under German hegemony. It turns out that Austrian culture is not just a local variation of other national cultures. The term "Austrian culture" has a much more emphatic significance. It means the absolute priority of a specifically cultural dimension over the secondary concerns of politics, the economy, and the military, and such a cultural privileging appears to be the prerequisite for the establishment of a coherent Central European confederation of nations.

Interestingly enough, Weber too insists on the crucial role of cultural legitimation, which does not eclipse political considerations but certainly overshadows economic factors, an aspect he deemphasizes as much in the 1916 speech as in his earlier study of the Protestant ethic. Yet now the geographical polarity undergoes an inversion. In Weber's eyes, Austro-Hungary is crippled by the lack of a uniform culture, a point he illustrates with reference to the situation of a German-speaking officer who shares no common language with the multinational soldiers under his command.[37] In contrast, it is now Germany that derives its strength from the vitality of its culture, in Weberian terms: the unity between the state, i.e., the political apparatus, and the nation, understood as the carrier of cultural identity.

While this unity between state and nation provided Germany, according to Weber, with a cultural consistency and a superiority over its enemies in the First World War, soon after the war, Thomas Mann appropriated precisely the same argument, the unity between state and nation as the source of culture, in order to defend the young Weimar Republic against its domestic opponents. Rebutting conservative groups who insisted that democracy was a foreign system, forced onto Germany by the Treaty of Versailles, Mann attempted to outline a specifically German version of democratic government, which he labeled "the German Republic." Thus he contrasts the republic with the Wilhelmine empire, judged inadequate because it excluded the nation from participating in affairs of the state, and then he proceeds to contrast it as well with genuinely foreign political forms, located in the by now familiar alternatives, East and West. In the Russian East, whether czarist or Bolshevik, he sees a penchant for mystical despotism, where the inaccessible state stands far above society and the individual disappears into the disenfranchised mass. He locates a diametrical opposite in the democratic West, where however the extreme atomization of capitalist self-interest ultimately prevents the individual from a genuine entry into a vital community. It is in the end only in Germany where state and nation, the individual and the collective, private values and public virtues coexist in a synthesis guaranteeing authentic humanity and culture. The German Republic, Mann argues, is the political expression of this synthesis.[38]

None of these different early twentieth-century conceptualizations of culture has immediate and direct significance today: too much history has intervened, and too radical metamorphoses have marked the collection of objects and practices called "culture." Nevertheless this intellectual-historical background indicates a constellation of questions within which the contemporary discussion of a Central European cultural identity is unfolding. Because reflections on the construction of German national identity intersect with visions of the East and the West, whenever the German question is raised the problem of *Mitteleuropa* is likely to follow soon. Because this *Mitteleuropa* lacks both dynastic continuity and ethnic homogeneity, it cannot rely for its legitimation on a monolinear historical narrative. Central Europe is no sceptered isle. Culture becomes the substitute, the stand-in for a really-existing political confederation as well as the motivation to bring one into being. This connection partially explains the special role played by cultural intellectuals and literary developments in recent formulations of Central European identity.

Certainly the neutrality discussion commenced as the response to a precise political event, the NATO double decision of 1979. Yet that single event could not have led to a reaction on the scale of the West German peace movement unless it touched deep cultural nerves. This cultural prefiguration can be found in the so-called *Tendenzwende,* the cultural turn, of the mid-seventies.[39] The *Tendenzwende* is in fact in many ways reminiscent of the new culture of fin-de-siècle Vienna, and it is perhaps no accident that it is precisely in this period that the West German reading public began to direct more of its attention to the Austrian literary scene, still partially embedded in the traditions of the early part of the century. One thinks of the proximity of the work of writers like Peter Handke and Thomas Bernhard to the language games of Wittgenstein.

In a rash of articles that began to appear around 1974, a single paradigm appeared repeatedly in many variations. The culture of the student movement of the sixties, allegedly marked by Enlightenment reason, political engagement, and aesthetic realism, was declared bankrupt. Its refusal to consider individual histories and emotional experience desiccated its literature, which was henceforth to be replaced by a different sort of text, given the label of the "new subjectivity." Whether this shift implied a retreat from politics into a quietistic privacy or, as feminists for example could argue, an extension of politics into a personal sphere is not of concern here. Nor does the dubious reduction of the sixties to radical reason, a description that omits all the extravagance of the counterculture, bear on the present argument. The issue is solely that a cultural program was launched which combined an explicit preference for irrationality with a fascination for personal identity understood as an original substance, prior to any social or historical mediations. I have therefore written about the *Tendenzwende* in terms of a "discourse of authenticity."[40]

It is this version of identity, grounded in an unquestionable personal specificity and constantly besieged by the threatening forces of external mediation, which provided the cultural prefiguration for the political response to the NATO double decision. After nearly a decade of a narcissistic insistence on private identity, the political context induced a collectivization of the discourse of authenticity, a transition from personal subjectivity to national identity. This particular psychological predisposition explains the peculiar formulations of the West German peace movement which, when compared with the parallel development in the United States, initially paid less attention to the natural scientific experts and their concerns regarding the ecological consequences of nuclear war than to a purported existential threat to the survival of German national identity. Ultimately it was therefore the subjectivist bias in the German movement, derived from literary culture, that pushed it toward a reexamination of the German question and from there to neutrality and Central Europe.

This transition from individual to national subjectivity also had literary ramifications. While the private personality cult of the seventies was accompanied by a wave of private forms—personal histories, autobiographical memoirs, accounts of family life—authors have more recently begun to present narratives of national history. Unlike the literature on the German past from the sixties, which focused on "uncovering" the Nazi past in order to differentiate the present from it or to denounce any unquestioned continuities (Böll's *Billiards at Half Past Ten*), more recent historical fiction insists on continuities with the German past with the goal of examining the specificity of the national culture. Thus Grass's *Meeting at Telgte* transposes contemporary questions into the seventeenth century, at the conclusion of the Thirty Years War. Similar shifts might be traced in the visual media from the still-engaged political melodramas of Fassbinder in the early seventies to the repeated thematization of national history and identity in recent years, most notably in the television series "*Heimat.*"

The point is not that all this material is terribly nationalistic (some of it is) but that the national question has come to be addressed with increasing frequency in literature and film. Just as the recent series of international exhibits indicates how turn-of-the-century Austria has displaced an earlier interest in the Weimar Republic, within Germany the earlier literature of memory, coming to terms with the events of the Third Reich, has been pushed aside by an interest in collective identity. These two shifts in matters of public interest are of course just two sides of the same question which used to be formulated with dramatic brevity: "What is German?"[41]—either the particularity of small nation-states or the aspiration for European hegemony. This ambivalence recurs throughout the literature of recent years and even marks the reading habits of the West German public which has begun to turn more and more to other German-speaking countries for its texts, not only Austria but East Germany and Switzerland as well, whose authors are read especially for their regional identity: culture provides the Central European unity which politics have failed to achieve.

One can therefore not be surprised when one encounters authors taking a leading role in the discussion of German or Central European identity. Literary developments have determined the direction of recent debates, and many of the arguments for a revision of the Yalta Conference and the creation of a Central European confederation have to do with claims regarding the specificity of European culture. Yet the arguments current in the political arena, the various proposals to redraw the map of Europe, are much more radical than the positions articulated by literary figures, most of whom seem relatively cautious. This differential is particularly apparent in the case of Peter Schneider, whose *Wall Jumper* was praised by Werner Herzog as a sign of a "new patriotism," as if Schneider were the proponent of a neo-nationalism. Herzog's extraordinary misreading misses the point fully. Schneider is certainly the case in point of the writer who moved from the new subjectivism of personal identity in *Lenz* to a discussion of German national identity, but despite Herzog's judgment, he does not conclude with an invocation of a Germanic revival. On the contrary, *The Wall Jumper* locates the particularity of German identity precisely in its divided character; the unified Bismarckian state represents the exception, not the norm, in German history. It is difficult to see how the establishment of an umbrella state in Central Europe, the core of which would necessarily be a reunified Germany, would guarantee either personal freedom or cultural vitality, both of which would more likely be crushed. A cultural discussion is all that links the two German states, but the political division remains indelible, perhaps the most salient feature of German identity. It is a legacy of history that cannot be wiped away without doing an injustice to the same national specificity the advocates of neutrality purport to defend.

Like Peter Schneider, an East German author, Rolf Schneider, also views the efforts to revise the political organization of Central Europe with an adamant skepticism. Because he insists that the division of Germany was not an arbitrary imposition by foreign powers but the consequence of German history itself—Hitler's war of aggression—he criticizes the German efforts to establish a Central European confederation for ignoring the real legacy of national history as well as urgent contemporary political projects that are sacrificed to the pursuit of the mirage of neutrality. In addition, he denounces the myth of a Central European mission, proof enough that the historical material discussed above, the cult of a *Mitteleuropa,* retains some currency among the proponents of neutrality. Central Europe was never a peaceful zone of mediation between north and south, east and west; on the contrary it was the expression of the hegemonic claims of the German elite of the Wilhelmine empire and Austro-Hungary, based on

> a racial doctrine of the biological superiority of the Germanic peoples. These dreams of omnipotence were shared by the Saxon Richard Wagner and the Hohenzollern Kaiser Wilhelm II, the Austrian knight von Schönerer and the mayor of Vienna Karl Lueger. In the person of Adolf Hitler, born on the German-Austrian border, this doctrine turned violent and swept all of Europe into a catastrophe. We still live in its wake. Whoever is nurturing Central European phantasies continues these rotten myths. I think it would be better if they stopped.[42]

For Peter Schneider, Germany's identity depends on its division, around which a cultural discussion could form. For Rolf Schneider, the division of Germany represents the defeat of National Socialism and therefore the prerequisite for any desirable cultural activity. While the political arguments for confederation are most articulate in Germany—they are barely found elsewhere, since only in Germany do

international borders seem to have a provisional character—the literary elite is most skeptical. The strongest cultural argument for the
notion of a Central Europe consequently is made by a Czech author,
for whom Yalta is not a result of a national guilt. Yet even for Milan
Kundera, there is no original Central Europe, only an East and a West,
heirs to the ancient division of the Roman Empire. Central Europe is,
if anything, a product of Yalta, the surrender of the border territories
of the West to the domination of the East, the character of which owes
more to the legacy of traditional czarist despotism than to modern
Soviet communism. Composed of the successor states of the Hapsburg
Empire—Czechoslovakia, Poland, and Hungary—Central Europe
tragically emerges as a specific region only at the historical moment
when it is separated from the West to which it historically belonged
and subjected to a foreign control bent on the eradication of the local
cultures.[43]

According to Peter Schneider, the notion of an undivided Central
European culture is an impossibility; for Rolf Schneider, it is an un-
desirable program to revive an imperialist German project; for Kundera, Central European culture operates only in the mode of reminis-
cence. The Soviet Union pursues a policy of destroying the culture of
the small European nations, and the West, the original home of the
specific sensibility he values as "culture," has abandoned its commitment and entered a postcultural phase of postmodernity. Weber's pre-
diction in 1916 appears to have come true: a world divided between
"the boredom of Anglo-Saxon conventionality" and "the desolation
of Russian bureaucracy," but the quandary is felt more direly in the
Czechoslovakian exile than in the two Germanys, each comfortably
integrated into its respective block.

If culture is incompatible with either of the superpowers, neither
does Kundera locate it in a populist national identity. The plausibility
of a grounding of culture in some ethnoracial identity ended with the
Third Reich, if not earlier, but rejecting that sort of irrationalism does
not necessarily allow for an easy return to the progressivist optimism
of the nineteenth century. The proponents of dialectical materialism
and socialist realism have taken care of that, and in any case, it would
entail giving up the culture of Viennese modernism which Kundera so
treasures as the final brilliance of Central Europe. The dilemma of
culture in postmodernity means the impossibility of either solution:
the inadequacy of any totalizing rationalism, always stifling and intolerable, as well as the evanescence of any regional specificity that

promises local identity only to disappear into the logic of domination. The oscillation between these nonpositions defines the motion of Kundera's prose, his narratives of desire that are never completed, since any conclusion would imply a closure inimical to the very project of modern culture, always existing at a penultimate moment, just before destruction. Such a definition of culture holds, more than anywhere else, in the Central European realm of Austro-Hungary, the cultural legacy of which has disappeared more from neutral Austria than even from the successor states in the Soviet sphere. Where has the culture of Austria, so vaunted in the recent exhibits, disappeared to? Perhaps we should ask the Austrian president.

The Case of Kurt W.

Instead of adding to the debate on the degree of Waldheim's legal culpability for war crimes, I want to inquire into the connection between the mobilization of anti-Semitism during the presidential election and the Vienna fascination, understood as a corollary to the renewed interest in Central Europe and the question of neutrality. The manifest connections are in fact so thick that one is tempted to speak of an overdetermination, in the Freudian sense of the word. The Austro-Hungarian Jews were the primary carriers of a multinational Central European loyalty, but precisely the effort to establish a Central European world power between East and West led to their annihilation as well as to the division of Central Europe at Yalta. While Waldheim himself has attributed his desire to pursue a diplomatic career to reminiscences of the multinational culture of the past, the National Socialist regime which he considered it his patriotic duty to serve dealt a final blow to the cultural vitality of Vienna and contributed to the final provincialization of Austria, a neutral dwarf state between East and West.[44] The centrality of anti-Semitism in Nazi ideology hardly needs to be pointed out; its virulence in the same turn-of-the-century Vienna which gave birth to the cultural wealth now making its way through the museums of the world is more significant. Waldheim is a direct heir to Lueger, both exponents of an Austrian political anti-Semitism framing the Vienna fascination.[45]

If there is a deeper connection between the Waldheim affair and the Vienna of 1900, it will not be found in any particular cultural preferences on the part of the Austrian president, who, as far as anyone can tell, has none.[46] It is more fruitful to approach the problem by paying close attention to Waldheim's own words and deeds within the context of the public debate in order to examine the psychological foundation for his political character. The explanation in his autobiography of his early interest in politics and diplomacy discloses a strong identification with postimperial Austria; he underscores how he was born in 1918, the same year as the "infant republic," described in a revealing manner as hopelessly weak: "Set adrift, its mighty parent dead, its expectations crushed, the new republic could not sustain itself."[47] Thus abandoned by its parent, the young state, onto which Waldheim projects his own psychological drama, becomes a victim of the threatening forces of a hostile world. The political content of the threat is clarified by a passage in the German text which was omitted from the English translation:

> At least since my fifteenth year, I have dreamed of becoming a diplomat. I thought this would give me the chance to serve my fatherland and to contribute to repairing the injustice done to my country. Like many of my generation, I considered the fate unjust that the allied powers decided for Austria after the fall of the monarchy.[48]

In political terms, Waldheim bases his career on a desire to revise the Treaty of St. Germain (the Austrian counterpart to the Treaty of Versailles for Germany), which implies a critique of the dismemberment of the Hapsburg Empire and of the territorial integrity of the successor states. In psychological terms, Waldheim recalls a personal and national trauma associated with the death of the "mighty parent" and the loss of the vital organs of the collective body.

In the case study of little Hans of 1909, Freud suggests that the fear of castration is the psychological root of anti-Semitism, a fear based unconsciously on the image of circumcision.[49] Given Waldheim's explanation of his original political motives (interestingly suppressed in the English version), it is noteworthy that the anti-Semitic rhetoric of the presidential campaign included a set of terms current in the right-wing stab-in-the-back propaganda against the political arrangements in Germany and Austria after the First World War: "infamous treachery" (of the World Jewish Congress), "dishonorable journeymen," etc. Thus the current political language borrows from an earlier right-wing radicalism that was itself a response to a trauma of personal and national impotence. In other words, the language of the Waldheim campaign against the World Jewish Congress is in many ways identical to the language of the post-1918 right-wing agitation against the treaties of Versailles and St. Germain, sharing the same fascination with international machinations and Jewish treachery as threats to national cohesion.

The psychological derivation from a fear of castration is confirmed by two further pieces of evidence. The many Austrian justifications for Waldheim's participation in the war in the Balkans indulged in extensive accounts of brutal atrocities allegedly commited by the Yugoslav partisans, including the repeated claim that the partisans regularly cut off the genitals of the German soldiers.[50] The popular imagination could therefore defend any activity by the soldier Waldheim as a sort of defensive gesture against the threat of dismemberment. Waldheim himself resorted to a similarly motivated claim, exaggerating the importance of the leg wound he received on the Russian front. In an early version, he returned to Vienna because of the wound and was therefore no longer involved in the war. Later, faced with new documents, he changed the story but still pointed to the scar: it was the wound that prevented him from participating in genuine fighting on the front and restricted him to office work.

The leg wound is an old topos: the scar of Odysseus, Jacob's struggle with the angel, some figures in Kafka. It evidently represents a displacement of circumcision, the ritual scar of the male and the sign of Jewish identity.[51] Waldheim's insistence on the wound betrays a conscious effort to exculpate himself and an unconscious admission of his fixation on a threat to his personal and national identity, a threat he associates with Jews who are so dangerous not only because of the international network of power Waldheim ascribes to them but because he can barely separate himself from them. His lapsus in his unsuccessful 1971 Austrian presidential campaign is symptomatic: "I must decisively reject the accusations that I am a National Socialist or even a Jew."[52] In the 1986 campaign, the same identification with international Jewry on the part of Waldheim was evident in the choice of the theme song "New York, New York," a symbol that mixed the boasting of the former secretary-general with cynicism, nostalgia, and resentment. Waldheim's memory functions well, but only through displacement, and he is therefore terrified of the placeless eternal wanderer, his *Doppelgänger,* his patriarch, flesh of his flesh, too close for comfort for a labile psyche. The Jew appears to exercise hypertrophic strength because the political anti-Semite, traumatized by a profound sense of helplessness, has been unable to construct an autonomous personality capable of independent decisions. The subjective ego weakness is fertile ground for violent fantasies and images of persecution: it is Waldheim, and not the Jews, who is the victim. The eternal child is in constant danger. Only a "mighty parent" might protect the "infant republic," victimized by the Western powers, but the parent is dead, and the son responds to this abandonment with melancholic resentment rather than with mourning.

This resentment first turned up in the rhetoric of the 1971 campaign which the supporters of Waldheim enacted as a generational conflict, the rebellion of the son against the father. Thus Waldheim promises to be a "president of a new style" who will bring about "a modern Austria," while his opponent, the incumbent President Franz Jonas, is derided as "a representative of the old system." Waldheim is "dynamic" and had "initiative," and, above all, he is "not yet ready for retirement." In contrast, the aged Jonas is allegedly "a lover of ceremonies," "dependent on Kreisky," the socialist chancellor, and tainted by party loyalties, unlike Waldheim, who stands above the party differences inherited from the past.[53]

The youthful challenger is therefore the agent of innovation, even though he is conservative, while the paternal incumbent defends the established status quo, even though he is a socialist. The attack on the "system" is both a repetition of the Nazi language of the twenties and a symptom of the weak personality structure: the son fears the all-encompassing system of the father rather than any particular policy issue. In the language of the campaign, genuine political differences were displaced by an oedipal drama, which however was not enough to win the election for Waldheim. The 1971 rhetoric of generational conflict is nevertheless significant because it echoes the experience of cultural modernity in turn-of-the-century Vienna and, more germane, because it anticipates the 1986 campaign which the unattractive candidate was able to win so resoundingly only by directing public attention away from internal Austrian disputes and toward the alleged threat of international intervention in Austrian affairs. In 1971 he attacked the old socialist Jonas; in 1986 he attacked the elders of Zion, in Waldheim's words, "the World Jewish Congress, Herr Singer, Herr Steinberg, Herr Rosenbaum."[54] In 1971 his campaign complained that the major political offices in Austria were controlled by socialists; in 1986, the argument was changed into the allegation that the world press was controlled by a Jewish mafia, which Waldheim opposed in the name of a Christian *Weltanschauung* and a moral rearmament.[55]

The vision of persecution and encirclement has undergone an extraordinary distortion and magnification, based on an oedipal imagery of the overwhelming power of a conspiracy of Jewish patriarchs.

The unattractive candidate Waldheim probably opted for this strategic use of political anti-Semitism in order to generate an otherwise unlikely emotional mass appeal. Yet precisely this emotional success indicates his psychological predisposition to attack the Jewish patriarchs because of an ambivalence toward the father. In fact Waldheim repeatedly invokes his own father, whose association with the clerical fascism of the Christian Socialists during the thirties led to conflicts with the Austrian Nazis; hence Waldheim's dubious anti-Nazi pedigree. Yet in his autobiography he describes his rejection of his father, the "mighty parent," i.e., his rejection of his father's political partisanship, instead of which he chose to pursue a path of political neutrality outside of party strife:

> Despite the affection and respect that I felt for my father, I had already begun to exercise a certain intellectual independence, which he was the first to encourage. He was strong in his convictions and concerned that I should be so in mine, whatever these might be. One issue on which we disagreed was political affiliation. Where he was active in the Christian Socialist party, I remained aloof. I could never bring myself to give allegiance wholly to any single party, since I was already convinced that I could better serve the interests of my country by staying free of partisan obligation.[56]

Waldheim confuses "intellectual independence" with a refusal to engage in concrete disputes that might require the strength of character he never developed. Closing his eyes to real conflicts, he adopts a model of neutrality that is not conciliatory but at best vacillating, at worst solipsistic. Instead of carrying out the conflict with the father, which might have endangered his already labile identity, he opts for a strategy of conflict avoidance and an accommodation with authority that can never be critiqued. This model of nonpartisan authority determines the trajectory of his political career, including his understanding of the presidential office he pursued, described as "the father of the fatherland."[57] The ambivalence of the son toward the father points the son on the road to domestic nonpartisanship as well as to his peculiar understanding of international neutrality, remaining "aloof" on principle.

The relationship between this psychology and Waldheim's anti-

Semitism comes to the fore in another passage of the autobiography which was deleted from the English edition. Eager to underscore the importance of his own contributions to world affairs, Waldheim takes pains to describe his collaboration with Kissinger in the Middle East negotiations. Waldheim's account betrays a desire to identify with Kissinger, stronger than with any other figure in the book; Kissinger represents an indisputable authority as well as proof of Waldheim's goodwill—one of his best friends is a Jew. Yet Waldheim lets the cat out of the bag in the deleted passage: "After an incident in Tel Aviv, where he had been sharply attacked by demonstrators, he said to me jokingly, 'Thank God there is one thing the Israelis can't accuse me of— that I am an anti-Semite.'"[58] The passage not only displays Waldheim's fascination with the authority Kissinger as a Jew. It also suggests the unspoken extrapolation: it is not Kissinger who could be labeled an anti-Semite but rather Waldheim himself. As if eager to gloss the unconscious admission, Waldheim proceeds with a bit of family drama. Because of Kissinger's affection for his parents, he often invited them to the United Nations to hear his speeches. On these occasions, Waldheim and his wife had the opportunity to speak with them "in their mother tongue—German." Yet for reasons that Waldheim treats as unfathomable, Kissinger himself would not speak German. Hence the following anecdote: "Kissinger prefered to speak English with me. During a dinner party with mutual friends, a Swiss lady, who was also a guest, remarked that she would get Kissinger to speak German. In fact she addressed him in German. Without blinking an eye, Kissinger answered—in English."[59]

Aside from the banality of the story, characteristic of Waldheim's memoirs in general, one is struck by the feigned naïveté: why on earth might Kissinger not want to speak German with Waldheim? The implied critique of Kissinger's intransigency is coupled however with a clear sexual rivalry. While Waldheim is off making small talk with Kissinger's parents, Kissinger stands his man in the encounter with the Swiss woman. Clearly the suggestion is that Waldheim, presenting himself in the role of the child, would not have the strength, i.e., potency, to meet the challenge, which he can only watch as a voyeur, whose castration anxiety leads him to envy and resent the prowess of the likeliest candidate, the international Jew. Waldheim plays the good son, sitting with the parents, whose authority he never questions, since parents are "mighty." But he wishes he could be the bad boy, who goes out into the world. Because of his timidity, the trauma of weakness, the oedipal ambivalence is never resolved. Because he speaks the "mother tongue," he can never achieve the power of the father, which he detests and fears but can never embody. He chooses instead the role of passive vacillation, a result of his own psychopathology of neutrality.

Of course the legal category of neutrality is not associated universally with the Waldheim model, but it is evident that Waldheim's neutrality derives from particular cultural and psychological predispositions to respond to conflicts by avoiding them. Thus in 1968 as Austrian foreign minister, he refused to allow the Austrian embassy in Prague to grant asylum to Czech citizens fleeing the Russian invasion. It is this decision which probably earned him the support of the Soviet Union in his successful 1972 effort to become the secretary-general, as well as Moscow's opportunist position on the 1986 controversy.[60] Waldheim's proud comment: "Since the signing of the [1955] treaty and the adoption of the Austrian constitutional law on permanent neutrality there has been no serious strain on amicable relations [with the USSR], not even under such difficult external conditions as during the Hungarian rising or the Czechoslovak crisis. The relationship of trust between Vienna and Moscow has been further strengthened by a number of official visits."[61]

The refusal to make difficult decisions "even under such difficult external conditions" is a feature of Waldheim's personality, trenchantly analyzed during the campaign in a brilliant essay by Peter Handke.[62] It is moreover a consequence of Waldheim's particular understanding of international politics and neutrality. The initial desire to revise the Treaty of St. Germain and retrieve the multinational Europe lost in 1918 led him to his dissertation topic of 1944, the study of the confederation principle (*Reichsidee*) in the work of Constantin Frantz. He concludes with a glorification of "the magnificent collaboration of all the peoples of Europe under the leadership of the Reich" in the battle against the threat of external powers. Germany will become, in Waldheim's view, the vehicle for a resurrection of Europe, as if the "mighty parent" had returned to save the beleaguered son.[63]

Whether the vitriolic language in the Nazi dissertation of the student Waldheim is relevant to President Waldheim is a less urgent topic than the degree to which Waldheim's postwar political conceptions continue to display a strong indebtedness to the problematic notion of confederation inherited from Frantz. As in Frantz, one finds a political relativism that refuses to judge local political cultures in terms of some universal norms. Hence Waldheim's notorious ability to get along in a jolly manner with dictators: Syrian President Assad is "always kind and listens patiently and sympathetically to others, even when he does not share their views." [64] Marshal Tito "is basically a man of simple tastes and pleasures [who] spends his free time walking, swimming and working at various handicrafts." [65] Not a word of criticism is added regarding domestic affairs, since the multinational model demands an agnosticism in order to respect local particularity. Thus Waldheim's conception of the United Nations echoes Frantz's model for a European confederation: in both cases, the establishment of a supranational administration implies a tolerance for authoritarian regional powers. In particular, it leads to Waldheim's explicit apology for nondemocratic regimes and human rights abuses in the third world. Waldheim's answer is only to remind us "that violations of human rights are not restricted to the Third World," and that democracy is not "automatically valid for all peoples." It is particularly inappropriate "in a social order based on tribal principles or among groups that have not achieved even a minimum of national cohesion." [66] The implication is that political formations lacking a single cohesive national identity cannot have a democratic character: in other words, tribal peoples cannot rule themselves; *ergo,* more dictators for Africa. Frantz certainly would have agreed. One wonders if it applies as well to Waldheim's multinational "grand design of a global community." [67]

This curious international tolerance for local intolerance recurred as well in Waldheim's definition of Austrian neutrality during his brief tenure as foreign minister. In a speech on June 12, 1968, he dismissed charges of a "tilt toward the East," a claim that was perhaps belied by his response to the Russian invasion in August. He equally rejected foreign policy activism because of the need to respect all national sovereignties, a principle adhered to so rigidly that he attacked the Israeli rescue mission at Entebbe in 1976 as "a serious violation of the national sovereignty of a United Nations member state." [68]

This sort of world vision put Waldheim repeatedly at odds with the press, long before the 1986 campaign. As secretary-general, he complained that the coverage of the United Nations in the West was too critical, insensitive to the accomplishments of the organization and providing too much scrutiny of bad details. "Sometimes I feel that the trivia of international life—spy stories, so-called personnel scandals, diplomatic license plates and such—are disproportionately covered in the media to the exclusion of more important, though doubtless less newsworthy, activities. . . . But the public should also have access to the broader picture of the work we try to do here."[69] Similarly, in his autobiography, Waldheim complains of "unwarrented or reckless criticism."[70] Again, the German version includes a passage absent in the English edition that conveys a fuller sense of Waldheim's antipathy toward the press: "The Western press in particular spares me no criticism. As great as my respect for the freedom of the press is—one of the most precious achievements of mankind—the newspapers and mass media do not always make my job easy. Of course I can understand that owing to financial difficulties and the struggle with competition, certain newspapers try to increase their readership with sensational reports."[71] In Waldheim's view, the press appears as a perpetual threat, driven solely by insatiable greed to persecute the honest diplomat, who, despite his "respect for the freedom of the press," makes it perfectly clear that he wishes that "certain newspapers," especially in the West, would shut up. The new information order?

Yet Waldheim's hostility to the press in fact predates his activity in the United Nations. In *The Austrian Example,* the German original of which appeared in 1971, the year of his first presidential campaign, he devotes considerable space to the conflict between foreign policy and public opinion. The career diplomat expresses a deep distrust of public opinion but recognizes that, given the power of the mass media, the government has to remain open: not however in order to encourage public discussion but as a sort of public relations campaign.[72] Nevertheless, he fears that the press might, in certain circumstances, encourage public criticism that would put pressure on the government and impinge on the policy of permanent neutrality: "Wild or unbridled criticism, unfounded sensational reports and personal insults merely serve to intensify existing tension in the event of critical situations in foreign policy." Following his former dissertation advisor Verdross, the commentator on Austrian neutrality, Waldheim therefore deduces that "situations may arise . . . in which the information media should impose voluntary restrictions on themselves for the common good."[73] One presumes such situations would include events like the Soviet invasion of Czechoslovakia, since Waldheim's decision to close the embassy doors in Prague to refugees was severely attacked. He would obviously prefer a press that would not provoke the public to respond vigorously to any foreign event, i.e., a press ready to subordinate itself to the calculations of the government.

This illiberal readiness to modify the freedom of the press resonates with the unwillingness to criticize undemocratic practices abroad. Both echo features of Frantz's confederation, and both depend on Waldheim's construction of neutrality: if criticism thrives on partisanship, then impartiality necessitates a restriction of critical discussion. Frantz is echoed as well to the extent that Waldheim has compounded his critique of the press with an anti-Semitic fantasy, his own claim that "international journalism is dominated by the World Jewish Congress." [74] In fact Waldheim is afraid of Jews for the same reason that he is afraid of the press, and, for that matter, any public debate. The weak ego surrounds itself with fantastic nightmares of alien power, international conspiracies, and bloodcurdling encirclement. It responds by claiming the absolute innocence of a child. Hence the compulsive insistence on forgetting. Like the "infant republic," the child has no memory, and therefore the leader of the conservative People's party, Alois Mock, derided discussions of "our so-called past." The infant is unmarked, uncircumcised, and neutral, but, just as Frantz's confederation threatens to engulf surrounding nations, it is the infantile neutrality that knows no borders and makes limitless demands. Hence the campaign slogans "Österreich über alles" and "We Austrians do what we want to do."

It is noteworthy that, with one exception, all the established newspapers supported Waldheim's campaign and participated in the denunciations of foreign journalism. In any case, the model of neutrality he offers, drawing on political traditions, a cultural heritage, and a particular social psychology, remains extraordinarily problematic. A century ago, the limitations of bourgeois liberalism gave way to a generational revolt out of which grew the culture of fin-de-siècle Vienna. Its mythic sensibility was not restricted to the painting Klimt provided for the ceiling of the university, in which conceptual knowledge appears as a tiny footnote to an irrational cosmos. The same sensibility recurred in a new political culture that combined radical gestures of revolt with a new rhetoric of myth. That turn-of-the-century culture is not only being celebrated today in the great museums; it is also being appropriated by the Austrian conservatives and turned into nationalism.

The Austrian paradigm today means the transformation of the neutrality of 1955, a legal international standing, into a radical insistence on insularity, a hysterical fear of an imagined international intervention, a fear of the world. The Austrians may be insisting on their freedom from international pressure in an "*Österreich über alles,*" but their foreign policy is in fact strictly limited by the 1955 treaty. Yet if the neutral Austrians find their international status difficult, one can only wonder how a neutral Germany—if such an unlikelihood should ever occur—would fare with a pledge to avoid an alliance with either East or West. The probable result would be either the gradual incorporation of a reunified Germany into the influence sphere of either the East or the West, or the emergence of Germany at the head of a European confederation as a third superpower, for which the term "neutral" ceases to be appropriate. Therefore the Waldheim model certainly sheds a new light on the West German fascination with "the Austrian example" as a version of neutrality and Central European confederation. The connection between Waldheim and the West German neutralists is not at all absurd, given the fact that in the runoff election the Austrian Greens tilted more toward Waldheim than toward his socialist opponent.[75] The question—the new version of the German question—is how many of its principles the German left will surrender in order to achieve neutrality, reunification, and a confederation. There is an Austrian answer, and it is the specter haunting the Vienna fascination.

Notes
Index

Notes

Introduction

1 Jean-François Lyotard, *The Postmodern Condition: A Report on Knowledge*, trans. Geoff Bennington and Brian Massumi (Minneapolis: University of Minnesota Press, 1984), p. 49.

2 Max Horkheimer and Theodor W. Adorno, *Dialectic of Enlightenment*, trans. John Cumming (New York: Seabury Press, 1972), p. 45.

3 Lyotard, *Postmodern Condition*, pp. 19, 91 n. 68.

4 Horkheimer and Adorno, *Dialectic of Enlightenment*, p. 78.

Chapter One
Is Liberty an "Invention of the Ruling Classes"?

1 Michel Foucault, "Nietzsche, Genealogy, History," *Foucault Reader*, ed. Paul Rainbow (New York: Pantheon Press, 1984), p. 78.

2 Theodor W. Adorno, "Zu einem Porträt Thomas Manns," *Noten zur Literatur*, vol. 3 (Frankfurt: Suhrkamp, 1973), pp. 19–29.

3 Max Horkheimer and Theodor W. Adorno, *Dialectic of Enlightenment* (New York: Seabury Press, 1972), p. 241 (this section bears the title "A Personal Observation," which is an unfortunately imprecise rendering of "*Gezeichnet*," i.e., marked).

4 Theodor W. Adorno, *Prisms* (Cambridge: MIT Press, 1972), p. 30.

5 Ibid., pp. 21, 23, 25.

6 Horkheimer and Adorno, *Dialectic of Enlightenment*, p. 182.

7 Ibid.

8 Ibid., p. 183.

9 Foucault, "Nietzsche, Genealogy, History," pp. 93–94.

10 Michel Foucault, *The Order of Things* (New York: Vintage Books, 1973), p. 387.

11 Ernst Jünger, *Der Arbeiter, Werke* (Stuttgart: Ernst Klett Verlag, n.d.), 6: 119, 250.

245

Chapter Two
The Aestheticization of Politics

1   Rudolf Borchardt, *Prosa,* vol. 3, ed. Marie Luise Borchardt (Stuttgart: Ernst Klett Verlag, 1960), p. 38.

2   Ibid., p. 40.

3   Ibid., p. 43.

4   On modernism and opposition to modernization, see T. J. Jackson Lears, *No Place of Grace: Antimodernism and the Transformation of American Culture, 1880–1920* (New York: Pantheon Books, 1981).

5   See Peter Bürger, *Theory of the Avant-garde,* trans. Michael Shaw (Minneapolis: University of Minnesota Press, 1984).

6   Borchardt, *Prosa,* p. 47.

7   Ibid., p. 42.

8   D. H. Lawrence, *Lady Chatterley's Lover* (New York: Grove Press, 1959), pp. 180–84.

9   D. H. Lawrence, *A Propos of Lady Chatterley's Lover* (London: Mandrake Press, 1930), pp. 54–55.

10   Lawrence, *Lady Chatterley's Lover,* pp. 117–18.

11   Kate Millett, *Sexual Politics* (New York: Doubleday, 1970), pp. 237–45.

12   Max Weber, *The Protestant Ethic and the Spirit of Capitalism* (New York: Charles Scribner's Sons, 1958), pp. 181–83.

13   See Martin Green, *The von Richthofen Sisters: The Triumphant and Tragic Modes of Love* (New York: Basic Books, 1974); Marianne Weber, *Max Weber: Ein Lebensbild* (Tübingen: J. C. B. Mohr, 1926), p. 468.

14   Georg Lukács, *The Theory of the Novel: A Historico-Philosophical Essay on the Forms of Great Epic Literature,* trans. Anna Bostock (Cambridge: MIT Press, 1971), pp. 38–39.

15   See Martin Jay, *The Dialectical Imagination: A History of the Frankfurt School and the Institute of Social Research, 1923–1950* (Boston: Little, Brown, 1973); Eugene Lunn, *Marxism and Modernism: An Historical Study of Lukács, Brecht, Benjamin, and Adorno* (Berkeley: University of California Press, 1982); Richard Wolin, *Walter Benjamin: An Aesthetic of Redemption* (New York: Columbia University Press, 1982).

16   Walter Benjamin, *Illuminations,* ed. Hannah Arendt, trans. Harry Zohn (New York: Schocken Books, 1969), p. 221.

17   See Laura Mulvey, "Visual Pleasure and Narrative Cinema," *Screen* 16, no. 3 (Autumn 1975): 8f.; and my "Recipient as Spectator: West German Film and Poetry of the Seventies," *German Quarterly* 55 (1982): 499–510.

18   See Walter Benjamin, "Krisis des Romans: Zu Döblin's *Berlin Alexanderplatz*," *Gesammelte Schriften*, vol. 3, ed. Hella Tiedemann-Bartels (Frankfurt: Suhrkamp, 1972), pp. 230–36.

19   Benjamin, *Illuminations*, p. 231.

20   Walter Benjamin, *Gesammelte Schriften* 1/3, ed. Rolf Tiedemann and Hermann Schweppenhäuser (Frankfurt: Suhrkamp, 1974), p. 1055.

21   Alfred Kurella, *Mussolini ohne Maske: Der erste rote Reporter bereist Italien* (Berlin: Universum-Bücherei, 1931).

22   Benjamin, *Illuminations*, p. 241.

23   See Carl E. Schorske, *Fin-de-siècle Vienna: Politics and Culture* (New York: Vintage Books, 1981), pp. 116–46.

24   Walter Benjamin, *Briefe*, ed. Gershom Scholem and Theodor W. Adorno (Frankfurt: Suhrkamp, 1964), p. 323.

25   Benjamin, *Illuminations*, p. 242.

26   See Walter Benjamin, "Theorien des deutschen Faschismus," *Gesammelte Schriften*, 3: 238–50; Ansgar Hillach, "'Ästhetisierung des politischen Lebens': Benjamins faschismustheoretischer Ansatz—eine Rekonstruktion," in *"Links hatte noch alles sich zu enträtseln . . ."* in *Walter Benjamin im Kontext*, ed. Burkhardt Lindner (Frankfurt: Syndikat Autoren- und Verlagsgesellschaft, 1978), pp. 127–67.

27   See Egon Schwarz, "Fascism and Society: Remarks on Thomas Mann's Novella 'Mario and the Magician,'" *Michigan Germanic Studies* 2 (1976): 47–67.

28   Thomas Mann, "Mario and the Magician," *Death in Venice and Seven Other Stories*, trans. H. T. Lowe-Porter (New York: Vintage Books, 1954), pp. 140–41.

29   Jürgen Habermas, *Strukturwandel der Öffentlichkeit: Untersuchungen zu einer Kategorie der bürgerlichen Gesellschaft* (1962; Neuwied and Berlin: Luchterhand, 1974), pp. 233, 273.

Chapter Three
Consumer Society

1   See Jürgen Habermas, "Neoconservative Culture Criticism in the United States and West Germany: An Intellectual Movement in Two Political Cultures," in *Habermas and Modernity*, ed. Richard J. Bernstein (Cambridge: MIT Press, 1985), pp. 78–94; Peter Steinfels, *The*

Neoconservatives: The Men Who Are Changing America's Politics (New York: Simon and Schuster, 1979); Daniel Bell, *The Cultural Contradictions of Capitalism* (New York: Basic Books, 1976); Hilton Kramer, "The MLA Centennial Follies," *New Criterion* 2, no. 6 (February 1984): 1–8.

2   Jürgen Habermas, "Modernity versus Postmodernity," *New German Critique,* 22 (Winter 1981): 13–14.

3   William J. Bennett, "To Reclaim a Legacy: A Report on the Humanities in Higher Education" (National Endowment for the Humanities, 1984); Jean-François Lyotard, *The Postmodern Condition: A Report on Knowledge* (Minneapolis: University of Minnesota Press, 1984); John Rajchman, "Foucault, or the Ends of Modernism," *October* 24 (Spring 1983): pp. 37–62.

4   Heinrich Mann, "Geist und Tat," *Essays* (Hamburg: Claassen, 1960), p. 14.

5   Robert Musil, *Young Törless,* trans. Eithne Wilkins and Ernst Kaiser (New York: Pantheon Books, 1955), p. 115.

6   Peter Bürger, *Theorie der Avantgarde* (Frankfurt: Suhrkamp, 1974), pp. 21–22.

7   Thomas S. Kuhn, *The Structure of Scientific Revolutions* (Chicago: University of Chicago Press, 1962).

8   Friedrich Schiller, *Sämtliche Werke* (Berlin and Weimar: Aufbau Verlag, 1980), 1: 272.

9   Thomas Mann, "Tod in Venedig," *Die Erzählungen* (Frankfurt: Fischer, 1967), 1: 345–46.

10   Theodor W. Adorno, "Auf die Frage: Was ist Deutsch," *Gesammelte Schriften* 10/2, ed. Rolf Tiedemann (Frankfurt: Suhrkamp, 1977), p. 695.

11   See the more extensive discussion in Russell A. Berman, *The Rise of the Modern German Novel: Crisis and Charisma* (Cambridge: Harvard University Press, 1986), pp. 205–86.

12   Bürger, *Theorie der Avantgarde,* p. 72.

13   Ferenc Feher, "Was ist jenseits von Kunst? Theorien der Nachmoderne," in *Tendenzwenden: Aspekte des Kulturwandels der Siebziger Jahre,* ed. David Roberts (Frankfurt: Peter Lang, 1984), pp. 91–105.

14   See Richard Wolin, "Modernism vs. Postmodernism," *Telos* 62 (Winter 1984–85): 9–29.

15   Max Horkheimer and Theodor W. Adorno, *Dialektik der Aufklärung* (Amsterdam: Querido Verlag, 1947), pp. 144–98.

16   William Leiss, *The Domination of Nature* (New York: Braziller, 1972).

17   James Clifford, "Histories of the Tribal and the Modern," *Art in America* (April 1985), pp. 164–77, 215; Russell A. Berman, "Beauty in the Age of Pollution," *Telos* 37 (Fall 1978): 132–44; *La Biennale di Venezia. Section of Visual Arts and Architecture. General Catalogue* (Venice, 1978).

18   Theodor Adorno, *Philosophy of Modern Music* (New York: Continuum, 1973), p. 30.

19   Fredric Jameson, "Postmodernism, or the Cultural Logic of Late Capitalism," *New Left Review* 146 (July/August 1984).

20   Bürger, *Theorie der Avantgarde*, p. 73.

21   Paul Piccone, "From Tragedy to Farce: The Return of Critical Theory," *New German Critique* 7 (Winter 1976): 104; Andrew Arato, "Critical Theory in the United States: Reflections on Four Decades of Reception," in *America and the Germans*, ed. Frank Trommler and Joseph McVeigh (Philadelphia: University of Pennsylvania Press, 1986), 2: 282–85.

22   Guy Debord, *Society of the Spectacle* (Detroit: Black and Red, 1977).

23   Stuart Ewen, *Captains of Consciousness: Advertising and the Social Roots of the Consumer Culture* (New York: McGraw-Hill, 1978); Albrecht Wellmer, "Art and Industrial Production," *Telos* 57 (Fall 1983): 53–62; T. J. Jackson Lears, *No Place of Grace: Antimodernism and the Transformation of American Culture, 1880–1920* (New York: Pantheon, 1981); Peter Gorsen, "Zur Dialektik des Funktionalismus heute: Das Beispiel des kommunalen Wohnungsbaus im Wien der zwanziger Jahre," in *Stichworte zur "geistigen Situation der Zeit,"* ed. Jürgen Habermas (Frankfurt: Suhrkamp, 1979), 2: 688–705.

Chapter Four
Writing for the Book Industry

1   Ernst Fischer, "Der 'Schutzverein deutscher Schriftsteller,' 1909–1933," *Archiv für Geschichte des Buchhandels (AGB)* 21 (1980), col. 14.

2   Quoted in Hans Widmann, ed., *Der deutsche Buchhandel in Urkunden und Quellen* (Hamburg: Hauswedel, 1965), 1: 68.

3   Ilsedore Rarisch, *Industrialisierung und Literatur: Buchproduktion, Verlagswesen, und Buchhandel in Deutschland im 19. Jahrhundert in ihrem statistischen Zusammenhang* (Berlin: Colloquium Verlag, 1976), p. 35.

4   See Peter Bürger, *Theorie der Avantgarde* (Frankfurt: Suhrkamp, 1974), pp. 57–63.

5   See Jean Baudrillard, *The Mirror of Production* (St. Louis: Telos Press, 1975).

6   Max Weber, *The Protestant Ethic and the Spirit of Capitalism* (New York: Charles Scribner's Sons, 1958), p. 17.

7   Fischer, "'Schutzverein deutscher Schriftsteller,'" col. 12.

8   See Jürgen Habermas, *Theorie des kommunikativen Handelns* (Frankfurt: Suhrkamp, 1981), 1: 49ff.

9   Theodor W. Adorno, "Culture Industry Reconsidered," *New German Critique,* 6 (Fall 1975), p. 12.

10 See Daniel Bell, *The Cultural Contradictions of Capitalism* (New York: Basic Books, 1976), and Jürgen Habermas, "Die Kulturkritik der Neukonservativen in den USA und in der Bundesrepublik," *Merkur* 36, no. 11 (November 1982): 1047–61.

11 Friedrich Uhlig, *Geschichte des Buches und des Buchhandels* (Stuttgart: C. E. Poeschel, 1953), pp. 39–49.

12 Rarisch, *Industrialisierung und Literatur,* p. 12.

13 Ibid., p. 83.

14 Ibid., p. 18.

15 Ibid., p. 19.

16 Ibid., p. 21.

17 Ibid.

18 Uhlig, *Geschichte des Buches und des Buchhandels,* pp. 64–66.

19 Rarisch, *Industrialisierung und Literatur,* p. 28.

20 Ibid., p. 35.

21 Ibid., pp. 38, 85.

22 See Gerhard Friesen, "Karl Gutzkow und Heinrich Hoff: Zu einer vormärzlichen Kontroverse über Preisherabsetzungen im Buchhandel," *AGB* 21 (1980), col. 749–68.

23 Ibid., col. 751.

24 Ibid., col. 758.

25 Rarisch, *Industrialisierung und Literatur,* pp. 41–43.

26 Uhlig, *Geschichte des Buches und des Buchhandels,* p. 70.

27 Fischer, "'Schutzverein deutscher Schriftsteller,'" col. 17.

28 Ibid., col. 18.

29 Rarisch, *Industrialisierung und Literatur,* p. 61.

30 Ibid., p. 63.

31   Ibid., p. 64.

32   Fischer, "'Schutzverein deutscher Schriftsteller,'" col. 19.

33   Theodor Fontane, *Literarische Essays und Studien,* ed. Kurt Schreinert, *Sämtliche Werke,* vol. 22 (Munich: Nymphenburg, 1963), p. 491.

34   See Ferdinand Tönnies, *Gemeinschaft und Gesellschaft: Abhandlung des Communismus und Socialismus als empirischer Kulturformen* (Leipzig: Fue's Verlag, 1887).

35   Friedrich Schulze, *Der deutsche Buchhandel und die geistigen Strömungen der letzten Hundert Jahre* (Leipzig: Verlag des Börsenvereins der deutschen Buchhändler, 1925), p. 18.

36   See Brigitte Verdolfsky, "Klassenkämpfe innerhalb des Leipziger Buchgewerbes in der zweiten Hälfte des 19. Jahrhunderts," in *Beiträge zur Geschichte des Buchwesens,* 8:44–93.

37   See Schulze, *Deutscher Buchhandel,* p. 98.

38   Uhlig, *Geschichte des Buches und des Buchhandels,* pp. 61–62.

39   See Schulze, *Deutscher Buchhandel,* pp. 82–83.

40   See Karl May, *Mein Leben und Streben,* ed. Hainer Paul, rpt. ed. (Hildesheim and New York: Olms Press, 1975), pp. 178–207.

41   Schulze, *Deutscher Buchhandel,* p. 180.

42   See Herbert G. Göpfert, *Vom Autor zum Leser: Beiträge zur Geschichte des Buchwesens* (Munich: Hanser, 1977), p. 45.

43   Conrad Alberti, "Paul Heyse als Novellist," *Die Gesellschaft* 5, pt. 2 (1889): 968.

44   Ibid.

45   Ibid., pp. 970–71.

46   See Wilhelm Schäfer, *Der Schriftsteller* (Frankfurt: Rütten und Loening, 1910), p. 23.

47   See Thomas Mann, *Death in Venice and Seven Other Stories* (New York: Vintage, 1954), p. 14.

48   See Uhlig, *Geschichte des Buches und des Buchhandels,* pp. 80–82; Eugen Diederichs, *Aus meinem Leben* (Jena: Diederichs, 1938), p. 49; Schulze, *Deutscher Buchhandel,* p. 256.

49   See Ronald Fullerton, "The Development of the German Book Markets, 1815–1888," Diss. University of Wisconsin–Madison 1975.

50   Levin Ludwig Schücking, *The Sociology of Literary Taste* (Chicago: University of Chicago Press, 1966), pp. 36–40.

51   See Rudolf Wilhelm Balzer, "Aus den Anfängen schriftstellerischer Interessenverbände. Joseph Kürschner: Autor-Funktionär-Verleger," *AGB* 16 (1976), col. 1517ff.

52   See Schulze, *Deutscher Buchhandel,* p. 208.

53   Ibid., pp. 166ff.

54   See Widmann, *Deutscher Buchhandel in Urkunden und Quellen,* pp. 131–48.

55   See Schulze, *Deutscher Buchhandel,* p. 168.

56   Cited in Gerd Schulz, *Zeugnisse und Programme zur Geschichte des deutschen Buchhandels* (Stuttgart: Poeschel, 1964), p. 88.

57   See ibid., pp. 93–101.

58   See Michael Kienzle, *Der Erfolgsroman: Zur Kritik seiner poetischen Oekonomie bei Gustav Freytag und Eugenie Marlitt* (Stuttgart: Metzler, 1975), p. 62.

59   See Adolf Bartels, *Geschichte der deutschen Literatur* (Leipzig: Avenarius, 1902), 2: 575–78.

60   Cited in Widmann, *Deutscher Buchhandel in Urkunden und Quellen,* p. 397.

61   See Susanne Jährig-Ostertag, "Zur Geschichte der Theatervereine in Deutschland bis zum Ende des Dritten Reiches," *AGB* 16 (1976), col. 185–205.

62   Michael Georg Conrad, "Kritik: Romane und Novellen," *Die Gesellschaft* 8, pt. 1 (1892): 642.

63   Balzer, "Aus den Anfängen schriftstellerischer Interessenverbände," col. 1542.

64   See Thomas Mann, "Rede zur Gründung der Sektion für Dichtkunst der Preussischen Akademie der Künste," *Gesammelte Werke* (Frankfurt: Suhrkamp, 1974), p. 213.

65   See Hermann Kinder, *Poesie als Synthese: Ausbreitung eines deutschen Realismus-Verständnisses in der Mitte des 19. Jahrhunderts* (Frankfurt: Athenäum, 1973).

Chapter Five
Modern Art and Desublimation

1   Thomas Mann, *Death in Venice and Seven Other Stories* (New York: Vintage Books, 1954), p. 3.

2   Ibid., p. 65.

3   James Joyce, *Ulysses* (New York: Vintage Books, 1961), pp. 366–67.

4   The reference to Mann and Joyce as representatives of an avant-gardist project diverges from current terminological distinctions between the avant-garde per se and modernism. One version, advocated above all by Matei Calinescu, differentiates among the avant-garde with its confluence of aesthetic revolt and political revolutionism, the modernists committed to major literary production, and postmodernism as a third and privileged mode of contemporary aesthetic innovation. Peter Bürger separates modernism as a radicalized insistence on autonomy (Valéry) from the avant-garde and its attack on the bourgeois institution of art, while he remains sensitive to the limitations of this conceptual separation. Both Calinescu and Bürger distinguish between the avant-garde and modernism in order to circumscribe strictly the significance of modernism and consequently legitimate aesthetic innovation in the wake of modernism's alleged obsolescence, i.e., a "post-modernism." The tendency to denigrate modernism can lead to a periodization identifying the modernists as largely nineteenth-century figures. The break with the liberal bourgeois culture of the nineteenth century thereby dwindles in significance. It is precisely this break however which is of concern in this essay; "modernism" and "avant-garde" are therefore used interchangeably to refer to the full range of tendencies commonly identified as "modern" art and literature. Cf. Matei Calinescu, *Faces of Modernity* (Bloomington: University of Indiana Press, 1977) and Peter Bürger, "The Decline of the Modern Age," *Telos*, no. 62 (Winter 1984–85), pp. 117–31.

5   Jürgen Habermas, *Theorie des kommunikativen Handelns* (Frankfurt: Suhrkamp, 1981), pp. 205–366.

6   See Fredric Jameson, *Fables of Aggression* (Berkeley: University of California Press, 1979), and Henry Sussman, *The Hegelian Aftermath* (Baltimore: Johns Hopkins University Press, 1982).

7   Michel Foucault, *The Order of Things* (New York: Vintage Books, 1973), p. 387.

8   Christa Bürger, *Der Ursprung der bürgerlichen Institution Kunst* (Frankfurt: Suhrkamp, 1977), and Peter Bürger, *Theory of the Avantgarde* (Minneapolis: University of Minnesota Press, 1984).

9   Maurizio Calvesi, "Arte e arti: Attualita e storia," in *XLI Esposizione Internazionale d'Arte: La Biennale di Venezia* (Venice: Electra Edetrice 1984), p. 13.

10 Hermann Hesse, *Steppenwolf* (New York: Holt, Rinehart, and Winsten, 1957), pp. 168–69.

11 See Lucien Goldmann, "Interdependences between Industrial Society and New Forms of Literary Creation," *Cultural Creation in Modern Society* (St. Louis: Telos Press, 1976), pp. 76–88.

12 Georg Lukács, *The Theory of the Novel* (Cambridge: MIT Press, 1971), pp. 29–39.

13   Walter Benjamin, "Krisis des Romans," *Gesammelte Schriften,* vol. 3 (Frankfurt: Suhrkamp, 1972), pp. 230–31.

14   Walter Benjamin, "Oskar Maria Graf als Erzähler," ibid., p. 310.

15   Peter Brandt and Herbert Ammon, *Die Linke und die nationale Frage* (Reinbek: Rowohlt, 1981).

16   Ernst Jünger, "Der Kampf als inneres Erlebnis," *Werke* (Stuttgart: Ernst Klett Verlag, n.d.), 5: 107.

17   Walter Benjamin, *Illuminations* (New York: Schocken Books, 1969), pp. 241–42.

18   Ibid., pp. 107–8.

19   Ernst Jünger, *Der Arbeiter: Herrschaft und Gestalt, Werke* (Stuttgart: Ernst Klett Verlag, n.d.), 6: 228.

20   On the vicissitudes of the individual in the Weimar period, see Leo Lowenthal, "Die biographische Mode," *Sociologica,* vol. 1 (Frankfurt: Suhrkamp, 1955), pp. 363–86; on Jünger's "heroic realism," see Herbert Marcuse, "Der Kampf gegen den Liberalismus in der totalitären Staatsauffassung," *Kultur und Gesellschaft,* vol. 1 (Frankfurt: Suhrkamp, 1965), pp. 17–55. The ease with which Jünger moves from the aristocratic image of the soldierly elite to the proletarian virtue of the "worker" indicates that the seemingly antithetical figures derive from the same social substance. Both of course are antisubjective terms (a feature which explains the current renaissance of Jünger who can easily appeal to poststructuralist taste). Both moreover are produced by the same self-destructive logic of bourgeois individuality. The presubjective elite and the postsubjective proletarian are less external challenges to bourgeois identity than the externalized personae that it chooses when, experiencing itself as an alienated other, it assumes the masks of its historical competitors: Nietzsche's aristocratic gestures, or the mimicry of the proletariat popular in the bourgeois intelligentsia at least since naturalism (see Walter Benjamin, "Bücher, die übersetzt werden sollten," *Gesammelte Schriften,* 3: 175). In either case, the imitation of the deadly antagonist represents the culmination of a fundamentally self-destructive urge that was present from the start in the emancipated bourgeois, trapped in his own guilt—vide the paradigmatic suicide of Werther and Emilia Galotti's sacrifice. Because it buries traditional society beneath the tabula rasa of its ego (the reign of terror) and occludes concrete exploitation with the categories of exchange (Manchester), the bourgeoisie attempts an atonement in the form of a perpetual reenactment of its own death. After the prototypically bourgeois revolt, Brutus reveals the proximity of violence and freedom:

> And let us bathe our hands in Caesar's blood
> Up to the elbows, and besmear our swords:
> Then walk we forth, even to the market-place,

And waving our red weapons o'er our heads,
Let's all cry, "Peace, freedom, and liberty!"

Cassius' reply indicates a compulsion to repeat, an eternal return, that in fact belies the claim that a substantive freedom has been attained:

Stoop then, and wash. How many ages hence
Shall this our lofty scene be acted over,
In states unborn, and accents yet unknown!
(*Julius Caesar* 3.1.106–13)

Crime and exculpation converge in the same ritual of washing because both are part of a revolt in the name of freedom but designed to preserve hierarchy. The real suffering however cannot be simply denied, so the penance takes the form of theatrical repetition. The bourgeois subject stages its own *démontage* of this "lofty scene": from Brutus' suicide to Jünger's worker.

21   Jünger, *Der Arbeiter,* p. 232.

22   On "repressive desublimation," see Herbert Marcuse, *One-Dimensional Man* (Boston: Beacon Press, 1964).

23   Theodor W. Adorno, *Philosophy of Modern Music* (New York: Continuum 1973), p. 30.

24   The aestheticization of politics is evident not only in the spectacular character of political conventions (from Nuremberg to Dallas) but in the increasing contamination of political discourse with cultural material. "Of all the phenomena of Mr. Reagan on the stump, none are so fascinating as his ability to generate emotional effects from the distinct areas of fact and fiction. In addressing the American Legion convention in Salt Lake City, the President created a patriotic surge in the hall by alternating between such reference points as the joyous homecoming of the Iranian hostages ('that unforgettable moment') and the commercialism of television military fiction ('Maybe you've seen the television show "Call to Glory" that celebrates Air Force officers serving in "the twilight struggle" of the cold war?')" *New York Times,* September 8, 1984, p. 9. The infusion of the categories of the culture industry into politics is pursued consciously, with strategic precision. Appearing in Nashville at the Grand Old Opry, Reagan claimed the Bayreuth of country music for himself and Republican nationalism: "The event in the packed Opry theater was one of the more spectacular efforts from the Reagan campaign engineers, ending in a storm of confetti and a mass rendition of 'God Bless the U.S.A.,' the red-white-and-blue song used on Reagan television commercials." From within the staged unanimity of the love feast, the orator produces a pejorative image of his opponents by mixing political characterization and racial slur with a musicological category: "Mr. Reagan, who sang along with his partisans, earlier had said the Opry was no place for his opponents. 'They'll just sing the blues,' he said as the crowd laughed and

applauded" (*New York Times*, September 14, 1984, p. 12). The opponents are associated with an aesthetic form suggesting both black culture (as opposed to the white country music) and pessimistic critique (as opposed to the upbeat optimism of the festival).

25   Theodor W. Adorno, "The Idea of Natural History," *Telos* 60 (Summer 1984): 111–24.

26   Mann, *Death in Venice,* p. 68.

27   See Christa Wolf, *Cassandra* (New York: Farrar, Straus and Giroux 1984); Michael Ende, *The Never Ending Story* (Garden City: Doubleday, 1983); Marion Bradley, *The Mists of Avalon* (New York: Knopf, 1983); Michel Tournier, *The Ogre* (Garden City: Doubleday, 1972); J. R. R. Tolkien, *The Lord of the Rings* (Boston: Houghton Mifflin, 1965). See also Charlene Spretnak, *Lost Goddesses of Ancient Greece* (Boston: Beacon Press, 1978).

28   Beuys comments: "Oak trees had a specific role to play not only during the Nazi period but even before then in the Wilhelmine era; it is certainly possible to misuse all these traditions but even when abused they do reveal another kind of factor and that is the polarity between the culture of the North and that of the South. Once again, under the sign of the oak, flowers the ancient contrast between the decentralized, almost barbarous culture of the Germanic peoples and the Celts, and the Latin conscience of urban character. The decentralized, itinerant and nomadic element in the Celtic and Germanic nature is today current once again.

"It will naturally now be possible to prevent there being initiated any manipulation intent on opening the way to a historical and regressive conquest of a barbarous and inhumane past. We, on the contrary, intend with a new production of organic architecture to take action devoted to the future. We are perfectly aware that the most remote past and the most distant future come together under this sign." Joseph Beuys–Bernhard Blume, "Interview on Trees," *Quartetto* (Milan: Arnoldo Mondadori, 1984), p. 105.

Henning Eichberg criticizes the constellation of patriarchy, monotheism, and Christianity (which appears to be a sort of Roman colonialism when viewed from a neo-German perspective) and points out the current ubiquity of myth even within the allegedly progressive subculture: "The renaissance of Celtic druids and Indian medicine men corresponds to the reappearance of witches in Germany (and elsewhere). Beside its liberal egalitarian wing, the feminist movement has generated a decidedly anti-egalitarian perspective, based on female specificity. Consequently the witches of the past recur as midwives and popular healers. The suppression of their paganism by Christianity (the father religion) and the science of male experts turns out to be a chapter in a comprehensive battle of the sexes." Eichberg goes on to point out how formerly leftist publishing houses have traveled from Marxism via anarchism and third-worldism to popular religions, shamanism, and myth. See his "Kommen die alten Götter wieder? Germanisches Heldentum im 18./20. Jahrhundert—Zur Genese alternativer Mythen," *Unter dem Pflaster liegt der Strand* 13 (1984): 9–10.

29   Russell Jacoby, *Social Amnesia* (Boston: Beacon Press, 1975); Jean Baudrillard, *La société de consommation* (Paris: Gallimard, 1974).

30   "In the midst of a half-hour of American good feeling and praise for Ronald Reagan that the Republican campaign aired on television this week, there was one woman who looked into the camera with a sun-struck conviction and summed up the impression that is the strength of the Reagan Presidency, and the way the President creates it.

"'I think he's just doggone honest,' she said. 'It's remarkable. He's been on television—what have I heard, about 26 times, talking to us about what he's doing? Now he's not doing that for any other reason than to make it real clear. And if anybody has any question about where he's headed, it's their fault. Maybe they don't have a television'" (*New York Times*, September 14, 1984, p. 12). In fact, Reagan had fewer televised interviews and news conferences than his predecessors. The point is rather that aestheticized politics tends to drop the traditional dialogic forms, remnants of a liberal parliamentary ethos of political responsibility, and replaces them with the power of the cosmetic image.

31   Max Weber, *The Protestant Ethic and the Spirit of Capitalism* (New York: Charles Scribner's Sons, 1958), p. 182.

32   Thomas Mann, *Doctor Faustus* (New York: Vintage Books, 1971), p. 322.

Chapter Six
Written Right Across Their Faces

1   Ernst Jünger, *Der Arbeiter, Werke* (Stuttgart: Ernst Klett Verlag, n.d.), 6:13.

2   Ibid., pp. 38–39.

3   Ibid., p. 227.

4   Ibid., p. 219.

5   Ibid.

6   Ibid., p. 250.

7   Ibid.

8   Ernst Jünger, "Der Kampf als inneres Erlebnis," in *Werke*, 5:41–42.

9   Jünger, *Der Arbeiter*, p. 119.

10   Ibid., p. 129.

11   Richard Wagner, "Judaism in Music," *Stories and Essays,* ed. Charles
      Osborne (London: Peter Owen, 1973), p. 27.

12   On the cover of Albert Parry, *Tattoo: Secrets of a Strange Art* (1933;
      New York: Collier Books, 1971).

13   See Konrad H. Jarausch, *Students, Society, and Politics in Imperial
      Germany: The Rise of Academic Illiberalism* (Princeton: Princeton
      University Press, 1982), pp. 244–49.

14   See John Freccero, "Manfred's Wounds and the Poetics of the 'Purga-
      torio,'" in *Centre and Labyrinth: Essays in Honour of Northrop Frye,*
      ed. Eleanor Cook et al. (Toronto: University of Toronto Press, 1983),
      pp. 69–71.

15   See Philip P. Hallie, *The Scar of Montaigne: An Essay in Personal Phi-
      losophy* (Middletown: Wesleyan University Press, 1966).

16   Ernst Jünger, introduction to Richard Junior, ed., *Hier spricht der
      Feind* (Berlin: Neufeld u. Henius, n.d.), pp. 11–12.

17   Ernst Robert Curtius, *Europäische Literatur und lateinisches Mittelal-
      ter* (Bern: A. Francke AG Verlag, 1948), pp. 75–76.

18   George Kurman, "Ecphrasis in Epic Poetry," *Comparative Literature*
      26, no. 1 (Winter 1974): 1.

19   Eleanor Winsor Leach, "Ekphrasis and the Theme of Artistic Failure
      in Ovid's Metamorphosis," *Ramus* 3, no. 2 (1974): 104.

20   Ibid., p. 105.

21   Jünger, *Der Arbeiter,* p. 221.

22   Interview in *Der Spiegel,* no. 33, 1982, p. 160.

23   Jünger, *Der Arbeiter,* p. 225.

24   Max Horkheimer and Theodor W. Adorno, *Dialectic of Enlighten-
      ment* (New York: Seabury Press, 1972), p. 3 (translation modified).

Chapter Seven
The Routinization of Charismatic Modernism

1   Thomas Mann, "Death in Venice," *Death in Venice and Seven Other
     Stories,* trans. H. T. Lowe-Porter (New York: Vintage Books, 1954),
     p. 14.

2   See Dorrit Cohn, "The Second Author of 'Der Tod in Venedig,'" in
     *Probleme der Moderne: Studien zur deutschen Literatur von Nietzsche
     bis Brecht. Festschrift für Walter Sokel,* ed. Benjamin Bennett, Anton
     Kaes, and William J. Lillyman (Tübingen: Max Niemeyer Verlag,
     1983), pp. 223–45.

3   Max Weber, *The Protestant Ethic and the Spirit of Capitalism,* trans. Talcott Parsons (New York: Charles Scribner's Sons, 1958), p. 182.

4   Max Weber, *Wirtschaft und Gesellschaft: Grundriss der verstehenden Soziologie,* 4th ed. (Tübingen: J. C. B. Mohr, 1956), pp. 140–42.

5   Marianne Weber, *Max Weber: Ein Lebensbild* (Tübingen: J. C. B. Mohr, 1926), pp. 220–21. For an extended reading of this material, see my *Rise of the Modern German Novel: Crisis and Charisma* (Cambridge: Harvard University Press, 1986, pp. 25–54.)

6   Henry Adams, *Novels, Mont Saint Michel, The Education* (New York: Literary Classics of the United States, 1983), pp. 440–41.

7   Ibid., p. 1067.

8   T. J. Jackson Lears, *No Place of Grace: Antimodernism and the Transformation of American Culture, 1880–1920* (New York: Pantheon Books, 1981), pp. 261–97.

9   Peter Bürger, *Theory of the Avant-garde,* trans. Michael Shaw (Minneapolis: University of Minnesota Press, 1984).

10 Kurt Sontheimer, *Das Elend unserer Intellektuellen: Linke Theorie in der Bundesrepublik Deutschland* (Hamburg: Hoffman und Campe, 1976). Cf. Jürgen Habermas, "Neoconservative Cultural Criticism in the United States and West Germany," *Telos* 56 (Summer 1983): 75–89.

11 Hans Magnus Enzensberger, "The Aporias of the Avant-garde," *The Consciousness Industry: On Literature, Politics and the Media,* ed. Michael Roloff (New York: Seabury Press, 1974), pp. 15–41.

12 Levin L. Schücking, *The Sociology of Literary Taste* (Chicago: University of Chicago Press, 1966).

13 Peter Jelavich, "Popular Dimensions of Modernist Elite Culture: The Case of Theater in Fin-de-siècle Munich," in *Modern European Intellectual History: Reappraisals and New Perspectives,* ed. Dominick La Capra and Steven L. Kaplan (Ithaca and London: Cornell University Press, 1982), pp. 220–50.

14 Stanley Fish, *Is There a Text in This Class? The Authority of Interpretive Communities* (Cambridge and London: Harvard University Press, 1980), p. 321.

15 See my "Rambo: From Counterculture to Contra," *Telos* 64 (Summer 1985): 143–47.

16 See Teresa De Lauretis, *Alice Doesn't: Feminism, Semiotics, Cinema* (Bloomington: Indiana University Press, 1984).

17 See Fredric Jameson, "Postmodernism, or the Cultural Logic of Late Capitalism," *New Left Review* 146 (July/August 1984).

18   Lucien Goldmann, *Cultural Creation in Modern Society* (St. Louis: Telos Press, 1976), pp. 53–54.

Chapter Eight
Myth and Modernity in Der Park

1   William Shakespeare, *A Midsummer Night's Dream,* 1.1.1–6, cited in the edition by Madeleine Doran (New York: Penguin Books, 1971). Subsequent references to act, scene, and verse will be included in the text.

2   Botho Strauss, *Der Park* (Munich: Carl Hanser Verlag, 1983), [p. 7]. Subsequent page references will be included in the text.

3   Theodor W. Adorno, "Lyric Poetry and Society," *Telos* 20 (Summer 1974): p. 65.

4   See Jean-François Lyotard, *The Postmodern Condition: A Report on Knowledge* (Minneapolis: University of Minnesota Press, 1984), pp. 72–73.

5   Stefan George, *Das Jahr der Seele* (Düsseldorf and Munich: Helmut Küper vormals Georg Bondi, 1964), p. 12.

6   Paul Celan, "Todesfuge," *Ausgewählte Gedichte,* ed. Beda Allemann (Frankfurt: Suhrkamp, 1970), p. 19.

7   Theodor W. Adorno, "Kulturkritik und Gesellschaft," *Gesammelte Schriften* 10/1 (Frankfurt: Suhrkamp, 1977), p. 30.

8   G. W. F. Hegel, *Phänomenologie des Geistes* (Hamburg: Felix Meiner Verlag, 1952), p. 148.

Chapter Nine
Imperial Encounters

1   See Peter Bürger, *Theory of the Avant-garde,* trans. Michael Shaw (Minneapolis: University of Minnesota Press, 1984).

2   Robert Musil, *Young Törless,* trans. Eithne Wilkins and Ernst Kaiser (New York: Pantheon Books, 1955), p. 115.

3   Hugo von Hofmannsthal, "Wir Österreicher und Deutschland" (1915), *Reden und Aufsätze,* vol. 2: *1914–1924,* ed. Bernd Schoeller (Frankfurt: Fischer, 1979), p. 394.

4   Adalbert Stifter, *Nachsommer* (Munich: Winkler, 1978), p. 459.

5   For an account of the political ramifications of Stifter's text, see my *Rise of the Modern German Novel: Crisis and Charisma* (Cambridge: Harvard University Press, 1986), pp. 105–33.

6   Stifter, *Nachsommer,* p. 459.

7   Ibid.

8   Karl Emil Franzos, *Halb-Asien: Land und Leute des östlichen Europa,* 3d. ed., vol. 1 (Berlin: Concordia Deutsche Verlags-Anstalt, 1888), pp. xxiii–xxiv.

9   Ibid., p. xxvii–xxviii.

10   Franzos, "Schiller in Barnow," ibid., p. 206.

11   Ibid., p. 189.

12   *Die Österreichisch-ungarische Monarchie in Wort und Bild,* vol. 20: *Bukowina* (Vienna: Kaiserlich-königliche Hof- und Staatsdruckerei, 1899), p. 377.

13   Ibid., p. 376.

14   Ibid., Vol. 15: *Böhmen,* pt. 2 (Vienna: Kaiserlich-königliche Hof- und Staatsdruckerei, 1896), p. 126.

15   Hofmannsthal, "Österreich im Spiegel seiner Dichtung" (1916), *Reden und Aufsätze,* 2:13.

16   Hofmannsthal, "Boykott fremder Sprachen" (1914), ibid., 354.

17   Hofmannsthal, "Wir Österreicher und Deutschland," pp. 393–94.

18   Hofmannsthal, "Österreich im Spiegel seiner Dichtung," pp. 13–14.

19   Ibid., p. 25.

20   Ibid.

21   See Walter Benjamin, "The Work of Art in the Age of Mechanical Reproduction," *Illuminations,* trans. Harry Zohn (New York: Schocken, 1969), p. 242.

22   Michael Haberlandt, *Österreich: Sein Land und Volk und Seine Kultur* (Vienna and Weimar: Verlag für Volks-und Heimatkunde, 1927), p. v.

23   Ibid., p. xii.

24   Ibid., p. 465.

25   Ibid., p. 207.

26   Ibid.

27   Sigmund Freud, *Civilization and Its Discontents,* ed. James Strachey (New York: Norton, 1961), p. 92.

28   Musil, *Young Törless,* p. 1.

29   Elias Canetti, *Auto-da-Fé,* trans. C. V. Wedgwood (New York: Continuum, 1982), pp. 410–11.

30   See Kalervo Hovi, *Cordon Sanitaire or Barrière de l'Est?: The Emergence of the New French Eastern European Policy, 1917–1919* (Turku: Turun Yliopisto, 1975).

Chapter Ten
The Peace Movement and the Avant-garde

1   *Peace Education at Stanford* 2, no. 1 (Autumn 1984): 1.

2   Ibid., p. 5.

3   Georg Lukács, *Essays on Realism,* trans. David Fernbach (Cambridge: MIT Press, 1981), p. 91.

4   Ibid., p. 96.

5   Ibid., pp. 112f.

6   See Theodor W. Adorno, "Zur Schlusszene des Faust" and "Balzac-Lektüre," both in *Noten zur Literatur,* vol. 2 (Frankfurt: Suhrkamp, 1970), pp. 7–18 and 19–41, respectively.

7   Theodor W. Adorno, "Rede über Lyrik und Gesellschaft," in *Noten zur Literatur,* vol. 1 (Frankfurt: Suhrkamp, 1971), p. 92.

8   Theodor W. Adorno, *Ästhetische Theorie* (Frankfurt: Suhrkamp, 1974), p. 387.

9   Theodor W. Adorno, "On the Question: What Is German," in *German Mosaic: An Album for Today,* ed. Christopher Howe (Frankfurt: Suhrkamp, 1972), p. 332.

10   Ibid., pp. 332f.

11   Peter Bürger, *Theory of the Avant-garde,* trans. Michael Shaw (Minneapolis: University of Minnesota Press, 1984), p. 49.

12   Kurt Hiller, *Geist werde Herr: Kundgebungen eines Aktivisten vor, in und nach dem Kriege* (Berlin: Erich Reiss, 1920), p. 37.

13   Heinrich Mann, *Diktatur der Vernunft* (Berlin: Die Schmiede, 1923), p. 21.

14   Thomas Mann, "Rede zur Gründung der Sektion für Dichtkunst der Preussischen Akademie der Künste," *Werke,* vol. 5: *Das essayistische Werk,* ed. Hans Bürgin (Frankfurt: Fischer, 1968), pp. 157f.

15   V. I. Lenin, "What Is to Be Done? Burning Questions of Our Movement," *Selected Works in Three Volumes* (New York: International Publishers, 1967), 1:117f.

16   Ibid., p. 122.

17   Cited in *Arbeiterdemokratie oder Parteidiktatur,* ed. Frits Kool and Erwin Oberländer (Freiburg im Breisgau: Walter-Verlag Olten, 1967), p. 25.

18   Ibid., p. 18.

19   Lenin, "What Is to Be Done?" p. 163.

20   Ibid., p. 244.

21   See Cornelius Castoriadis, *Devant la guerre: Les réalités* (Paris: Fayard, 1981).

22   V. I. Lenin, "The Military Programme of the Proletarian Revolution," *Selected Works*, 1:778.

23   Ibid., p. 780.

24   Ibid., p. 784.

25   A. Kollontai, "Die Arbeiteropposition," in *Arbeiterdemokratie oder Parteidiktatur*, p. 184.

26   Ibid., pp. 185f.

27   Alice Cook and Gwyn Kirk, *Greenham Women Everywhere: Dreams, Ideas, and Actions from the Women's Peace Movement* (London: Pluto Press, 1983), p. 4.

28   See Sigrid Meuschel, "Neo-Nationalism and the West German Peace Movement's Reaction to the Polish Military Coup," *Telos* 56 (Summer 1983): 118–30.

29   See my "Opposition to Rearmament and West German Culture," *Telos* 51 (Spring 1982): 141–48.

30   Cited in my "The Peace Movement Debate: Provisional Conclusions," *Telos* 57 (Fall 1983): 137.

31   Cook and Kirk, *Greenham Women Everywhere*, p. 29.

32   Ibid, pp. 76f.

33   Ibid, pp. 30f.

Chapter Eleven
The Vienna Fascination

1   *Le arti a Vienna: Dalla secessione alla caduta dell'impero Asburgico* (Edizioni La Biennale di Venezia, 1984); *Traum und Wirklichkeit: Wien, 1870–1930* (Eigenverlag der Museen der Stadt Wien, 1985).

2   See Walter Z. Laqueur, "The Tucholsky Complaint," *Encounter*, (October 1969): 76–80.

3   Peter Handke, "Horváth ist besser als Brecht," in *Theater im Umbruch: Eine Dokumentation aus "Theater Heute,"* ed. Henning Rischbeiter (Munich: Deutscher Taschenbuchverlag, 1970), pp. 62–63.

4   Kurt Waldheim, *The Austrian Example*, trans. Ewald Osers (New York: Macmillan, 1973).

5   Halliday in *tageszeitung,* June 13, 1986; Jochen Löser and Ulrike Schilling, *Neutralität für Mitteleuropa: Das Ende der Blöcke* (Munich: Bertelsmann Verlag, 1984), pp. 9, 170, 194, 206; for an anti-Soviet version from Eastern Europe, see Braxator et al., *Selbstbestimmung für Mitteleuropa,* Schriftenreihe Sloboda 3 (Brugg: Verlag Adria, 1979).

6   Carl E. Schorske, "Österreichs ästhetische Kultur, 1870–1914," in *Traum und Wirklichkeit,* pp. 12–25.

7   See the remarks by the foreign policy speaker of the CDU/CSU, Otto Rühe, in "Das Korsett der NATO wird den USA zu eng," *tageszeitung,* June 10, 1986.

8   Rudolf Augstein in *Der Spiegel,* November 28, 1983; Werner Herzog, "Absurde Anfälle der Ordnung," *Der Spiegel,* no. 21, 1982, p. 210; Löser and Schilling, *Neutralität für Mitteleuropa,* p. 111.

9   On Schily, see Wilfried von Bredow and Rudolf H. Brocke, "Dreimal Deutschlandpolitik: Deutschlandpolitische Ansätze der Partei der Grünen," *Deutschland Archiv,* January 1986, pp. 59–60; Löser and Schilling, *Neutralität für Mitteleuropa,* p. 142.

10 Constantin Frantz, *Die Genesis der Bismarckschen Aera und ihre Zeit* (Munich: M. Huttler, 1874), p. 25.

11 Constantin Frantz, *Der Bankrott der herrschenden Staatsweisheit* (Munich: M. Huttler, 1874), pp. 20–22.

12 Constantin Frantz, *Das neue Deutschland* (Leipzig: Rossberg'sche Buchhandlung, 1871), p. 402.

13 Friedrich Naumann, *Schriften zum Parteiwesen und zum Mitteleuropaproblem, Werke,* vol. 4 (Cologne and Opladen: Westdeutscher Verlag, 1964), pp. 375, 377.

14 Ibid., p. 453.

15 Ibid., p. 523.

16 Ibid., p. 552.

17 Ibid., pp. 563–65.

18 Ibid., pp. 735–36, 755.

19 Frantz, *Genesis der Bismarckschen Aera,* p. 22; see also his *Bismarckianismus und Friedricianismus* (Munich: M. Huttler, 1873).

20 Kurt Waldheim, *The Challenge of Peace* (New York: Rawon, Wade, 1980), pp. 102–3.

21 Max Weber, *Zur Politik im Weltkrieg: Schriften und Reden, 1914–1918* (Gesamtausgabe 1/15), ed. Wolfgang J. Mommsen (Tübingen: Mohr, 1984), p. 192.

22 Ibid., pp. 193–94.

23   Ibid., pp. 162–63.

24   See the dispute around the 1981 Havemann letter to Brezhnev, in Hermann Gremliza, "A German Document," *Telos* 51 (Spring 1982): 97–100.

25   See Reinhard Frommelt, *Paneuropa oder Mitteleuropa: Einigungs-streben im Kalkül deutscher Wirtschaft und Politik, 1925–1933* (Stuttgart: Deutsche Verlags-Anstalt, 1977).

26   See Löser und Schilling, *Neutralität für Mitteleuropa*, pp. 111–13.

27   Peter Schneider, "Warnung vor diesem Frieden," *Kursbuch* 68 (June 1982): 180–81, 185; see also Sigrid Meuschel, "Neo-Nationalism and the West German Peace Movement's Reaction to the Polish Military Coup," *Telos* 56 (Summer 1983): 119–30.

28   See *Berliner Begegnung zur Friedensförderung: Protokolle des Schrift-stellertreffens am 13./14. Dezember 1981* (Darmstadt: Luchterhand, 1982).

29   Alfred Verdross, *The Permanent Neutrality of the Republic of Austria* (Vienna: Österreichischer Bundesverlag, 1967), pp. 19–20. See also Karl Zemanek, "Der völkerrechtliche Status der dauernden Neutrali-tät und seine Rückwirkungen auf das interne Recht des dauernd neu-tralen Staates," *Juristische Blätter* 89 (1967): 281–98.

30   Waldheim, *Challenge of Peace*, pp. 10–11; the full critique of the press that was included in the earlier German version has been deleted from the English edition, therefore cf. Kurt Waldheim, *Der schwierigste Job der Welt* (Vienna: Molden, 1978), pp. 28–29.

31   Weber, *Zur Politik im Weltkrieg*, p. 164.

32   Ibid., p. 181.

33   *Traum und Wirklichkeit*, pp. 14–22.

34   Ibid., p. 20.

35   Naumann, *Schriften zum Parteiwesen*, p. 627.

36   Hugo von Hofmannsthal, "Wir Österreicher und Deutschland," *Re-den und Aufsätze*, vol. 2: *1914–1924*, ed. Bernd Schoeller (Frankfurt: Fischer, 1979), pp. 393–94.

37   Weber, *Zur Politik im Weltkrieg*, p. 181.

38   Thomas Mann, "The German Republic," *The Order of the Day: Polit-ical Essays and Speeches of Two Decades*, trans. H. T. Lowe-Porter (Freeport: Books for Libraries Press, 1969), pp. 29, 45.

39   Russell Berman, "Opposition to Rearmament and West German Cul-ture," *Telos* 51 (Spring 1982): 143–45.

40   Ibid.

41   Richard Wagner, "What Is German?" *Stories and Essays*, ed. Charles Osborne (London: Peter Owen, 1973).

42   Rolf Schneider, "Vor 'Mitteleuropa' wird gewarnt," *tagesezeitung*, June 10, 1986.

43   Milan Kundera, "The Tragedy of Central Europe," *New York Review of Books*, April 26, 1984.

44   Waldheim, *Challenge of Peace*, p. 28.

45   See Gregor von Rezzori, "Viennese Style," *Vanity Fair*, July 1986, pp. 66–73.

46   Cf. Peter Handke, "Gegenstimme," *Profil*, May 26, 1986, pp. 20–22.

47   Waldheim, *Challenge of Peace*, pp. 17–18.

48   Waldheim, *Schwierigster Job der Welt*, p. 38.

49   Sigmund Freud, "Analyse der Phobie eines fünfjährigen Knaben," *Studienausgabe* (Frankfurt: S. Fischer, 1969), 7:36 n. 2.

50   Peter Michael Lingens, "Unter Partisanen," *Profil*, May 26, 1986, p. 10.

51   See Erich Auerbach, *Mimesis* (Bern: Francke Verlag, 1946), and John Freccero, "Manfred's Wounds and the Poetics of the 'Purgatorio,'" in *Centre and Labyrinth: Essays in Honour of Northrop Frye*, ed. Eleanor Cook et al. (Toronto: University of Toronto Press, 1983), pp. 69–71.

52   Cited in Handke, "Gegenstimme," p. 21.

53   From a pamphlet of Freie Österreichische Studentschaft in Hoover Library (Stanford, California) documentation of the Austrian 1971 campaign (Waldheim file).

54   Kurt Waldheim in *Die Presse*, April 22, 1986.

55   Hajo Funke, "Hass auf Juden ist wahlentscheidend in Wien," *tageszeitung*, June 7, 1986.

56   Waldheim, *Challenge of Peace*, p. 21.

57   Funke, "Hass auf Juden."

58   Waldheim, *Schwierigster Job der Welt*, p. 137.

59   Ibid.

60   Serge Schemann, "Moscow defends Waldheim, Denounces U.S. and Zionists," *New York Times*, June 9, 1986.

61   Waldheim, *Austrian Example*, pp. 97–98.

62   Handke, "Gegenstimme," pp. 20–22.

63   Cited in Mark Wurm, "Waldheim's Thesis," *Nation*, May 17, 1986, pp. 684–85. See also Michael Siegert, "Das deutsche Reich laut Waldheim," *Profil*, June 2, 1986, pp. 56–57.

64   Waldheim, *Challenge of Peace*, p. 86.

65   Ibid., p. 102.

66   Ibid., pp. 102–3.

67   Kurt Waldheim, *Building the Future Order: The Search for Peace in an Interdependent World*, ed. Robert L. Schiffer (New York: Free Press, 1980), p. 242.

68   Kurt Waldheim, "Möglichkeiten und Grenzen der österreichischen Aussenpolitik," address to the Akademische Vereinigung für Aussenpolitik in Vienna, June 12, 1968; cited in Elaine Sciolino, "Waldheim's U.N. Tenure Seems to Show No Pattern Favoring East or West," *New York Times*, June 13, 1986.

69   Waldheim, *Building the Future Order*, p. 242.

70   Waldheim, *Challenge of Peace*, p. 10.

71   Waldheim, *Schwierigster Job der Welt*, p. 28.

72   Waldheim, *Austrian Example*, p. 185.

73   Ibid., p. 188.

74   *Le Monde*, May 3, 1986.

75   See Funke, "Hass auf Juden," and *New York Times*, June 9, 1986, pp. 6, 9.

Index